# THE LOIRE

Arthur Eperon is one of the most experienced and best-known travel writers in Europe. Since leaving the RAF in 1945 he has worked as a journalist in various capacities, often involving travel. He has concentrated on travel writing for the past twenty-five years and contributed to many publications including *The Times*, *Daily Telegraph*, *New York Times*, *Woman's Own*, *Popular Motoring* and the *TV Times*. He has also appeared on radio and television and for five years was closely involved in Thames Television's programme *Wish You Were Here*. He has been wine writer to the RAC publications and a number of magazines.

He has an intimate and extensive knowledge of France and its food and wine as a result of innumerable visits there over the last forty years. In 1974 he won the *Prix des Provinces de France*, the annual French award for travel writing. In 1991 the French Government awarded him the Médaille de Mérite (Tourisme). His *Travellers' France* topped the paperback bestseller list for eleven weeks.

# EPERON'S FRENCH REGIONAL GUIDES

# THE LOIRE

ARTHUR EPERON

PAN BOOKS
LONDON, SYDNEY AND AUCKLAND

First published 1992 by Pan Books Ltd
a division of Pan Macmillan Publishers Limited
Cavaye Place, London SW10 9PG
1 3 5 7 9 8 6 4 2
© Arthur Eperon 1992
Illustrations © Mary Fraser 1992
Maps © Ken Smith 1992

The right of Arthur Eperon to be identified as author of this
work has been asserted by him in accordance with the Copyright,
Designs and Patents Act 1988.

ISBN 0 330 32222 2

Designed by Peter Ward
Photoset by Parker Typesetting Service, Leicester
Printed in England by Clays Ltd, St Ives plc

# C O N T E N T S

# PLACES
115

## MAPS

# INDEX
277

1   *Departments of France*

# KEY TO PRICES

| ROOMS | | MEALS | |
|---|---|---|---|
| A = | Under 100F | A = | Under 75F |
| B = | 100–150F | B = | 75–100F |
| C = | 150–250F | C = | 100–130F |
| D = | 250–350F | D = | 130–165F |
| E = | 350–450F | E = | 165–220F |
| F = | 450–550F | F = | 220–300F |
| G = | over 550F | G = | over 300F |

Room prices per night for double room without breakfast.
Meal prices include tax and service.

# INTRODUCTION

For centuries the Loire valley has been the playground of Parisians and the market garden of Paris. Its mild climate, well-watered meadows, flooded in winter, its wine slopes and its network of beautiful but moody rivers, all running into the majestic but capricious Loire, lured kings and courtiers to transport themselves there for months every year for their favourite sports of hunting, intrigue and adultery. From the time the English were finally thrown out in the fifteenth century until Louis XIV commanded the courtiers to stay in the discomfort of his beloved and hopelessly overcrowded Versailles, they not only moved to the Loire with their servants, retainers and remotest relatives, but many took their furniture and even their cooking utensils. To house them, they built the magnificent châteaux, so many of which have blessedly and miraculously survived. Unlike the castles of the Dordogne, which were built for war, the châteaux of the Loire were built mostly for pleasure and love, so there was little reason for warring kings and potentates to destroy them.

The most flamboyant of all French kings, François I, took so many people and so much baggage with him from Paris to the Loire each year that twelve thousand horses were used to carry them.

In time Parisian merchants and richer bourgeoisie took the place of the courtiers. The arrival of the motor car brought an invasion in summer of ordinary Parisian people on weekends and holidays, so that hotels and restaurants thrived. Parisians bought weekend cottages. Since the A10 motorway was built from Paris to Orléans and along the Loire Valley to Blois and Tours, Parisians drive to the Loire for a day's outing to see an historic château or for a bathe from one of the riverside beaches and a picnic. Orléans is only 130 kilometres from Paris, and Tours only 230 kilometres, so traffic can be formidable during

*Château de Chambord*

July and August and restaurants do better business than overnight hotels. But the great gîte movement has brought back
holidaymakers staying for a week or fortnight – especially visitors from the industrial cities of the north of France, from
Britain and from Belgium and Holland. Most of the gîtes are in
the comparatively unvisited farming villages to the north of the
Loire river, along its northern tributaries such as the Mayenne,
the Sarthe and that lovely little river the Loir without an 'e', and
into western Loire among the Muscadet vineyards. Others are in
the Sologne, the attractive but strangely melancholy flatland of
pools, heaths and forest stretching from south of Orléans to the
Cher and eastward to the wine hills of Sancerre. The central

Loire may be the fresh-air retreat of Paris but there are still secret places just away from the riverside tourist roads which are quiet, beautiful and a joy to discover.

The central Loire valley is blessed by gentle, kindly weather and through the ages invaders have coveted it. Winters are short and quite warm, spring arrives as early as March, bringing superb early vegetables and warm, gentle weather which, by July and August, can become very hot. May and early June are usually delightful. Once the early morning mists have cleared from the river valleys, autumn days can be comfortably warm, relaxing and calm. The western end of the river, Loire Atlantique, is different. Atlantic winds, which blow hard and sometimes very cold in winter, turn to gentle breezes which make even July and August refreshing.

Some years the rivers dwindle in summer to a narrow trickle, revealing a lazy landscape of riverside trees, beaches where children play and their elders sunbathe, and green islands that you can reach on foot. A French writer described the Loire in summer as 'wallowing in an oversized bed'. But beware – all the rivers in this central part of France – the Indre, Maine, Loire, Cher and Vienne – can play unpleasant tricks, with perverse currents around the islands. If you bathe, take advice where and when you do it.

If the Loire weather is gentle in spring, the rivers are not. As the snow melts in the Massif Central where the 1020-kilometre-long river Loire rises from a volcanic moll, Mont Gerbier-de-Jonc, the water can flood down in such torrents that trees are swept away, fields flooded and islands sunk so deep that only their tree-tops show above the savage water. In autumn rains, the rivers flood again, but without the intense rage of spring floods. Men have been fighting these waters since the Middle Ages and the fight was especially fierce when the people had to rely on the river for much of their transport. The Loire was notoriously badly off for roads, and people as well as goods had to take to boats, such as the flat-bottomed *chalands*, which had a sail and were steered by a pole, or the *coches d'eau*, which were rowed. Even royalty used these. Although the journey from Orléans to Nantes on the Atlantic Loire estuary took eight days and the return took a fortnight, it was often quicker, as well as safer and more comfortable, than going by springless coaches on the muddy, rutted roads.

Now roads from all parts of France meet at Tours, the hub of the Loire, and its bridges over the Loire and Cher are vital to the French road system. Armies that have been unable to cross the Loire have perished, even in 1940, when the French themselves were chased by the Germans, and 1944 when the Germans were chased by the Allies. Tours has long been chosen as a centre by tourists, for it is within easy reach of many of the most interesting and beautiful Loire châteaux. Amboise is the other convenient centre, for many of the châteaux lie east of here in the pretty wooded countryside between the Loire and the Cher. Château de Chenonceau, the loveliest of all, is on the river Cher, which flows south of Amboise and joins the Loire just west of Tours. Both Tours and Amboise are very attractive cities with beautiful old buildings, both are very busy and somewhat traffic-jammed. Both have very pleasant villages nearby where you can stay.

Tours has expanded industrially but industry has been carefully planned and is concentrated to the north near the A10 motorway to Orléans and Paris and to Bordeaux. The N152 north of the river is still lorry-ridden from Langeais to Amboise and often as far as Blois. In fact, from Langeais to Orléans, most of the best scenery is away from the river. It is southward towards the Cher and along the Loire west of Langeais on to Angers that you find the best river scenery. Westward it is attractive for long stretches both sides of the river. After Angers the small riverside roads on the south side are very attractive almost into Nantes. You find some of the nicest villages and most charming smaller châteaux northward from Angers along the Mayenne and Sarthe rivers, tributaries of the Loire. Few people know this almost secret area of pretty lanes, forests, and a web of pleasant rivers and streams, such as the Authion which follows the Loire for miles just to the north of it, the Cousnon which passes through the pleasant little town of Baugé where good King René d'Anjou's favourite little château is now the town hall, and the river Loir (with no e), which passes through as much attractive scenery as any river in France. La Flèche is built on its bank, and here is the château where France's favourite king, Henri IV, spent much of his time as a tiny boy. This is a land rich in likeable smaller châteaux and manor houses. There are still more than nine hundred of them in the area north of Angers around the Mayenne, Sarthe and Loir, some still lived in by their original families, others now hotels or guest houses. The Loire is rich in *Chambres d'hôtes* – private houses taking in bed and breakfast guests. Some offer dinner, too. Although a lot of hosts and hostesses speak English, not all do, and to enjoy staying you must be the sort of visitor who really likes mixing with strangers and following each twist and turn of French etiquette.

The country around the south bank of the Loire from Angers to Nantes is most attractive, and the river scenery, with a multitude of islands and pleasant villages, some still used by working fishermen, is the best on the river west of Orléans. Do take the D751 south of the river from Angers, along the Corniche Angevine, looking down on the vineyards of the river. Then you can follow the same delightful road almost into Nantes. It is a different world from the busy N23 and the A11 motorway along the north bank.

Eastward, I have finished this book at Sancerre and La Charité-sur-Loire on the border of Cher where it runs along the Loire's left bank and to the south-west at Bourges in Cher. The hilly, vineyard country of pretty roads and medieval villages west of Sancerre is so delightful that it is difficult to choose which of the small roads to take. I like to follow the D22 to Henrichemont then turn onto the D11 southward to Bourges or continue south-west on the D20 into the Forêt d'Allogny to the little town of that same name. Following the little white roads on the yellow Michelin map you can work your way through the Forêt de Vierzon and north-west to Nançay on D944, over the A71 motorway at Salbris into the mass of lakes and lagoons of the Sologne spreading all the way to Beaugency on the Loire, south-west of Orléans.

The rivers that feed the Loire are well worth exploring in their own right. The Cher rises in the north-west foothills of the Massif Central, quite near Aubusson and, except in spring floods, ambles quite gently on its 352-kilometre journey to the Loire, passing through Bourges and skirting the Sologne to join the Loire just after it has passed through Tours.

The Indre rises in the same foothills but north of Aubusson. It meanders slowly most of the year for 265 kilometres. Just before it reaches the Loire it turns away westward towards the sea for 16 kilometres, and this is one of its most attractive stretches as it washes the piles on which the beautiful Château of Azay-le-Rideau is built, then laps against meadows, orchards and woods to flow into the Loire near Neman. As it is gobbled up by the bigger, faster river, the waters are swallowed by the E.D.F Centrale Nucléaire, the first nuclear energy station in France, established in 1963 and still expanding. The French have no conscience about putting their nuclear plants in beauty spots.

The Vienne enters the Loire only 8 kilometres downstream. It rises south of Aubusson on the Milles Vaches plateau and travels much faster than the others on its 370-kilometre journey to the Loire. It is swollen by the waters of the Clain, which joins it at Châtellerault, and the Creuse, which joins it further downstream. The Creuse itself has already flowed for 255 kilometres, joined on the way by the waters of the river Gartempe which itself has flowed 181 kilometres. Yet in summer all this water often fades to a little narrow stream that can barely dampen the stone piles of the fine old bridge at Chinon.

The most eccentric and perhaps the most lovable river is le Loir, which could never be confused with la Loire except in conversation. It starts its 312-kilometre journey west of Chartres and winds and wiggles its way to Châteaudun and then through some beautiful stretches to Vendôme, then suddenly turns west through a series of large loops as if making for the Atlantic coast, pressing on through Château du Loir and La Lude to La Flèche and Durtal. Here it suddenly decides to wiggle southward towards Angers. But it never quite makes it. After two enormous loops, it collides with the Sarthe, an almost equally roving river. Just before the Sarthe gets to Angers, it runs into the Mayenne. That promptly runs into the Maine, an important river which is just 10 kilometres long, from Angers to the Loire.

The Mayenne and the Sarthe start in the hills south of Normandy and wander slowly, with many little rivers joining them, except in winter when they pour torrents into the Loire, creating the little isles and sandbanks that make the Loire so delightful up and downstream from Angers.

Of course, anyone seeing the Loire for the first time must not miss Chenonceau, a beautiful house with fascinating history; Azay-le-Rideau, which must have been heaven to live in; the ostentatious vastness of Chambord; the sumptuously furnished rooms of Cheverny; the charming and evocative old city of Amboise and, if possible, the Parc Floral at Orléans. I must have walked round Chenonceau at least eight times. Don't try to 'collect' châteaux. A few seen properly are more rewarding. And do find out a little of their history. People built the châteaux, loved, lived and died in them. The architecture is just their expression of life. You become addicted to the Loire. People go back year after year. There is always more and more to discover.

You will find true connoisseurs on the little roads near the lesser rivers, looking for interesting villages and minor châteaux and manor houses. There are plenty.

## HOW TO GET THERE

### ROAD

Motorway route from Channel ports is by A26 from Calais (from Boulogne join near St Omer) or A25 from Dunkerque to join A21 to Paris. Join A10 SW from Paris to Orléans, Blois, Tours. Or switch from A10 to A11 through Le Mans to Angers and Nantes. At Orléans, you can switch from A10 to A71 to Lamotte-Beuvron, Vierzon and Bourges.

### RAIL

Motorail car-carrying train Boulogne–Nantes – early July to early September.
London to Tours (via Paris) by ferry or Hoverspeed Hovercraft or Seacat via Calais or Boulogne Hoverspeed hovercraft via Boulogne.
TGV fast train Paris–Tours takes seventy minutes.

## AIR

Air France–Rail tickets take you Heathrow–Paris by air, then Paris–Tours by train.
Air France Heathrow–Nantes.
TAT Stansted–Tours (seasonal).

## FOOD

The fertile soil swept down by the Loire floods and warm early springs bring superb vegetables and fruit to the Loire a fortnight to a month earlier than further north, and so the Loire valley remains one of the chief suppliers to Paris, as it has been for centuries.

Since medieval times the Loire has been known for its game, poultry and fruit, and the excellent hunting helped to lure the French Court to spend summer in the valley and to build the superb châteaux. Few vegetables were eaten in medieval times, and when peasants were said to be reduced to eating grass, they were eating wild green vegetables.

Though rivers were rich in salmon, pike, carp, sandre, crayfish and little eels (*anguilles*), they were eaten mostly by the peasants except on Fridays, when the rich thought that they were fasting by eating fish instead of meat. Fish-eating became more fashionable in the reign of the hunting addict François I. A favourite dish was *chaudemer* – fish grilled, then stewed in wine, an ancestor of *matelote*. Catherine de' Medici, thinking ill of French cooking, brought her own chefs from Italy, with new recipes and above all new vegetables to grow. Among them were artichokes and what we now call French beans and the Americans call string beans.

Catherine also brought the famous Florentine pastry cooks, and the great French gâteaux were born. In rue Denis Papin in Blois you will see cakes which are works of art and beautiful chocolate concoctions, too, for Blois is famed for its chocolatiers. Le Mans produces superb gâteaux.

Market gardens of the Loire still grow some of Europe's most superb vegetables. Lettuce is particularly splendid. It is grown covered for eating from March, in the open from April to autumn, in several varieties – the round batavia, cabbage lettuces, iceberg and curly. Loiret (around Orléans) is France's biggest producer of cucumbers. Loir-et-Cher (around Blois) is the second biggest area for growing asparagus. It is also grown around Angers and Saumur. The season is April to June, and they grow mostly the big white asparagus, which is served with hollandaise sauce or just with melted butter (*beurre fondu*), or cold with vinaigrette. The asparagus from Candes, where the

Vienne meets the Loire north-west of Chinon, is claimed to be the best in France. The Loire is by far the most important area in France for producing radishes and celery. Tours has a famed *celeri violet*. Leeks are grown all the year, including a large winter variety called Malabare. Artichokes, cabbages, carrots, cauliflowers, fennel, courgettes, shallots, turnips (*navet*) and large Marmande tomatoes are all grown extensively, so are beans, including French beans and broad beans (*fèves*), which are either served very young or, when bigger, stripped of their tougher outer skin, which changes their taste and makes them tender. They are superb dressed with butter and cream after cooking (*mougettes*). Very young *fèves* are sometimes served raw and salted with aperitifs. Touraine leeks stewed in butter with a béchamel sauce added are used as sauce for chicken.

There is very little salmon left in Loire valley rivers but the lakes and streams of the Sologne, as well as the rivers, are rich in pike (*brochet*), perch (*perche*), delicate *sandre* (a sort of pike-perch), gudgeon (*goujon*), shad (*alose*), tench (*tanche*), little eels (*anguilles*) and freshwater crayfish (*écrevisses*). Shad arrives in early spring and is often stuffed with sorrel (*oseille*) and baked. *Friture*, a mixed fry of freshwater fish, is very popular – usually of perch, tench and gudgeon. But the classic way of serving fish, which has spread all over France, is in *beurre blanc*, claimed to have originated in Nantes. It is butter whisked into white wine with chopped shallots. *Carpe à la Chambord* is carp cooked in red wine. It's nicer with salmon. Eels are cooked in red wine with prunes, onions and mushrooms to make *bouilliture*. *Quenelles de brochet* are pike-flavoured tiny mousse – delicate and tasty.

Champignons de Paris are grown in the Loire valley. Until the last century they were grown in the caves under what is now the suburbs of Paris. They were moved to the Loire's riverside caves and the quarries dug out for stone to build the châteaux. There has been a small Loire mushroom industry since the seventeenth century. Caves unsuitable for maturing wine are used. The quarries at Chênehutte-les-Tuffeaux, west of Saumur, dug out for tufa stone, produce some of the best mushrooms.

Poultry is excellent. Bourges is a big centre. Nantes duck are famous. *Poulet Locheoise* from the delightful town of Loches is delicious – chicken with onion, brandy and thick cream sauce. Another excellent dish is *poulet aux chipolatas* – chicken stuffed with small smoked sausages. The first incubator for rearing chickens was used in Amboise in 1496.

The pastures of the Touraine are very rich and produce excellent veal and beef from the fields. Veal from the Saumur areas is good. Pork is used extensively. Amboise hams are excellent. But the pride of the area is the pork charcuterie called *rillettes*. It is made of fairly fatty pork cooked for many hours with salt, then shredded. I love it spread on toast. My friend Glyn Christian thinks that it tastes of overboiled , underseasoned meat. *Rillettes de lapin* – rabbit *rillettes* – is preferred by most gourmets, but not by me. But I *do* like *rille d'oie* – the same thing made with goose. Tours is renowned for *rillettes*. Le Mans, Blois and Saumur believe that theirs are even better. *Quiche Tourangelle* is *rillettes* in an open tart. *Rillons* are very different. Sometimes called *grillons*, they are pieces of pork fried until their fat has melted and they are crisp. They are good with aperitifs.

For centuries the Orléans area has been known for pâtés and terrines, mostly from game. So has the Sologne, which once supplied the tables of France with game. It still has the best winged game in France and excellent deer and wild boar. Duck, hare, partridge and quail abound in season and hare pâté is a Sologne speciality. Much of the boar is now produced domestically on farms and you can find plenty of boar (*sanglier*) pâté. You will often find pheasant casserole (*fasison en barbouille*) but less often *chevreuil poivrade* (venison cutlets marinaded in vinegar, with pepper sauce) because it takes five hours to prepare and cook. Chitterling sausages (*andouille* and *andouillettes*), once a peasant dish but now fashionable with French food and restaurant guide writers, but not with me, are a speciality of Tours. Le Mans in Sarthe, where you can eat very well, is proud of its *boudin blanc*, the white version of black pudding, made with chicken, onions, eggs, fat, herbs and spices. Le Mans is known, too, for *poulet gris* – chickens fed on wheat and milk. Nantes produces *saucisses au Muscadet* – pork sausages with Muscadet wine added, and *lard Nantais* – pork chops served with a fry of pork rinds, pieces of pork and lungs chopped in fine pieces, which is much nicer than it sounds.

The whole region is rightly proud of its fruit. Le Mans has even survived the French national obsession with Golden Delicious apples, imported from America, and still grows successfully its famous Reinettes (little queens), for long a rival to the British Cox's. Reinette d'Orléans are splendid, too, and do try if you get the chance Reine de Reinette. An expert from the great Angers fruit market told me that these came originally from Britain.

The Loire's greatest contribution to French national cooking is an apple tart produced in the Sologne town of Lamotte-Beuvron. In their little inn, the Tatin sisters, making an apple-pie (or upside down apple tart) accidentally allowed the sugar to caramelize, and there was born the tarte Tatin which appears on menus everywhere from Dunkerque to Perpignan, the Alps and Cannes. It must be made from firm eating apples and served fresh – *not* heated up. I complained for years that there was no mention of the Tatin auberge in Michelin. It has made it now – in the 1991 edition. You will find it opposite the station, and it looks smart these days.

There are plenty of peaches and melons in season, excellent pears and plums. The great philanthropist St François de St Paul is said to have created the Bon Chrétien plum five hundred years ago in Touraine, but you will now find more in Australia than France. You will still find plenty of Comice pears, developed in the Comice horticultural gardens in Angers around 1849. William pears appear from early August until the end of September, and you will be able to buy the huge Louise-Bonne pears, named after an unknown lady in Poitou.

The famous greengages, Reine Claude, were named after François I's wife.

The Loire and Cher valleys and the Sologne grow strawberries for the Paris market. They are sold from April to early August, and Angers, Saumur and Romorantin in Sologne are important centres.

Tours makes prunes from damsons (*damas* in French because the plums came originally from Damascus) and claims that they are the best in the world. Gros damas de Tours are certainly the best I have tasted. They should, of course, be soaked overnight in white Touraine wine! Long before the nouvelle cuisine popularized temporarily the serving of fruit with most meats, prunes were served with pork in France. *Noisette de porc aux pruneaux* is big pork chops simmered with prunes which have been soaked overnight in white (or sometimes red) wine and served with a sauce of the juices and cream.

Angers produces a variety of cherry called Guigne from which is made a liqueur called Guignolet.

Orléans's wine vinegar is much praised in Paris. So is its mustard.

In the 1920s and 1930s a man named Maurice Sailland, who called himself Curnonsky, was called the Prince of Gastronomes. His main book, *La France Gastronomique*, ran to thirty-two volumes. He taught the French that the complicated Grande Cuisine was not the only great cooking. The simpler Cuisine Bourgeoise and Cuisine Régionale had their joys, too. He was especially impressed by Loire cooking: 'It is a cuisine of chefs and its preparation requires time, patience and a little genius. Nothing replaces butter and things are in their natural state.'

Especially he praised Anjou (around Angers): 'The cooking is forthright, reasonable, good-natured and does not strive for effects. Anjou is the Paradise of easy digestion.'

But perhaps he was prejudiced. He was born and brought up in Angers!

## CHEESES

Although they cannot compare with Normandy in number and variety, Loire cheeses are good and some excellent, especially goats' cheese. Many you will find only at markets. You will also find on market stalls and in shops many superb cheeses from Poitou, which is just to the south, and is one of the greatest goats' cheese areas of France.

*Chabichou* (Poitou) is a strong, sharp, cone-shaped goats' milk cheese, made by farms and dairies.

*Chabris* is a type of Valençay (see below).

*Chavignol-Sancerre* is a small disc of mild goats' cheese which becomes crottin when old and dark-coloured (see *Crottin de Chavignol* below).

*Chouzé* is made by dairies in Touraine – heavily crusted.

*Crémet d'Anjou*, formerly made with goats' milk, now with cows', is a mild, creamy cheese used for making a dessert served with fruit and cream. Drain 250 grammes of cheese, whisk in 100 millilitres of thick cream until smooth, beat in 60 grammes of fine sugar, whip three egg whites with salt until stiff, fold into mixture. Hang to drip in muslin in a refrigerator for twenty-four hours. Cottage cheese can be used but is not so good. Crémet Nantais is similar.

*Crézancy-Sancerre* is a mild goats' milk cheese from farms around Crézancy and Sancerre.

*Crottin de Chavignol* has been made by farmers of Sancerre area since the sixteenth century; now, like Sancerre wine, it is protected by an official AOC (appellation contrôlée) to discourage imitations. Made from full-cream goats' milk, white at first, but goes dry, with a dark-brown rind, and achieves a slightly rancid taste with a powerful smell. *Crottin* means goats' dung! A gourmet's delight, but not everyone's. When young it is superb grilled or fried as a starter or savoury.

*Entrammes* is an unpasteurized cows' milk cheese rather like St Paulin, with an ochre rind and almost-white centre, made in the monastery of Port-du-Salut in the Mayenne valley south of Laval where the monks first made Port Salut. They sold the Port Salut formula and it is now made in a factory.

*Frinault* is an Orléans cows' milk cheese, strong, in small discs; sometimes matured in wood ash.

*Fromage Fort de Berry* is a strained cheese, dried, mixed with garlic, finely chopped herbs and dry white wine, then fermented in a closed vessel for several weeks. Often eaten with shallots.

*Gien* is a super cheese with a lovely nutty taste, made only on farms in the Gien area, either from goats' milk or goats' and cows' milk mixed, and dried in leaves of plane trees or in ashes. It is eaten from the end of spring to autumn and is not easy to get far from Gien.

*Graçay* is a goats' cheese from the Arnon valley in Berry in the shape of a truncated cone. It is dusted with charcoal dust and looks dark blue.

*Laval* is a cows' milk cheese made by Trappist monks at Laval

Monastery in Mayenne. Little holes and a pleasant sharp taste.

*Levroux*, from Châteauroux-Valençay area, was traditionally made by farmers from goats' milk but is now also made in factories from goats' and cows' milk mixed. The best has a satisfying nutty, savoury flavour. Rather like Valençay.

*Ligueil and Loches* are commercial variations of Ste Maure goats' cheese (see below). From Touraine.

*Montoire* is a nice fruity goats' milk cheese in cone shape. Also called Troo.

*Olivet bleu* is a super blue cheese made from cows' milk, matured in Olivet chalk caves. Mouth-filling flavour.

*Olivet cendré* is a firm supple cows' milk cheese made in farms and small dairies. Coned and coated with ashes. Very pleasant, interesting flavour, fairly low fat.

*Pannes cendré* is a very low fat cheese of the Orléanais, made of skimmed cows' milk, cured for three months in wood ash, giving it a strong flavour. Very palatable. Seen mainly in latish summer and autumn.

*Patay* comes from the village where Joan of Arc thrashed the English in 1429. Softish, eaten fresh in early spring, cured in ashes in summer and autumn.

*St Benoist*, from St Benôit-sur-Loire, is made on farms from partly skimmed cows' milk. Lovely fruity flavour.

*Ste Maure* – the *Fermier* version made on farms has straw running through it, a goat smell, very strong flavour and is a gourmet's joy. It spends a month in caves. *Laitier*, factory produced, is sometimes called Chèvre Long to distinguish it from the real thing. Verneuil makes it well. Pleasant but not the same.

*St Cyr* (Poitou) is a good industrially produced goats' cheese.

*Santranges* is the biggest of Sancerre-style cheeses. Tangy goats' milk produced on farms around Santranges in Berry.

*Selles-sur-Cher* is another goats' milk cheese protected by an appellation contrôlée. Manufactured originally in the Sologne and still called sometimes Romorantin. Unbroken curds, lightly renneted, are put in moulds, salted, coated with ash and left to mature in caves for about three weeks. At its best from late spring to autumn.

*Valençay*, made on farms around the Loire and also in factories, is a goats' milk cheese, dusted with charcoal, kept five to six weeks; at its best in spring to autumn, though kept in crocks in winter. The *Laitier* (factory) version is made all the year, by using deep-frozen curds and powdered milk. It smells stronger and to me is rather sour and sharp.

*Vendôme bleu* from around Vendôme. Soft 'paste' cheese with natural blue rind. Dry-matured in tuffeau caves for a month. Farmers' version is becoming scarce.

*Vendôme cendré* is a fatty, mouth-filling and satisfying cheese matured in ash, eaten summer and autumn into winter.

*Villebaron* is a disc of soft cheese on plane-tree leaves from the Blois region, summer and autumn.

*Villiers-sur-Loire*, is an ash-matured, delicate cheese from Orléanais, wrapped in a vine leaf.

## WINE

The flowery white wines of the Loire have justifiably been popular for centuries, especially in Paris. Vouvray alone can make wines of a delicacy and finesse unmatched in France from the Chenin Blanc grape, which can produce some sharp, acidy wines in other places. The best makers of Sancerre and Pouilly produce fruity, slightly smoky wines with a delightful and long-lasting flavour rarely equalled in wines from the Sauvignon grapes grown elsewhere.

The red wines of the Loire have had a more up-and-down history, and have not been helped by Paris fashions, like the recent belief that almost all red wine should be light and drunk young and acidic to go with nouvelle cuisine.

There was such a mad rush by Parisian 'modern cooking' enthusiasts for red Sancerre quite recently that it was almost unobtainable, for it is made with the Pinot Noir grape only in good years. The grape is grown here to make rosé and only on soil that cannot grow the Sauvignon for making white. Furthermore, young Parisians were drinking the red young and cold. It tastes really raw that way. Any grower around Dijon or Beaune will tell you that you cannot make Pinot Noir reds for drinking very young. But they *are* producing reds for drinking young

*Old-fashioned wine press*

now in Chinon using the Gamay grape, from which Beaujolais is made.

Pouilly-Fumé of the Loire is totally different from Pouilly-Fuissé from Mâcon. The Loire wine is made from Sauvignon grapes, Fuissé is made from Chardonnay, the classic Burgundy white grape. Both whites, Pouilly-Fumé and Sancerre, which is a

little fruitier, have become very popular and much dearer.
Pouilly-sur-Loire does produce a cheaper light wine from the
Chasselas grape which is much sharper, but palatable. Two of
the very best Sancerre are produced by Guy Paget and the
Blondelet family. For years we drank the dry white wine of
Quincy, west of Bourges, as a cheaper substitute for Sancerre –
softer, aromatic, fruity but not quite so smooth. Now Quincy
itself is so popular that it can cost more than Sancerre or Blanc
Fumé. White Reuilly is not so smooth but very aromatic and is
still cheaper.

But the Sauvignon grape has spread along the Loire to
Tours, and Touraine Sauvignon dry white wines are spreading
around Europe. They are fairly cheap, and good value, but do
vary greatly. Demi-sec (semi-sweet) and sweet wines are made,
too, in Touraine and also wines from the major white grape of
the Loire, Chenin Blanc (usually known here as Pineau de la
Loire). Touraine-Amboise and Touraine-Mesland white wines
are stronger than the others and have more personality. They
also age better. Touraine-Azay-le-Rideau, that pleasant little
town on the Indre river with one of the loveliest and most
interesting châteaux in Europe, produces white wine that is
fruity but non-acidic, and rosé made mostly from Groslot, the
Loire grapes used for that charming, popular, slightly sweet
Anjou rosé. Both Azay wines are scarce, but do try to get a bottle
or two. Gaston Pavy makes a good white.

Anjou vineyards fan out from Angers along the Loire
towards the Muscadet country and eastward along the south
bank to beyond Saumur, where they make dry and sweet white
wines and some red which is light in colour, low in alcohol, fruity
and pleasant. Saumur's semi-sweet whites have a touch of Vouvray's honey bouquet and crisp fruity flavour and go well with
fish and with pork.

Saumur was the first area outside Champagne to make
sparkling wines by the Champagne method. The secret was
brought there by an Alsatian called Ackerman in 1811. Though
made with a completely different grape from Champagne
(Chenin Blanc) it is very pleasant – one of the better sparklers.
Nearby dry and semi-sweet wines from the steep north bank
slopes of Savennières are very scarce but outstanding, especially

if kept about four years. Delicate, aromatic and fruity, they are perfect with chicken.

If you like sweet wines for elevenses, or to drink with rich pâtés or desserts, try wines of Coteaux du Layon from the Layon river south of Angers. Drink them cold but not iced or you may lose their honey bouquet and rich flavour.

Vouvray wines are a joy. Many of the families have been making wines there for centuries and still keep them in the same cellars cut into the chalky hillside which are so convenient. When the great vintage of 1985 was bottled and deserved to be kept from five to ten years or more, I found Daniel Jarry solving the problem by cutting deeper into the chalk hillside to make his caves longer! The French are so rightly proud of their fast TGV trains that new routes are almost sacrosanct. No one can get them moved here, there and everywhere as happens to British Rail. That is, they couldn't until French Rail tried to run a line near to those Vouvray caves. The progressive time-savers and the traditional wine-lovers met in fierce verbal combat – and the wine-lovers won. How could a good Frenchman shake up and ruin wines that would keep for thirty years just to save a few minutes on a journey? The sweeter wines of Vouvray *will* keep thirty to forty years, and the best will certainly keep for sixty years. I have tasted one. They become as luscious as the finest Sauternes, with the Vouvray bouquet of heavenly honey. The old *moelleux* (sweet) wines of Gaston Huet have been described as 'like having a bouquet of flowers in your mouth'. But it is the demi-sec wines by which most people know Vouvray and they, too, are a delight at their best. I have tasted Jarry's demi-sec from the 1960s and 1970s and they are magnificent now. So is his 1985, but it will keep and improve much longer. Already it has a lovely mixture of fruit and nectar and a long-lasting flavour. Vouvray demi-sec wines can be drunk young but it seems a waste when they age beautifully. You can also keep the dry wines which have a clean fruit flavour to follow their smell of honeysuckle on a warm summer's evening.

Vouvray Mousseux, the sparkling wine made by the Champagne method, is mostly dry or demi-sec and is a very pleasant wine. A very good one is now produced by the house of Marc Brédif of Rochecorbon, who are *éleveurs*, buying wine to blend, bottle and mature. You can tour their cellars at 87 quai de la Loire, Rochecorbon, on N152 just outside Tours (Monday–Friday, 10.30 a.m. or 4 p.m.). Vintages in their caves date back to the last century. Wine presses and bottles are older, for the company was formed in 1550. It was bought in 1980 by Patrick Ladoucette, producer of Pouilly-Fumé.

Wines of Montlouis, over the Loire, were passed off as Vouvray until 1938, then were regarded as inferior and drunk young. They had less taste or character. Now they have improved, and although the dry and demi-sec do not become so luscious as Vouvray with age, the very good sweet wine is soft with a delightful lemon and honeysuckle taste. Caves line the N751 riverside road and offer tastings.

Muscadet wine from the western Loire is in a world of its own. It is named after the grape from which it is made and which wandered here from Burgundy, where it was called Melon de Bourgogne and is no longer grown. It is almost everybody's idea of a dry white wine, harvested early to keep fresh and fruity, dry but not acidic, very pale, and a definite character. Once, it was rather despised by wine snobs, and many still think that it is fit only to drink with shellfish. But the world doesn't. It has become so popular that nearly ninety million bottles were produced last year, and it is catching the world's favourite, Beaujolais. It has become a very popular aperitif, and is drunk with hors d'oeuvres, fish and white meats. Try it with fresh, sharpish cheeses, especially goats' cheese.

Muscadet should be light, fresh, bone dry and drunk young. The trouble is that some is being sold too young – *pétillant* (slightly bubbling with fermentation) and not having reached its full fruit. Good Sèvre-et-Maine Muscadets from Vallet and Clisson improve with a little age – at least two years, up to four years – and their flavour lasts much longer. Some people now drinking it don't really like its acidity and to please them some makers are producing dull and bland wines – called 'collapsed' or 'over the top'. It is well worth paying a little more for a good wine. Try Château Galissonnière from the family of the French admiral who managed to escape a battle with Admiral Byng during the British siege of Menorca in 1745 causing poor Byng to be shot for failing to engage the enemy and Voltaire to say that in England it is necessary to shoot an admiral from time to time '*pour encourager les autres*'. The neighbouring domaines of Château Jannière and Maisonnière produce excellent Muscadet – vital, lively, flowery; so do the Sauvion family at Château de Cléray, which once belonged to the comtes de Malestroit. The present Count, a writer, lives the other side of Vallet in the elegant Palladian-style Château Noë de Bel Air. The family have made good wine there since 1741. Muscadet-sur-lie means that it had been matured on its lees (99 per cent dead yeast) until bottled, which must take place before 30th June of the year after fermentation. This gives it much more flavour.

Gros Plant wine is made in the Muscadet country from a grape of the same name. In good years when the grapes ripen well it is light, dry and fruity and some Frenchmen prefer it to Muscadet with shellfish. In many years it is tart and acidic.

Cabernet-Sauvignon and Cabernet Franc (on which many Bordeaux reds are based) are the main grapes used for red wine in the Loire, with wines for earlier drinking made from Gamay, the Beaujolais grape.

Touraine Gamay reds are not as good as most Beaujolais, being more acidic and less fruity. Mesland, one of the villages allowed to add its name to the appellation Touraine, produces one of the better Gamay wines – fruitier than Touraine-Amboise. But the best Loire Gamay is made at Chinon. The fashion in Paris is to drink it young and lightly iced with light 'modern' dishes. With Bourgueil and perhaps Saumur-Champigny, Chinon produces the best red wine of the Loire, which befits a charming little town that also produced Rabelais. Champigny makes its red from Cabernet Franc. Chinon makes wines from both Cabernet Franc and from Cabernet Sauvignon, and Bourgueil does the same but also blends the two very successfully.

Bourgueil has two different soils, producing different styles of wine – one light and fruity with a lovely smell of raspberries, the other heavier and needing time to mature. When the two are blended you get a deep ruby-coloured wine, though almost violet when new. It can be kept for ten years or more and matures superbly – clean, no tannin taste but enough acid to save it from collapsing. Some years back it was blended into good Médoc wine. Paris fashion put up prices a few years ago, but now it is very good value again. St Nicolas-de-Bourgueil produces some Bourgueil to be drunk young and iced.

Chinon has improved greatly and is not only fashionable but much loved by real winesmen. The Cabernet Franc wines are clean and fruity with the flowery smell that salesmen call *violets*. They are smooth, ruby-coloured and dearer than most Loire wines. Drink them young at cellar temperature, but better after five years at room temperature. A real taste of the Loire.

### WINE TASTING

In many wine areas, such as Vouvray and Montlouis, you will see many *Dégustation* signs. These tastings are free, but you cannot blame the wine producers if they hope that the tasters are real wine drinkers, willing to buy a bottle or two. Here are some rewarding places to taste. Most are shut 12–2 p.m. for lunch.

### POUILLY-SUR-LOIRE

*Caves de Pouilly*, Le Moulin à Vent, 9 ave de la Tuilerie – an old road through the village. Fumé, plus reds from Gien and Cosne.

### SANCERRE

*Henri Bourgeois*, Chavignol, 2km W of Sancerre. White and red. Famous old vineyards.

### QUINCY

*Raymond Pipet*, Quincy. From N76 Bourges–Vierzon road, turn W at Mehun on D20.

### REUILLY

*Claude Lafond*, Le Bois St Denis. Good young grower. White Sauvignon, red Pinot Noir.

### TOURAINE

*J. P. Monmousseau*, route de Vierzon, Montrichard. Big modern caves on road out of Montrichard to St Aignan. Cellar tours possible (telephone 54.32.07.04). Owned by Taittinger.

*J. C. Poupault*, 1 rue La Loire, Chargé. Cave in rock on D751 NE of Amboise towards Chaumont.

*Château du Petit-Thouars*, St Germain-sur-Vienne. Take D751 W from Chinon along south bank of Vienne river for 10 kilometres. Château of Comte du Petit-Thouars marked on yellow Michelin. Red Touraine wine.

### VOUVRAY AND MONTLOUIS

*Marc Brédif*, 87 quai de la Loire, Rochecorbon. From Tours follow N152 under motorway. Rochecorbon is 3km further on left. Brédif is on Vouvray road. Open 10.30 a.m.–4 p.m. weekdays.

*Daniel Jarry*, la Caillerie, route Vallée Coquette. After N152 going E dips under motorway at Tours, drive on for 6km looking for small road on left marked 'Vallée Coquette'. Jarry is 1000 metres along it. My favourite Loire white.

*Cave Co-operative*, Montlouis. On corner of D751 and D40 road to Chenonceaux, just after passing Montlouis on way to Amboise.

### CHINON, SAUMUR, BOURGUEIL

*Château de Ligré*, Ligré. Take D749 across river at Chinon, follow E 9km towards Richelieu. Turn right on D26 for 2km, then left for château. Great Chinon wines. Shut Sundays.

*Gratien et Meyer*. On D947, south bank of Loire, 3km E of Saumur on Chinon road. Highly organized. English-speaking guides. Sparkling Saumur.

*Maison Audebert*, ave Jean Causeret, Bourgeil. English spoken. Good Bourgueil red, plus Chinon and Saumur wines.

### MUSCADET

*La Galissonnière* (Pierre Lusseaud), le Pallet. Take N149 NW from Clisson for 7km or D116 from just south of Vallet for 6km.

*Guilbaud Frères*, Mouzillon. On D763, 4km S of Vallet. Very good wine.

## HISTORY

For centuries, the Loire was centre-stage for European history. Even in the New Stone Age (20,000 to 2000 BC) it was a major centre for exporting tools and weapons. Mined in yellow clods, the flint was easily split into sharp blades which were carved and polished, then exported all over Europe and North Africa. You can see a superb collection of these instruments of war and peace – flint tools , daggers, arrowheads and hand axes, in a Museum of Pre-history in the tiny market town of Le Grand-Pressigny, where the two small Loire tributaries, the Claise and Aigronne, meet, 48 kilometres south of Tours.

Until flint tools were produced, the people of the Loire had been fishermen and huntsmen using deer antlers as harpoons. Then settlers who came from the Danube basin via Provence introduced domesticated animals. They raised sheep, cattle, pigs and goats.

With the Bronze Age, trade started with faraway people. The Phoenicians from what is now Lebanon and from their big colony of Carthage in what is now Tunisia led the great new international trade drive and came up the Loire to trade for copper, which was mined near Bourges and at Azay-le-Rideau. Loire craftsmen travelled all round Europe.

The big, blond Celtic tribes then arrived – a warrior race, difficult to control. Their leading tribe, the Carnutes, were soon controlling the Loire valley, showing their importance by wielding highly decorated shields and throwing insults at the Roman legions of Julius Caesar, which were moving north to conquer Gaul. They attacked Orléans (Genabum) and Caesar himself had to return to put down their rebellion. But the Loire began to prosper under Roman law as domestic agriculture became safe from wandering tribes and Roman roads linked communities. The great highway between Paris (Lutetia) and Orléans was a vital link. But the rivers were the main highways for moving goods. Bridges were built over them and towns grew up alongside the bridges. Caesar made the Loire the boundary between Aquitainia in the south and Lugdunensis in the north, and it stayed that way for three hundred years.

The Christian evangelists came in the third century – St Maurice, St Gatien and St Martin, the Roman army officer who is said to have split his military cloak in two to give half to a beggar and deserted. He became a hermit in the chalk caves of Marmoutier near Tours until he was elected Bishop of Tours and built Marmoutier Abbey in 372. But Christianity was confined to towns, and when the Romans went, they left the fertile valley in the hands of Romanized Gauls and a prey to the tribes of Germany and Asia. Attila the Hun was beaten at Orléans by Bishop St Aignan in AD 451. But the Frankish tribes, who had come across the Rhine as mercenaries to the Gallo-Romans to help them defeat other invaders, turned on the Gauls, beat them, and took over the valley. The strongest Frankish tribe was the Salians, named Merovingians after their leader Merovius. His grandson Clovis, who became leader at the age of fifteen, defeated the Gallo-Romans at Soissons, and made Orléans his capital. Clovis, cynical and cruel, had married a Christian Catholic, Clotilda, who was very strongwilled and persuaded him to become a Christian. This suited him because the Roman Christian Church was becoming powerful and was a good ally. He has been aptly described by André Maurois in his *History of France* as 'a royal gangster who did his country a great service'.

The south of France had been taken over, after the Romans left, by Germanic Visigoths from north Italy, with their capital in Toulouse. Clovis halted his advance at the Loire at Amboise because the Visigoths, under Alaric, were on the other side. The two kings met in the centre of the river on the Île St Jean (Île d'Or) which you can see under the bridge at Amboise – a swimming beach. They feasted and swore eternal friendship, then built earth mounds (*donges*) to mark the frontier. But soon Clovis attacked the Visigoths near Poitiers, killed his 'eternal friend' Alaric, and drove the Visigoths almost to the Pyrenees. His lands, still ruled from Orléans, were almost as extensive as modern France and soon Gaul was being called France – land of the Franks.

The Merovingian kings ruled for three hundred years, longer than the Valois or the Bourbons. But family quarrels, murder by kings of their wives and sons, debauchery and decadence led to weak rule and frightful savagery. The royal concubines fought and murdered each other to come the official queen. Even the 'good King Dagobert' who ruled from 628 to

639, died at the age of thirty-four of old age, exhausted by his numerous wives and concubines. But the most brutal story of the Orléans court was of the beautiful servant girl Fredegunde, who tempted the king to marry her, strangled her rivals and hounded their children. Her greatest enemy was her sister-in-law Brunhilde, daughter of the Spanish Visigoth king. They feuded for thirty years. Brunhilde managed to outlive Fredegunde, but Fredegunde's son, King Clotaire II, captured her, had the old woman tied to the tail of a horse and torn to pieces by its angry hoofs. At least it provided us with a classic opera!

The most dangerous invasion came from the south. The Moors had captured most of Spain and moved over the Pyrenees into Languedoc, crept up the Rhône valley as far as Autun and reached Poitiers on their way to Orléans. But in 732 Charles Martel crushed them at Poitiers and although they still made sorties into the south they never reached the Loire. Charles' son, Pepin the Short, shut the last Merovingian king in a castle and got his friend St Boniface, a missionary from England, to persuade the Pope to crown him king. The Pope needed Pepin's army to help him fight invaders. That was the end of Orléans as capital of France. In fact, Pepin's wife, Bertha Broadfoot, set up the court for a while at Laon, north of Paris. Their child was Charlemagne, who spread his rule over France, Germany and Italy and was crowned Emperor of the West.

Under Charlemagne, who ruled from 768 to 814, churches and abbeys were built in the Loire and literature and learning flourished. Much was due to the influence of a Yorkshireman, Alcuin, born at York and later headmaster of the cloister school of York cathedral. Alcuin was called to Rome to fetch the pallium of the new Archbishop of York. Charlemagne met him in Parma and was so impressed by his learning that he asked him to be teacher to the Emperor's whole family, from children to Charlemagne himself. Nobles sent their sons to him and pupils came from far and wide. Finally he became tired and dreamed of retiring to an abbey. So Charlemagne made him abbot of the Benedictine monastery and school at Cormery, near Tours, and when he died in 804 it was the most influential place of learning in Europe, spreading culture which influenced the next one hundred years. He advanced human knowledge particularly by his 'scriptorium' where monks were taught to copy books.

The setback to the flowering of knowledge promoted by Alcuin came when the Norsemen sailed up the Loire to loot, rape, kill and destroy. They came each spring and returned to the north before winter with their booty and women as slaves, leaving behind dead men and burned towns, villages and churches, from Nantes to Orléans. The rich abbeys with their treasures were their favourite prey. They looted the treasure of St Martin from Marmoutier and killed a hundred monks. They stayed at Angers for six years and used it as a base to raid the whole valley, almost destroying, among other buildings, the abbey of St Benoît where St Benedict's bones lay.

Charlemagne's Empire had been divided among his sons after his death, as was customary, and they fought among themselves, as was also customary, so that soon the power was in the hands of feudal counts who had been Charlemagne's representatives. These ambitious, warlike men put up the only effective resistance to the invading Norsemen, particularly the Counts of Tours and Blois. The feudal lords warred among themselves, too, building forts and castles in the Loire valley to defend their territories. The fight between the Counts of Anjou and Blois in the tenth and eleventh centuries gradually became mixed up with the history of England and the whole of what is now France.

A particularly brilliant but greedy and violent man, Foulques Nerra or Foulques the Black, ruled Anjou from 987 to 1040 and spent the time fighting the counts of Blois. Blois lands separated his own and he was expected to pay tolls for anything passing through. He chose to fight his way through. His special enemy was a Count of Blois called Thibault le Tricheur – the Trickster. Foulques built a lot of castles and donjons (forts). But like so many medieval thugs he was deeply religious. Almost certainly they feared hell-fire. In moments of repentance he gave wealth to churches, he built abbeys, and he made three pilgrimages to Jerusalem. Eudes, Count of Blois, ravaged his lands while he was on a pilgrimage, which made Foulques very angry indeed and he set about even more destruction.

In the next century, the eleventh, changes started in the

Loire that revolutionized life and the landscape. Farmers started to clear the forests, plough the heathland, and improve the land. The clearing continued for three centuries, turning the land into the garden of France and the larder of Paris. Landowners became wealthier. The land supported more people.

Then Count Geoffroy V of Anjou made a marriage which gained him most of Normandy. Geoffroy wore a sprig of broom in his hat (*plante de genêt*) and was called *le bel Plantagenêt*. In 1128 he married Matilda, granddaughter of William the Conqueror and daughter of Henry I of England. The rival Duke of Blois had married the daughter of William the Conqueror and sister of Henry I, and they had a son, Stephen.

When Henry I died in 1135, Stephen and Matilda claimed the English throne. The English lords backed Stephen, so the Counts of Blois now ruled Blois, Champagne and England.

Geoffroy and Matilda of Anjou had a son, Henry Plantagenet, who by the age of eighteen had grown into a handsome ginger-haired lusty lad. His father and mother took him to Paris when they went to make a treaty with Louis VII of France. They were hoping to get young Henry betrothed to the French king's fourteen-year-old daughter. But it was Louis' twenty-nine-year-old wife Eleanor who had her eye on him.

Louis' marriage was a complete mismatch. He had married the beautiful, intelligent fifteen-year-old Eleanor of Aquitaine, who had brought as her dowry the Duchy of Guyenne, Périgord, Limousin, Poitou, Angoumois, Saintonage, Gascony, the Auvergne and the County of Toulouse – in fact, the south-west to the Pyrenees. She loved having fun, patronized the arts, liked to surround herself with troubadours. In modern terms, she was fun loving. Louis was extremely pious and dull. He liked to dress in the simplest clothes, to eat the simplest food, and little of it, and spent hours on his knees in prayer. 'I have married a monk', she said. He took her on a Crusade to fight the Saracens in the Holy Land for two and a half years. There they soon began to live apart. She was accused of having affairs and had to be hustled away from Antioch after scandal over a Saracen slave. She had committed an even greater sin in the eyes of French politicians – she had produced two daughters and no heir to the throne.

Back in France, Louis set about getting rid of her. He pulled down fortresses in Aquitaine, withdrew his army from it, then called an ecclesiastical court at Beaugency on the Loire to call on the Pope to dissolve the marriage. The Pope obliged. Louis was so anxious to get rid of her that he let her keep her lands in the south-west. Others wanted them and her. She was thirty, still beautiful and rich. Louis's sixteen-year-old brother tried to kidnap her. Then the son of the Count of Champagne tried to do the same at Tours. Eleanor slipped back to Aquitaine by night. She knew whom she wanted. Young Henry Plantagenet was now nineteen and already Duke of Normandy, Count of Anjou and Lord of Maine and Touraine. He was also heir to the English throne. Eleanor married him eight months after her divorce. Two years later he became King Henry II of England. His empire stretched from the Scottish borders to the Pyrenees. He ruled far more of France than the French king did.

They were happy at first. Eleanor indulged her love of parties. They even held a sort of 'pop concert' to which troubadours came from all over Europe. They had five sons, one of whom died, and five daughters. But they were both wayward and had affairs on the side. Among Henry's loves was Rosamond Clifford, the Fair Rosamond. They had two sons. Eleanor was accused of sleeping with a troubadour. Henry had the Plantagenet quick temper, which had already got him into disgrace with the Church when his exasperated outburst of 'Who will rid me of this turbulent priest?' had led to overzealous knights murdering Thomas à Becket, the Archbishop of Canterbury, on the altar steps of his cathedral. He lost patience with Eleanor and confined her to a castle. Her dignity was very badly hurt and she turned her sons against him.

Henry's eldest son and favourite was called Henry Courtmantel because he started a fashion for short jackets. Eleanor's favourite was Richard Coeur de Lion (Lionheart). Henry Courtmantel, already named as associate and heir by his father, was impatient to rule and started a revolt, to the joy of the new clever young King of France, Philippe-Auguste. Eleanor incited Richard to join him. After committing sacrilege by robbing abbeys and even the holy shrine at Rocamadour to pay his troops, Henry Courtmantel became desperately ill and died believing that he had been struck down by God. But Richard continued the revolt, allying himself with the King of France. Then the youngest son and Henry II's new favourite John joined in the revolt, too, and Henry was forced at his castle in Chinon to sign a humiliating treaty. He gave up and died. Richard then turned on the French king and fought him successfully until he was killed by a stray arrow while besieging a minor castle. The new Plantagenet king was John, who was weak, vacillating and no match for the cunning Philippe-Auguste. He gradually lost his lands in Normandy and the Loire, though the English held the south-west, Aquitaine.

In the Hundred Years War between 1337 and 1453, started when Edward III of England claimed the throne of France through his mother's line, fighting took place over most of France, but not the Loire Valley, until 1428. Most fighting was in the North (battles of Crécy and Agincourt), Poitou (the Black Prince won a great victory for the English at Poitiers in 1356), the Dordogne and Gascony. After the remarkable English victory at Agincourt in 1415, Henry V of England married King Charles VI of France's daughter, and on the Charles's death was recognized as King of France. But he died shortly after. The Dauphin, the eldest son of Charles, weak and indecisive, refused to be crowned. He scuttled round the Loire châteaux, setting up court at Chinon and Bourges, and was scathingly called King of Bourges. Henry V's son, Henry VI of England, claimed the French throne.

In 1428 the English army were besieging Orléans, but with a force too small to blockade it. At that moment the peasant girl Joan of Arc went to the Dauphin's Court at Chinon, told him that God had sent her voices telling her that he was the true King of France and to give her an army to drive out the English and put him on the throne. Probably in desperation the Dauphin gave her troops and with the help of Dunois, called the Bastard of Orléans because he was the illegitimate son of the Duke of Orléans, she slipped into Orléans city with a food convoy, roused the spirits of the depressed French garrison and led them to victory.

After more victories she almost forced the Dauphin to be crowned Charles VII. Yet when she was captured by the Burgundians, sold to the English, found guilty of heresy by churchmen and burned, he did not raise a finger to help her. Joan's friend Dunois did much to drive out the English finally. But the new king continued to spend much of his time in the Loire valley, not in Paris, setting up luxurious courts in Chinon and Loches. His new-found wealth came from a shrewd reorganization of taxation by Jacques Coeur, the Bourges merchant and financier who had backed the campaign of Joan of Arc. Charles rewarded Coeur by banishing him on a trumped-up charge of poisoning Charles' mistress, Agnès Sorel.

Charles was of the Valois family and it was under the Valois kings, who ruled from 1328 to 1589, that the Loire became a playground for the rich and powerful. The Court moved there for the summer and they were followed by the bourgeoisie, the bankers and merchants who had become financial experts to the kings and who lent them money. Châteaux and hunting lodges as big as châteaux were built by everyone with pretensions to importance. Hundreds of wagons and coaches carried the families, their relatives, retainers and servants, baggage and household chattels. François I needed 12,000 horses to carry his household, servants, furniture, crockery and baggage. But François was a flamboyant lover of show. When in 1520 he met Henry VIII of England at Guines near Calais to discuss an alliance at the Camp du Drap d'Or (Field of the Cloth of Gold) his tents were hung in gold, his horses draped with gold cloth and some shod with gold shoes, and his courtiers dressed in the most extravagant costumes. It was the greatest picnic in history.

Charles VIII fought a big campaign in Italy and lost. But he gained a love of Renaissance art and literature and brought back Italian designers and craftsmen to transform the château at Amboise. It was the beginning of the great French Renaissance period in building and art, brought to fruition in the Loire by François I at Amboise and Chambord.

Louis XI, who had followed his father Charles VII to the throne in 1461, disliked pomp and ceremony and rarely went to the Loire, though he installed his wife with a small court at Amboise. But Charles VIII, Louis's successor in 1483, brought not only a love of Renaissance art and design but also a general love of luxury and rich furnishings. He filled Amboise with Eastern carpets, beds, chests and tables, Flemish and Parisian tapestries, superb silverware, a huge aviary of rare birds, a menagerie which included lions, and an armoury which included the battleaxes of Clovis and the great soldier Du Guesclin, the dagger of Charlemagne and the armour of Joan of Arc.

François I, who became king in 1515, brought elegance, taste and culture to Amboise as well as flamboyance. He released the women of the Court from subservience to become joint leaders with the men. He insisted that they wore beautiful clothes and dressed perfectly and that all men treated them with courtesy and respect. He threatened to hang any man who hinted of anything dishonourable about a woman. François loved hunting game and women.

He had loved Amboise since he was a child and gave magnificent festivals there, celebrating feast days, weddings, baptisms or welcoming important visitors. Then he started to build Chambord and was so obsessed by this enormous palace of 440 rooms that he bankrupted himself to build it. Six years after he started it in 1519 he was defeated in Italy and taken prisoner by the Emperor Charles V. To release himself he gave Charles Flanders and Burgundy and his two sons as prisoner-hostages in Spain. He claimed that he had no money to ransom his sons but he went on pouring it into Chambord, even raiding the treasures of churches to pay the bills.

Henri II of France held court at Blois when he was not at the Palace of the Louvre in Paris. So did his widow, Catherine de' Medici and his sons Charles IX and Henri III.

The horrors of the religious wars reached the Loire in 1560, with murder, abduction and atrocities on both Catholic and Protestant sides, and royalty and noblemen used religious zealots to gain power for themselves. Catherine de' Medici, who vacillated between support for each side, brought her boy-king son François II and his girl-wife Mary, later Queen of Scots, to Amboise in fear of Protestant uprisings. In 1560 foolish Protestants fell into a trap about an organized coup and were betrayed to the brutal, all-powerful Duke of Guise. They were tortured, broken on the wheel and strung out from the Amboise castle balconies. The Royal family and Court would come out after dinner to watch their agonies. The Duchess of Guise warned Catherine, 'What vengeance is here being stored for the future!'

She was right. The boy-king François died within months. His brother Charles IX died in terror and remorse after a blood-stained reign which included the mass murder of Protestants on St Bartholomew's night – massacres planned once more by Guise. The Duke of Guise plotted with Philip II of Spain against Henri III of France, intending to grab the French Crown. Then Philip's Armada was defeated by the Protestant English and Dutch. Philip's power waned and Henri III felt safe to have Guise and his equally powerful brother, the Cardinal of Lorraine, murdered. Mary was finally beheaded, at Fotheringay in England, in February 1587. Shortly after Guise's death, Catherine de' Medici died, too.

Henri III had come to the throne in 1574. An effeminate, sensitive man, he had tried to mediate between the Protestants and Catholics and received the scorn and hatred of Guise and the extreme Catholics. They had formed the Catholic League, which grew into a terrorist tool of Guise and his party rather than a religious force. In fear of losing his throne and his life, Henri III allied himself with the League's arch enemy, the Protestant leader Henri of Navarre, who himself was an heir to the throne. Eight months after Guise was killed a monk who was a League member murdered Henri III.

Henri of Navarre had won his battles. He was heir to the throne but as a Protestant he was barred. He needed the keys of Paris. 'Paris is worth a mass,' he said and became a Catholic – in theory, at least. His plan was to unite France. After he was crowned Henri IV, he chose Nantes, whose ordinary people had supported him against the League, to issue his Edict making Protestantism legal.

Henri's love of enjoyment, wine and women was famous. He was called Le Vert Galant. And his favourite mistress, the handsome and intelligent Gabrielle d'Estrées, came from Touraine. But he showed little interest in the Loire Valley. The Loire's age of glory was over. It became an agricultural land again. Young Louis XIV did, in fact, hide at Blois during the Fronde uprising of disgruntled lords. For a short while the Loire valley became the playground of the Court again. He visited Château Chambord, where Molière created plays to be performed for him. (*See* Chambord page 146.) But Louis was determined to break the power of the lords who held what amounted to private courts in their châteaux. He appointed his own civil servants, called Intendants, who had the King's power behind them, and ruled their areas completely. The monarchy was absolute. 'I *am* the State' (*L'État, c'est moi*) he said.

He built his magnificent but cramped palace at Versailles and the aristocrats and successful bourgeoisie he had created fought for space and favours. If you had no room there, not even a humble room by the latrines, you did not exist. To be rusticated at the King's whim to your château was to be disgraced and forgotten.

The Loire remained mainly rustic until the railways came. Then it became a weekend and holiday area for Parisians. More important, its goods could be moved to Paris and to Nantes and its port without the vagaries of the river.

The rivers, for three thousand years the main highways of the valley, gradually lost their importance. They had been in some trouble since Louis XIV's Intendants took control of the waterways from Loire merchants. They neglected the rivers, bureaucratic regulations made commerce more and more difficult, the rivers began to silt up with sandbanks. Levies increased so much and there were so many toll-points (where the tollkeepers had to be bribed) that the cost of a cargo could multiply by four between Nevers and Nantes.

Special boats had been designed for the Loire. *Sapines* were poled with the current to carry wine to Nantes, then broken up for their wood. Large light *coches d'eau* were rowed both ways. Orléans to Nantes took eight days and the journey back about a fortnight. But this was not much slower than going by the appalling roads, and was more comfortable and safer, so even kings and nobles used them. Most traffic was carried by *chalands* (also called *gabares*), which were flat-bottomed with no keel, with a draught of less than a metre when fully laden, and flat raised bows so that they slid like landing craft onto obstructions, such as sand banks. Most were about fifteen metres long, but big boats, thirty metres long with a five-metre beam, could carry sixty tonnes. They had a rectangular sail on a mast which was lowered at bridges. They steered with an oar and a *bâton* (long pole) which was used at the back, like a punt, by a strong man. To tack, they threw out a big anchor and poled the boat's head round, then upped anchor. If they ran aground at low water, they could be there until enough rain came. They carried to Nantes various cargoes, but especially wine, wool, timber, grain and coal, and returned with fish, fruit and salt and imported sugar, spices, tobacco and rum.

In 1844 steamboats started to run, but some blew up their boilers or got stuck in the sandbanks. The Paris–Orléans railway opened in 1846 and other lines followed fast. The Loire became a leisure river.

The valley did become a refuge for French governments in times of war setbacks.

During the Franco-Prussian War in 1870 when Napoleon III had capitulated to the Prussians, the political leader Gambetta escaped from Paris by balloon and set up a Republican French Government in Tours. A very small army of the Loire defeated the advancing Prussians at Orléans and Coulmiers but were hopelessly outnumbered and had to flee to Bordeaux.

In the First World War, the Americans (*les Sammies*) had their headquarters at Tours.

In 1940, as the Germans advanced on Paris, the French Government fled to Tours and discussed surrender. The Germans bombarded Tours and Orléans and French military resistance stopped except for the cadets of Saumur military school who held three Loire bridges for twenty-four hours until their ammunition ran out.

The French surrender was signed on 24 October 1940 between Adolf Hitler and Marshal Pétain, head of the Vichy Government, at Montoire-sur-le-Loir railway station in the same railway carriage in which the Germans had surrendered in 1918. The Loire was the main boundary between Occupied and Unoccupied (Vichy) France. Escaped airmen, prisoners of war, Resistance fighters and Allied spies used Catherine de' Medici's wonderful Gallery at Chenonceau Château as a major escape route!

Since motorways from Paris reached Orléans and Tours and the fast TGV train joined Paris to Tours in seventy minutes, the Loire valley has become even more popular as a fresh-air haunt for Parisians. They can drive down for lunch and to see a château or use the bathing beaches and return the same day. Orléans and Tours have become more heavily industrialized, too, but industry has been kept as far away from the old centres as possible.

## WRITERS AND ARTISTS

Pierre de Ronsard (1524–85), poet of love and romance and the greatest French poet of the sixteenth century, was born at Château de la Possonnière at Couture-sur-Loir, west of Vendôme, and died at the Priory of St Cosne near Tours. He was a soldier-diplomat who abandoned arms for letters when he went deaf (see Vendôme, page 261).

François Rabelais (about 1494–1553), satirist, monk, connoisseur of wine and respected physician, was born in a farmhouse just outside Chinon. His most famous work was *Gargantua*, the story of a giant who performed prodigious feats, especially in battle, and had a prodigious appetite. The story is told in a larger-than-life style with exaggerated adjectives and coarse stories, but was a satirical comment on the changing times from the Medieval to the Renaissance. Voltaire called him 'a drunken philosopher'. Another of his great characters was a monk, Brother Jean des Entommeures, who was rewarded for helping Gargantua by being allowed to set up his perfect Abbey de Thélème. It was pleasant and luxurious, had no enclosing walls, no clocks, no rules except 'Do what you will' and admitted women. Hardly the sort of abbey where Rabelais himself had served! He satirized pedants, religious zealots, whether Catholic or Protestant, intellectual snobs, garblers of the French language and fusspots. On a voyage of exploration, his hero reaches the isle of Papefigues (Protestants) and the isle of Papimanes (Catholics) but he prefers the isle of Messire Stomach (the Epicureans). (*See* Chinon, page 164).

François Villon (1431–about 1463), lyric poet of the

fifteenth century, is less known than he deserves. The French literary establishment likes to sweep him under the mat and some well-known guide books discreetly ignore him. For, although a good poet and a great wit, he was also a robber, vagabond and probably a murderer. Born in great poverty in Paris, he got to university and graduated as a Master of Arts in 1452 but killed a priest in a street brawl and was imprisoned. He was released and banished from Paris. He went to Angers, but was imprisoned again for robbing a church in Orléans. But he met the Duke of Bourbon and was entertained and welcomed at Blois by Charles, Duke of Orléans, who was also a poet and who welcomed to his Court writers, poets and artists. Villon got into trouble again for brawling and burglary and was tortured and imprisoned in an *oubliette* at Meung-sur-Loire (see Meung-sur-Loire, page 208). He was released during a Royal amnesty, and went back to Paris where he was sentenced to death in 1463 for another crime. The sentence was commuted to banishment and he disappeared – aged thirty-two.

To the French, his greatest poem is 'Epistle to his Friends' describing his suffering at Meung, but he is known in Britain and the US for 'The Ladies of Bygone Days' ('Where are the snows of yesteryear?'), because it was translated dramatically by Rossetti (see Blois, page 65).

Brantôme was the pseudonym of Pierre de Bourdeilles (1530–1614), abbot, wit, envoy of Henri II (he accompanied Mary Queen of Scots back to Scotland when her husband François II died), Chamberlain to Charles IX and Henri III. He appointed himself a sort of court reporter, telling witty, amusing and sometimes scurrilous stories of court scandals, intrigues and parties. But from his gossip the French have gained much knowledge of court life, people and history (see Chenonceau Château, page 104).

Jean-Jacques Rousseau (1712–78), the essayist, musician and political thinker from Geneva, lived in Chenonceau Château for some time as tutor to the children of the Dupin family, who then owned it. Rousseau wrote the masterpiece *Du Contrat Social* (the Social Contract) which, with its famous call for liberty, equality, fraternity, became the bible of the French Revolution. For a Revolutionary, he had a great liking for living the high life with marquises and princes in their châteaux. (As a Communist trade union leader of the 1940s–60s said to me as he wined, dined and smoked Havana cigars in the Savoy Grill: 'I've always said that nothing's too good for the workers.') Rousseau wrote of the fine food at Chenonceau: 'I became fat as a monk'. He wrote, too, of the music, of composing pieces for three voices, and writing a play called *The Dangerous Engagement* which was acted by the Dupin family (see Chenonceau Château, page 104).

William Wordsworth (1770–1850) took lodgings in rue Royale, Orléans, in 1791 when he was twenty-one. He was an admirer of the French Revolution and attended Revolutionary meetings. But he fell in love with a Royalist and counter-Revolutionary, twenty-five-year-old Annette Vallon. She had a baby and 'Mr and Mrs Williams' had their daughter christened Ann Caroline in Orléans Cathedral. Annette persuaded him to flee France when war broke out with England. But they kept in touch and met occasionally. Finally Wordsworth, his wife and sister Dorothy met Annette and Caroline, by now grown up, in Paris.

Max Jacob (1876–1944), artist friend of Picasso, Cocteau and Braque, who shared their poverty and Bohemian life in Paris, was also a poet, rediscovered in recent times. Son of a Jewish tailor from Quimper in Brittany, he became a Christian in 1915. Picasso was godfather at his baptism. Six years later he went to live in St Benoît-sur-Loire, complaining jokingly that life in Paris was no longer fun because, as a Catholic, he could not sin with pleasure. He lived in the main street of St Benoît until 1944, when the monks returned to the historic abbey and he retired there. But the Gestapo came for him. On the train to prison camp he persuaded his guards to post a letter he wrote to Cocteau. Cocteau got up a petition to the Germans for his release and all his famous friends signed it, except Picasso, who said that Max was too smart to need his help. Picasso was obviously afraid of Nazi reprisals. Strangely the petition was a success, but when Cocteau and his friends went to collect him from Drancy prison, they were told that he had died of pneumonia, a standard Nazi reply to enquiries about anyone whom they had killed. Orléans' Beaux Arts museum has an area devoted to his work, mostly water-colours of Brittany and sculptures.

# Amboise

[INDRE-ET-LOIRE, MAP 3, page 273]

Modern traffic converging to cross its important bridge has not spoiled the charm of Amboise. More than any other Loire town, it evokes the grand old days when the valley was the scene of splendour and love, pageantry, intrigue, feasting and murder. Most of it is on the south bank of the river and you must approach it from the north to see how the town and a whole stretch of the river are still dominated by what is left of the great old château perched on a hill opposite. In the Revolution, much of the outer fortress and most of the inner apartments, which were built round courtyards, were pulled down. But it remains more impressive than other Loire castles which are more complete, and from its Tour des Minimes are some of the best views along the Loire river. The centre support of the big river bridge rests on the rocks of an island, once called Île d'Or, now Île St Jean, and now one of the favourite places for camping and river bathing. The island ensured the importance of Amboise from earliest times. It had been important for centuries when Crassus, one of Julius Caesar's commanders, set up camp here for an attack on Tours. Crassus found a large fortified Gallic town there. And it was on the island that Clovis, King of the Franks, made a treaty in 503 with Alaric, King of the Visigoths, which he promptly broke to kill Alaric and become the first ruler of a country called France. (See History, page 33). Two medieval castles stood there, then through local fights the Counts of Amboise owned it and built it up as a fortress until 1434, when Charles VII claimed that Louis of Amboise had conspired against him. Kings often did that if they coveted a castle. Charles gave it to his wife, Charlotte of Savoy, to live in while he was busy with Agnès Sorel. Charles VIII, who was born there, went off to fight in Italy, taking on the Pope, the Emperor Charles V, Spain, Venice and Milan. He lost, but he brought back a passionate enthusiasm for Italian Renaissance architecture, furniture, textiles and works of art. He came back with furnishings, paintings and Italian architects and craftsmen. He had recently married Anne of Brittany and he started to rebuild Amboise with Renaissance influence, setting his men to work with enormous energy. Work went on all night by torchlight and in winter fire kept the stone warm enough to work. Charles went around one day to inspect the work and hit his head on a low lintel. He felt all right and went to watch a tennis match. At midnight he collapsed and died. Rumours spread at once. There was no bruise mark from the blow, and he had just eaten an orange brought to him by one of his Court. His cousin Louis, who was his heir, was impatient to be king and was in love with Charles' wife Anne. There was a rumour that Charles was about to have him arrested for plotting rebellion. Louis was suspected of poisoning Charles.

Louis became Louis XII but was more interested in Blois Château than Amboise. It was François I, who had lived at Amboise from the age of six and was educated there, who made it his Court when he became king, and who completed the Renaissance transformation. It was he who, in 1516, brought Leonardo da Vinci, the great Italian artist, to live in Clos-Lucé, a fifteenth-century manor house nearby. François was a strange mixture of raw, uncouth and ostentatious extrovert, addicted to 'hunting game and women' and cultivated lover of the arts. He kept lions, tigers, leopards and bears in the dry moat and let them sleep on his head. He pitted a bear against a lion so that the Court could watch the primitive spectacle. He introduced a wild boar into a wedding party, the guests stampeded and he killed it with his own sword.

Then came the appalling blood bath by the Duke of Guise in 1560 (see History, page 40). The Court were driven from Amboise by the stink of corpses, and no one wanted to live in it. It became a prison. Among the prisoners was Fouquet, Louis XIV's finance minister, who made the mistake of building the luxurious Château at Vaux-le-Vicomte and giving the most expensive party there, so that young Louis XIV guessed that he had his hand in the Royal purse. The Duke of Penthièvre bought it but it became a prison again in the Revolution. In 1816 it was returned to Penthièvre's daughter, the Duchess of Orléans, mother of the 'citizen king' Louis-Philippe who, with his accustomed lack of taste, made neo-Gothic 'restoration'. His friend Queen Victoria stayed there.

Amboise was not just a château where noblemen lived but a *cité* where a thousand servants lived, from valets and doctors to Scottish bowmen and Swiss guards. It had a church, law-courts and barracks. Much has been pulled down over the centuries, especially during the Revolution when there was no money for its upkeep. It was damaged by German bombing in 1940. What is left is preserved by a foundation set up by the Count of Paris, Pretender to the French throne, and is certainly worth seeing. It is open daily (9 to 12 p.m., 2 p.m.–5.30 p.m. or 7 p.m. – guided tours about one hour).

You enter by a ramp onto the terrace which has magnificent views over the Loire river and green valley and the old rooftops and walls of Amboise. You can reach the terrace gardens by a vaulted ramp, which once had a drawbridge at each end for defence.

Logis de Roi (the King's apartments) are in late Gothic style with signs of Renaissance. The side facing the Loire is ornate, the garden side simpler. On the lower floor is a long vaulted guards' room with a river view through a gallery. The State room is divided into two vaults by slender columns supporting elegant ribs. It is light and has an iron balcony from which the main leaders of the Protestant revolt were hanged. In the nineteenth century the State suites were converted into a prison for the great Algerian leader, Emir Abd-el-Kader, who fought for twelve years to resist the French annexation of his country before losing. He was here in Amboise from 1842 to 1852, became a lover of French culture and supported local charities. When Napoleon III was crowned Emperor, he was released. He went to live in Damascus and in 1860 when Christians were being massacred in Syria, he saved thousands.

At right angles is the Renaissance François I wing, actually started by Louis XII, but François added two storeys. It is restrained by the standards of Renaissance in full bloom, but is very elegant and attractive, and flanked on the garden side by two pointed towers containing staircases. Several rooms are furnished and hung with tapestries.

Tour des Minimes (Minimes Tower), 21 metres, (69 feet) in diameter, dominates the Loire and the old monastery after which it was named. It has a spiral ramp which climbs gently round a huge central pillar, finishing at the roof vault, so that knights could ride up on horseback and horse-drawn carts and sledges could bring up supplies. It used to be hung with tapestries. The Emperor Charles V was almost suffocated because the torch bearer had set light to a tapestry. The view from the top over the Loire and valley is attractive and extensive. The slightly fatter Tower of Hurtault looks forbidding, as if it is scowling down on the town, probably because it now stands alone at the back of the castle.

The joy of Amboise is the little oratory, the Chapel of St Hubert, peeping over the rampart at the edge of the terrace. It was built by Charles VIII for Anne of Brittany at the end of the fifteenth century and a beautiful tympanum above the superb doorway shows them praying to the Virgin – a mysterious sculpture because nobody knows when it was done although it is believed to have been carved by Flemish sculptors. My friend Vivian Rowe described the chapel years ago as 'a tiny work of absolute perfection; a jewel by Benvenuto Cellini magnified to the size of a small building would not be more perfect'. It has stood for five hundred years, surprising because in 1940 a shell exploded on a main cross-beam. On the lintel is carved St Christopher carrying the infant Jesus, who unfortunately received some head injuries from a German shell. On the other side is the legend of St Hubert, patron saint of hunters. A rakish Frank nobleman of the eighth century, he was out hunting in the forests of the Ardennes when a stag turned at bay to reveal a cross shining between its antlers. Hubert was convinced that if he did not mend his ways he would soon go to hell. So he kneeled and swore to devote his life to Christian service. He converted the pagan people of the Ardennes forests and was rewarded by being made Bishop of Liège. The Flamboyant-Gothic lace carvings of the frieze are delightful.

Though so small, the chapel was heated by corner fireplaces.

Royal worship was obviously more comfortable than common worship in freezing, draughty village churches. The true love between Anne, Duchess of Brittany, and Charles was strangely touching. Anne, intelligent and courageous, but far from beautiful, became Duchess of Brittany in 1488 when her father died. Charles had become King of France when he was only thirteen, and the Regent was his tough, hard-headed sister, Anne of Beaujeu. Anne had been betrothed by her father at five years of age to the Hapsburg Emperor Maximilian of Austria, a widower, whose own daughter Margaret had been betrothed as a child to Charles. But the French had no intention of letting the Austro–Spanish Hapsburg Empire get hold of Brittany. The French invaded Brittany and took all important places except Rennes, where they besieged Anne. In the face of pleas from her starving subjects, Anne was forced to make peace. Within four days of signing the treaty she agreed to marry Charles. She was only fourteen, but bright and strongwilled. He was twenty-three, described as 'a puny man with very little sense' but was a good horseman and jouster and dreamed of valour in battle.

Anne de Beaujeu stipulated in the wedding contract that if Anne were widowed, she must marry the next King of France. The French intended to hang on to Brittany. Charles and Anne were very happy except that all four of their children died. And when Charles hit his head and died, Anne did her duty and married his heir, Louis XII. To marry her, Louis had to get rid of his wife of fourteen years, Jeanne de France, who was lame and had a deformed shoulder, but was deeply religious and loved by the French people. She was the daughter of King Louis XI. Louis claimed that her father had forced him to marry her. He swore that he had never made love to her, that she could not consummate the marriage, perjured himself with his hand on the Bible and set up three ecclesiastical judges at a hearing at Amboise. They gave her the most disgusting cross-examination and declared that the marriage had never taken place. The people booed and insulted them. Jeanne retired to start a Holy Order of the Annunciation at Bourges. She was canonized in 1950 as Ste Jeanne de Valois. Anne and Louis had a daughter, Claude. She was heir to Brittany. Anne died before Louis. He made sure that Claude married François, heir to the French throne. He became François I.

Clos-Lucé, where da Vinci lived later, was Anne's summer residence. As a boy, the future François I played with his friends in the garden. It had direct access to the castle. In 1516 François invited da Vinci, who was over sixty, to live there. An arthritic right hand had forced the great genius to give up painting, though a sketch he made of Amboise from his bedroom window is now in the Royal collection at Windsor. François gave him the manor house and an income in return for the pleasure of his conversation. Leonardo travelled over the Alps on the back of a mule but surprisingly brought some of his masterpieces with him, including *Virgin of the Rocks* and *Mona Lisa*, which François bought after his death. Leonardo designed costumes for François's sumptuous fêtes, and he continued his engineering and scientific designing. He anticipated many later inventions, making designs for a helicopter, an air-conditioning fan, a car on springs, submarine, parachute and swing bridge. He made a plan to drain the Sologne by building a canal to join the Loire river. None was built, but you can see models created by the IBM Company. The furnishings of the house are beautiful – so is the Renaissance garden running down to a stream (house closed in December, January).

Da Vinci died in 1519. François installed his finance minister Philibert Babou de la Bourdaisière in the house. The King had good reason. He slept sometimes with Babou's wife, Marie Gaudin, known as 'La Belle Babou'. Court scandal claimed that he also bedded her three sisters! La Belle Babou was generous with her charms, but only to very important men. She shared the comfort of her bed with the Emperor Charles V on his visit. Her granddaughter Gabrielle d'Estrées was the lovely, intelligent favourite of Henri IV.

A son-et-lumière held daily at the castle in July and August features François I's merrymaking, not the Guise bloodbath.

Traffic can build up into jams at the south end of the bridge from the riverside D751, especially at rush hours and in July and August. There is little to see across the river, so try to park on the meters near the bridge or along the river a few hundred yards in either direction.

There are some fine old houses down here near the river, especially in rue Concorde between the Château and the river. Downstream the lovely Promenade du Mail passes the strange, almost jokey surrealistic fountain given to Amboise by Max Ernst in 1968. Turn left at the Post Office for the Romanesque basilica of St Denis, built in the twelfth century on the site of a colossal Roman statue to Mars, partly rebuilt and extended in the fifteenth and sixteenth centuries. The doorway is elegantly attractive. There is a fine sixteenth-century statue of Mary Magdalene reclining and seemingly reading a book, and in the opposite aisle, a most realistic and chilling marble statue called *Femme Noyée* (the drowned woman) of a naked, middle-aged woman. The sculptor is not known, but some have said that it was the great Primaticcio who came from Italy in 1531 to decorate Fontainebleau for François I. It is said that his wife was drowned in the Loire. It is also said that the model for the sculpture was La Belle Babou. The sculpture of the Entombment in the south aisle was presented by her husband. On a fresco of the Lady Chapel is poor Jeanne de France. This church was the scene of her humiliating cross-examination and the end of her marriage to Louis XII. The fine chandelier in the choir was a gift from the Algerian leader Abd-el-Kader, a devout Muslim. The narrow rue Nationale from place St Denis has some good shops. Turn right along rue Orange and in a truly distinguished sixteenth-century house, Hôtel Joyeuse, is an interesting Musée de la Poste (closed Tuesdays) showing the development of the postal system from the days of stage coaches. It has interesting prints, stamps and pictures. A set of nineteenth-century cards shows a hundred postmen from all nations. Sea, air and balloon posts are represented, with a good collection of posters of transatlantic liners. The museum in the sixteenth-century town hall (Musée de l'Hôtel de Ville) has some fine tapestries from the Chanteloup Pagoda, which stands alone now 3 kilometres south-west of Amboise by the route de Bléré (D31) and a signposted avenue. This dignified and attractive folly, thirty-six metres high, with six storeys, was once the pride of a luxurious château and estate. Now it stands in a woodland clearing, reflected in a pond. It was commissioned in 1775 by the Duke of Choiseul from the architect Louis le Camus, and started

*Chanteloup Pagoda*

as a copy of the pagoda in Kew Gardens but grew much bigger. As you climb the inner staircase of 142 steps each circular room gets smaller. There are superb views from four wrought-iron balconies. The Duke had it built as a gesture of gratitude to friends who had risked the wrath of Louis XV by visiting him when he was here in exile from Paris.

A favourite of the powerful royal mistress, Madame de Pompadour, he became Louis XV's most trusted minister. By arranging the Treaty of Paris with Britain in 1763 he extracted France from the Seven Years War, in which she had been roundly defeated, lost her American Empire and become virtually bankrupt. Pitt described the Treaty of Paris as 'Indeed the Peace of God for it passeth all understanding'. Pompadour had talked Louis into starting this war because Frederick the Great of Prussia had lampooned her.

Planning revenge on Britain, Choiseul modernized the French forces, and to gain the alliance of the Hapsburg Empire, arranged the marriage of Marie-Antoinette, the Empress's daughter, to the Dauphin of France.

Pompadour's official successor as Royal Mistress, du Barry, wanted to clear out anyone left over from the Pompadour reign and Choiseul became unpopular. Then, when France was still almost bankrupt, he tried to persuade Louis to declare war on Britain over the Falkland Islands. Louis had tired of wars. He rusticated Choiseul to the Loire. There he bought the massive Château and Domaine of Chanteloup and set out to rival du Barry's Court at Versailles. He spent his fortune on rebuilding, on lavish entertainment and expensive forest hunts, so that wits, cultured courtiers and many of the followers of fashion preferred to be on the Loire to the constrictions of the Royal Court at Versailles. He also started expensive experiments in farming and built what the English agriculturist Arthur Young called 'a noble cowhouse and the best sheephouse in France'. He kept his hunters in marble stables. One of Napoleon's ministers, a doctor from Montpelier School of Medicine, Jean-Antoine Chaptal, took over Chanteloup and there invented the process of extracting sugar from beet, thus doing a great service to Napoleon. The English naval blockade had stopped the French from bringing sugar from their West Indian colonies. Now, alas, too much of Europe is covered with dreary fields of sugar beet at the expense of the West Indian standard of living. Chaptal also introduced chaptalization, the process of adding sugar to wine-must to strengthen the wine. This quite sensible addition was much abused until recently in many parts of Europe, especially Germany. It was banned for Bordeaux wines. Now it is controlled at least in the EC area, and even Bordeaux allows it in strictly controlled quantities. An asset-stripper pulled down Choiseul's château last century.

TOURIST INFORMATION quai Général de Gaulle
(47.57.09.28)
MARKETS Friday, Saturday
FESTIVALS Melon Festival first Wednesday in
September; Wine Festivals Easter, mid-August

## HOTELS

*Château de Pray*, 3km NE on D751 (47.57.23.67). Enchanting château with two thirteenth-century round towers with pointed roofs joined by a Renaissance pavilion, perched in a delightful garden with views over the river. ROOMS D–G. MEALS E. Shut 1 January–15 February.

*Choiseul*, 36 quai Guinot (47.30.45.45). Eighteenth-century elegant mansion, facing the river, in charming Italian gardens. Fine view from the restaurant. Pool. Gardens lead to 'Greniers de César', caves used by the Romans to store grain. Relais et Châteaux. ROOMS G. MEALS F–G. Shut 4 January–early March.

*Lion d'Or*, 17 quai Guinot (47.57.00.23). Small hotel below château overlooking the river. Very good bourgeois cooking. ROOMS C–D. MEALS D–E. Shut 4 January–10 February; Sunday evening, Monday low season.

*Auberge du Mail*, 32 quai Général de Gaulle (47.57.60.39). Original restaurant of François Le Coz. Bedrooms improved. ROOMS B–C. MEALS B–E. Shut 1–15 December; Friday in winter.

## RESTAURANTS

Manoir St Thomas, place Richelieu (47.57.22.52). François Le Coz cooks here, formerly called Mail St Thomas. Superb classic cooking, not highly considered by Gault Millau but rightly starred by Michelin. Fine Renaissance house, attractive garden. Interesting wines, especially Touraine. MEALS E–F. Shut mid-January–mid-March; Sunday evening, Monday low season.

# *Angers*

[MAINE-ET-LOIRE, MAP 2, page 272]

Angers has little instant appeal. It is an industrial city, with a population of around one and a half million, and an agricultural market centre with a big export trade. But behind the newer city and the modern suburbs is a delightful old city. It is hardly hidden. Though Henri III had the seventeen bastion towers of the great castle cut down to the height of its curtain walls in 1585, the great stubs of the towers and awesome enclosure walls 600 metres long totally dominate the town. It looks down on the river Maine, the short river formed by the meeting of the Mayenne and Sarthe and joining the Loire a mere 10 kilometres later.

Henri had tired of squabbles between the Catholic League and Protestants and he ordered the château to be razed to the ground to stop either side using it. The Governor stalled, Henri died and the order was forgotten. In 1944 the RAF nearly carried out Henri's orders. The Germans were using the castle to store munitions, so the RAF bombed it. Luckily for the citizens of Angers, the Germans had hastily removed the explosives.

Philippe-Auguste took Anjou from King John of England but his grandson Louis IX (St Louis) feared that the English would come back. So he knocked down the old wooden fort in the capital, Angers, built by the fighting, fearsome Foulques Nerra around 1000 AD, and had built the strong fortress in stone. It took ten years from 1228, regarded as quick for building a big castle in those days, although Richard Coeur de Lion had the great Andelys castle finished in a year.

The truncated towers are still 40 to 50 metres high and from the tallest, Tour du Moulin, are good views over the city, the cathedral, the river banks and the attractive gardens laid out by the moats, where a herd of deer roam. You reach the gardens over a drawbridge. It is in medieval style, planted with marguerites, lavender, hollyhocks, vines and box, and is a joy in

Angers, which lacks flowers and greenery. Beyond the yew trees is the charming sixteenth-century-style chapel built by Louis, Duke of Anjou, for his wife Yolande, in white tufa stone – a pleasant relief from the black shale that alternates with light brown stone in the castle walls. Angers was once called Angers the Black until enthusiastic modernizers pulled down most of the old buildings and put up bigger and uglier ones.

The show of tapestries in a new building is the greatest joy of the château. In the Logis Royal, the royal apartments built by Duke Louis II, father of the last of Anjou's local rulers Good King René, are four superb fifteenth- to sixteenth-century tapestries. *La Dame à l'Orgue* (Lady at the Organ) was probably worked locally. The scenes of animals, birds and plants are from Audemarde.

*The Apocalypse Tapestry* in the Grand Gallery is the masterpiece of all tapestries. Duke Louis I of Anjou had it designed by Hennequin of Bruges and the originals are in the Bibliothèque Nationale in Paris. It was made in Paris by Nicolas Bataille between 1373 and 1380. It was 130 metres long and 5 metres high. What you can see today is about two-thirds of that length in seventy-five pictures.

When Louis XI turned out his uncle King René, who went south to rule Provence and to promote poetry and agriculture, René gave the tapestry to Angers Cathedral. For a while it was brought out for festivals, then put away and forgotten. In 1782 the church tried to sell it but nobody wanted it.

Angers joined the Revolution. The cathedral was stripped and made into a Temple of Reason. The tapestry was thrown into the streets and people helped themselves to it, cutting off strips to use as carpets, bedspreads and cart covers. Some cart horses were wrapped in tapestry blankets! A bishop started a search for the pieces in 1843. He recovered two-thirds, mostly from a rubbish dump.

The tapestry story follows fairly accurately St John's Revelation, with a relevant Bible verse opposite each picture. These are in French. You can hire a taped commentary in English. The medieval artists were certainly able to show terror on people's faces and one can imagine the fright they gave to simple people of the Middle Ages. The tapestry leads to the Victory of Christ.

*The Apocalypse*

The other great tapestry of Angers is over the river at the far end of boulevard Arago in the ancient Hospital of St Jean, founded in 1153 by Henry II, Plantagenet King of England, as part of his penance after his followers had murdered Archbishop à Becket at Canterbury. As in Beaune Hospice, beds were set so that all the sick and dying could see the altar. Now they would see *Chante du Monde* (The Song of the World), a tapestry by the man who revived the tapestry art, Jean Lurçat. When Lurçat died in 1966 he had completed a tapestry eighty metres long. He intended to design tapestries up to 125 metres long. Lurçat was a visionary and a humanist. His view of life and of death clashed with that of the traditional Catholics and his dramatic use of a riot of bright colours on a black background offended more traditional artists, so this work brought criticism near to abuse from both – and especially from Catholic art critics. They have accused him of trying to give his 'answer' to St John's Prophecy. One critic says that it is 'a mere riot of modernistic platitudes in a disordered dream.' Surely John's

Revelation was something of a disordered dream, too. The critics had praised Lurçat's less controversial work for years. He first saw the *Apocalypse* tapestry in Angers in 1938 when he was already forty-six, and was deeply impressed. He started his own in 1957. He held strong views on nuclear warfare and showed the atomic bomb as La Grande Menace. The first tapestries show the bomb itself, a man of Hiroshima, burned, stripped, emptied, all reason for living shattered. Then comes the *Charnel House of Death*, based on his experiences fighting in the trenches at the age of twenty in the First World War, and a remarkable tapestry called *The End of Everything*, shown by snow on a black background and the last plant in the world, broken and dying.

I talked to Lurçat and he was adamant that his was not a disdainful or gloomy view of life. His friends will tell you the same. And he showed that with the tapestries that followed, called *Man and Our Reasons for Living*, including *Man in Glory in Peace*, a happy, bubbly tapestry called *Champagne*, a superb *Conquest of Space* and a charming *Poetry*.

His first title for the whole work had been *La Joie de Vivre*. But he said: 'It did not take me long to be convinced that life for one who tries to live correctly is sweet and salted, mild and bitter, convulsive and serene.'

The form, beauty and the colours make it for me a work of genius. His black backgrounds accentuate splendidly the joyous colours of his reds, oranges, deep and bright blues and gold. The exhibition is shut on Mondays.

The old town of Angers was partly demolished in the last century but there is still much of charm and interest. From the side street opposite the castle you can climb steps and you are facing St Maurice's Cathedral.

Between its twin spires is a lantern tower hung with a great six-ton bell called 'Maurice', added to the church in 1535. The cathedral rebuilding started in 1140 and the great nave, a sensation in its day, was finished in 1162, the transept in 1240, the choir at the end of the thirteenth century, so although it was started before Notre-Dame in Paris, it was finished long after. The nave is still the widest of any French cathedral (16 metres, 54 feet). Its vaults in the Angevin style are supported by slim arches rising to 25 metres. The doorway in the unusual façade is a beautiful example of French Gothic, with figures of saints and angels, and a tympanum of the risen Christ. High above it is a frieze of St Maurice with his fellow soldiers dressed, rather strangely for Roman Legionaries of Diocletian's reign, in medieval military uniforms. I am told that the inscription, too high to see, reads: 'Bring peace in our time Lord and scatter nations who want war.' Maurice was an officer in Diocletian's elite Theban Legion, recruited from the East of the Roman Empire. They were ordered to attack a Christian area of Gaul and kill all its people. They all refused, so the Emperor had one in ten killed.

The stained glass of the cathedral is magnificent, especially the two beautiful rose windows lighting the vaults of the transept. The twelfth-century windows in the nave are preciously rare, the thirteenth-century windows in the choir are in glorious colours. There are a lot more windows, from two dozen medieval to modern windows in the chapel of Notre-Dame de Pitié. The window to the right of the chancel shows the life of Thomas à Becket. A green marble Roman bath was used by the Dukes of Anjou as a baptismal font. Behind the cathedral is Maison d'Adam, an attractive fifteenth-century half-timbered house, with posts decorated with curious small carved figures. Its name comes from an apple tree carved below a corner turret. Adam and Eve are there, but were vandalized during the Revolution. There are angels, shepherds, flute and bagpipe players, monkeys and pelicans and some funny and slightly risqué goings on. The Logis Pincé (rue Lenepveu), built in the sixteenth century for a mayor, houses the Turpin de Crissé museum, based on a fine personal collection of treasures belonging to a local painter (1772–1859) who was Chamberlain to Napoleon's Empress Josephine. It contains lovely ceramics, masks and Japanese engravings given by de Crissé's nephew, the Count of St Genys (closed Mondays).

The Beaux Arts museum is in a beautiful late-fifteenth-century mansion (Logis Barrault) built by the King's secretary who became mayor (shut Mondays). It was built as a square with an elegant tower with a superb staircase not now in use.

Guests there included Cesare Borgia, Mary Stuart and Marie de'
Medici (second wife of Henri IV).

The museum, which spreads to other buildings, has some
real treasures, including Renaissance furniture, medieval panels, primitive paintings from Italy, Switzerland and France, and
some major works of the seventeenth, eighteenth and nineteenth centuries. But first there is a *Holy Family* by Raphael from
the early sixteenth century. *Feast of the Gods* is by Hendrik Van
Balen, an underestimated contemporary of Rubens. There are
charming pastoral scenes by Antoine Watteau and his pupil
Jean-Baptiste Pater. Jongkind's *Estacade* is a fine painting of the
Seine in 1852. Jean-Jacques Henner has a very seductive woman
in black. He delighted our great-grandfathers at the turn of the
century with his sensuous nudes.

The best-known and best painting is Ingres's *Paolo and
Francesca*, showing the scene when Francesca da Rimini is caught
by her husband, Lanciotto Malatesta, in a passionate scene with
her brother-in-law. There are interesting works by Fragonard,
Corot (landscapes), Romney, Géricault and Delacroix, and a
particularly unexpected *St Barbara* by Millet, better known to us
for painting farm workers and landscapes.

To the annoyance of Angers's traditionalists, the thirteenth-
century abbey church of Toussaint was added to the museum,
given plain glass windows and a metal-supported glass roof and
is now the David d'Angers Gallery. In it are the works of the
local sculptor who loved to make huge statues of famous men.
He lived from 1788 to 1856 and was a contemporary of Jacques-
Louis David (1748–1825), the leader of the Neoclassical movement, a sort of dictator of the arts after the Revolution and then
Napoleon's official painter. They are still confused with each
other. David d'Angers, son of an Angers wood carver, was in
fact the pupil of Jacques-Louis David. He created fifty-five
statues, mostly huge, a hundred and fifty busts and many medallions and bas-reliefs, and he designed the front of the Panthéon
in Paris.

I find this exhibition fascinating. There are statues and busts
of famous people who almost all look quite different from how I
imagined them – except Jean Bart, the Dunkerque sailor whom
the rest of the world called a pirate and the French called a hero.

Here he is, about ten times life size, in seaboots astride a cannon. You'll find, too, more life-size busts of Châteaubriand, Victor Hugo, Goethe and Balzac (exhibition shut on Mondays).

Angers is a lively city, helped by many thousands of students from its historic university. Its shops are good quality, the cafés and bars of the place du Ralliement, the main square, are nearly always crowded and chatty. Many of the narrow old streets around the château are now blessedly closed to vehicles and although it is outside the centre, the big agricultural market adds considerably to the feeling of action and prosperity. So do the wine caves. Angers has always been a big marketing centre for Anjou wines. There is a shortage of old houses for such an historic town but the Anglicized American writer Henry James, who seems to have been in a bad mood in Angers, was exaggerating when he said that it had been 'stupidly and vulgarly modernized'. I have the impression that James did not travel well and went sour. Perhaps he should have stayed in his delightful house in Rye. One of the less disturbed old areas of Angers is the quartier of La Doutre (from d'Outre-Maine, 'beyond the Maine'), inhabited since the Middle Ages, a snob area until the Revolution, when it fell on hard times. Now the old timber-framed houses and fifteenth-century mansions of place Laiterie have been well restored and there are more old houses along rue Beaurepaire leading to Pont de Verdun. Look at No 67, the apothecary's house, decorated with statues. At Trélazé, 6 kilometres east from Angers, they still produce the pleasing grey-blue slate used for the roofs of the great châteaux of the Loire since the twelfth century, but now they quarry it underground, though they saw and split it on the surface. They have to split 100 tons of schist to get 15 tons of blue slate. You can see how the old Perreyeux (slate miners) lived.

Avrillé, 5 kilometres northwest, is restoring its Angevin windmills. Cointreau, the liqueur, is made in Angers-St Barthélemy. Adolphe Cointreau (1823–94) kept a sweetshop and made cherry brandy from an old family recipe. Then he started a distillery to make fruit alcoholic drinks. Then his son concocted a clear liqueur made from orange peel, which he called Triple Sec Curaçao, but so many companies stole the Triple Sec tag that they changed the name to Cointreau. It became very popular in the cocktail era. Most famous of its cocktails is still the Sidecar (one part Cointreau, one or two parts Cognac, one part lemon juice, shaken with ice). Use whisky for brandy and it becomes Silent Third. The popular White Lady is ½ gin, ¼ Cointreau, ¼ lemon juice. Cointreau's distillery is at Carrefour Molière (41.43.25.21). For visits, enquire at the Tourist Office (see below).

Angers is a centre for cruising on the Maine and Loire. Cruisers *Roi René I* and *II* are like the Seine's Bateaux Mouches, with huge panoramic windows, bar and gastronomic meals. They start from quai la Savette across the Maine from the château (41.88.37.47 March – November). Information on other boat trips and boat hire from the tourist office (see below).

TOURIST INFORMATION Tourist Office, place Kennedy
(41.88.69.93)
WINE TASTING Maison de Vin, 5bis place Kennedy
MARKETS Daily, rue St Martin. Avrillé – Tuesdays
FESTIVALS Mid-May Fair-Exposition. June Angers en
Fête, (includes music, drama, art). Early September
Autumn Fête

## HOTELS

*Anjou, Restaurant Salamandre*, boul. Mar. Foch (41.88.24.82). On busy crossroads but saved by triple-glazing. Modernized old hotel. Good value meals. ROOMS E. MEALS C–E. Restaurant shut Sunday.

*France, Restaurant Plantagenet*, place de la Gare (41.88.49.42). Modernized 'Grand' Hotel. ROOMS D–E. MEALS B–C. Restaurant shut Saturday.

## RESTAURANTS

*Rose d'Anjou*, 9 place Ralliement (41.87.64.94). Formerly Le Quéré. New young chef is talented. Classic and regional cooking. MEALS C–F.

*Le Quéré*, 3 boul. Foch (41.87.69.94). Paul Le Quéré has moved a few hundred yards to the nineteenth-century mansion. Bedrooms being restored in 1991. Superb cooking (he trained at Robuchon). His wife Martine is a renowned sommelier. Expensive. MEALS G.

*Le Logis*, 17 rue St Laud (41.87.44.15). Superb fish superbly cooked. MEALS C–F. Shut mid-July–early August; Saturday evening, Sunday in summer.

# *Blois*

[LOIR-ET-CHER, MAP 3, page 273]

Blois is a charming city. It is like a once-shining jewel which has become rather neglected and faded but is being polished to return its sparkle. Some traditionalists have complained that the château has been over-restored and repainted. François I, who did much to make it so magnificent, would not agree. He was not a man to admire faded elegance. Blois's one great problem is shortage of parking. Park where you can, grabbing any legal spot, and walk, though you'll need to be fit. You will climb steep streets, ramps and stairs through a muddle of twisting, narrow, medieval streets until your muscles ache. As a friend said to me: 'It's a wonderful place to get fit for skiing or rugby.' But it is superbly rewarding.

   Out of season, you could probably park by the château but in season the space is crammed with coaches and cars. Blois was set on fire by Stuka dive-bombers and a bombardment in 1940 but the restoration has been done with love and care, so that in the centre are fine timbered houses, old mansions where you can peep into their courtyards and find treasures like the lovely staircase in the seventeenth-century Hôtel de la Chancellerie and the Italian Renaissance galleries and sculptures in the courtyard of Hôtel d'Alluye in rue St Honoré, which can be seen during office hours. The mansion was built in 1508 by Florimond Robertet, Treasurer to Charles VIII, Louis XII and François I.

Approaching Blois from the south bank of the river, from which you can see the line of its towers and steeples, you cross the humped bridge built in 1717–26 by Jacques Gabriel, which rises in the middle to an elegant pyramid bearing a globe and cross. Engineers believed in those days that a flat bridge could fall down. Across the bridge is rue Denis-Papin, which runs up to the castle – a street renowned for food shops, but particularly for *chocolatiers*, artists in chocolate who make superb concoctions, and for pâtisseries, with gâteaux like little sculptures. Just before the road swings left you reach Denis-Papin steps, with a good view to the south. The honouring of Papin is ironic. Born nearby in 1647, he was a Protestant and had to flee persecution after the Edict of Nantes, giving some freedom of worship to Protestants, was revoked. He swore never to return to Blois. A doctor of medicine, engineer and inventor, he realized the power of steam a hundred years before Watt. In England, where he worked with Boyle, he invented the marmite de Papin, the first pressure cooker. Moving to Germany, he invented a steamboat, which he sailed on the river Weser, but local fishermen, fearing for their livelihood, broke it up. So he returned to England.

From the top of Denis-Papin steps, rue du Palais leads to the place St Louis, with St Louis cathedral, whose tower dominates the town. That is all that remains of the delicate cathedral built by François I in the fifteenth century and destroyed by a hurricane in 1678. The tower is crowned by a double lantern. After the destruction, Louis XIV's Minister Colbert, who had been married in the cathedral, persuaded Louis to let him pay from the Royal purse for the rebuilding. An original church on the site was dedicated to a Frankish priest named St Soulaine who was buried there. His name was muddled with *se soûler* (to get drunk) and alcoholics were sent to his tomb to be cured!

The church of St Nicolas, by the river end of the château, is lovelier. Built in the twelfth century as church to a Benedictine abbey, it has a delightful three-storeyed early Gothic nave

*Staircase of the château at Blois*

inspired by Chartres Cathedral. Its lantern tower was added in the seventeenth century. The old abbey is now part of the city hospital facing a river quay.

The massive château is an awesome muddle. Its mixture of thirteenth- to seventeenth-century styles, ornate decorations, doorways and carvings can be quite bewildering. I love the

magnificent outside staircase-tower built by François I – a fine
blooming of Renaissance. It is a sumptuously beautiful
octagonal cage, with three sides built into the château, the other
five looking into a courtyard through glassless windows between
pillars. These were used as viewing balconies for jousts and
receptions.

The Count of Blois, Thibault the Trickster, almost certainly
built the first castle here. The Chatillon family, who took over,
built a medieval fortress from which the Tour du Foix remains.
The last of the line, Guy II de Chatillon, married a much
younger girl. The story of how he sold the château could be
made into a farce worthy of the Regency theatre. Louis d'Orléans, brother of Charles VI, and a notorious lecher and
trickster, coveted Blois. He seduced the young Chatillon bride.
Pleading poverty, he persuaded his mistress to give him large
sums of money, which she wheedled out of her adoring husband. He ran out of money and had to sell the château. Then
the wife realized that she had been fooled. Orléans didn't need
the money. He had saved it – and he used it to buy the château!

Louis was married to his cousin Valentine, Viscountess of
Milan. Among his mistresses was the Queen, Isabelle of Bavaria,
while his wife Valentine went to bed with the King, Charles VI.
As the Marquis de Sade said, 'He had his cousin for a wife and
his sister-in-law as a mistress.' It did him no good. In his fight to
be Regent he was assassinated. Despite his infidelities, his wife
was so upset at Louis's death that she shut herself up for the rest
of her life in the château in a room draped in black. Her son,
Charles d'Orléans, was no soldier. He was a literary man and
poet. But a man in his position had to take up arms, and he was
taken prisoner by the English at Agincourt. He spent more than
twenty-five years as a prisoner in London. His miserable family
did nothing to ransom him. But he seems to have been well
treated, even though he was mostly in the Tower of London,
and he spent much of his time composing poems, roundels and
ballads. When he was freed in 1440 he found that his wife,
Isabella, who had been the widow of Richard II of England, was
dead. So he retired to Blois, married the fourteen-year-old
Marie of Cleves, knocked down much of the château to build
one bigger and more comfortable, and held a literary court. The

vagabond poet François Villon was one of his visitors (*see* page 44) and took part in his poetry competitions called 'Concours de Blois'. The good King René of Anjou, who also preferred culture to power and politics, visited him, too.

He wanted a son, and after twenty-one years, when his wife was thirty-five and he was seventy-one, a son was born. He ignored the bawdy jokes from Court and called him Louis. Thirty years later the boy became King Louis XII.

When Louis had got rid of Jeanne de France and married Anne of Brittany, he moved the Court on the Loire from Amboise, which Anne loved, to Blois, where he had spent his childhood. He was very anxious to make Anne forget Charles and he encouraged her to furnish the castle luxuriously. Their little daughter Claude had the most magnificent nursery while her governess slept on a camp bed nearby covered in black serge. After Anne died, Claude was Duchess of Brittany, so Louis quickly married her to his cousin François of Angoulême who Louis made Count of Blois and his heir. Louis was not going to let France lose Brittany at the last hurdle. Meanwhile he himself married Mary Tudor, sister of England's Henry VIII, a lively, strong-willed girl of sixteen who wore him out with balls, parties and late nights, so that he soon died, and François became King.

When he and Claude had married at St-Germain-en-Laye François had immediately gone off hunting and left her to return to Blois with a solitary wagon containing all her personal effects and wedding gifts. He gave her a bed. There was no wedding feast. Claude was a retiring, frail girl who spent her time between reading and working tapestries among her ladies-in-waiting and bearing children. She had seven in nine years and died young. They set up their court at Amboise but she loved Blois where she had spent her happy childhood and they moved there. Among her ladies-in-waiting was a girl called Anne Bullen from Blickling in Norfolk, daughter of a former English Ambassador to France. She returned to Hever Castle in Kent and went to Court calling herself Anne Boleyn, with polished French Court manners. The poor girl was spotted by Henry VIII.

As you would expect, the most magnificent wing of Blois castle was built by François I and is well worth all the time you can spare on it, for it shows the Italian Renaissance in bloom for the first time in France. It is gloriously sumptuous and imaginative, spurning exact symmetry and glorying in an abundance of carved decorations. The staircase tower is ostentatiously superb.

After Claude's death, François started to build Chambord in the heart of hunting country and his interest in Blois waned.

Henri II succeeded to the throne and Catherine de' Medici arrived in Blois. Her room is rather mysterious. It has 237 panels and four are secret doors to cupboards, opened by a pedal in the skirting board. The snobbish French Court despised Catherine for being Italian and a banker's daughter. They called her a 'tradesman's daughter' and they said later that these were her poison cupboards. Balzac wrote in his book *Catherine de' Medici* that she was caught hiding secret papers there by Mary Stuart, her daughter-in-law. My guess is that she hid money and jewels there. Just above her room are the apartments of her son Henri III, where he had the Duke of Guise murdered by eight armed men while he hid behind a tapestry. On Christmas Eve, he had Guise's brother, the Cardinal of Lorraine, murdered. Their bodies were burned and thrown into the Loire. A year later Henri was assassinated and the new King Henri IV had little interest in the Loire.

Louis XIII gave the château to his brother and presumed heir, Gaston d'Orléans, to keep him busy. He was a notorious conspirator, especially against the powerful Cardinal Richelieu. The King had no son and Gaston was sure he would inherit the crown. He borrowed the royal architect Mansard and in 1635 they set about pulling down the whole château to put up an enormous four-sided classical building. Happily he had only destroyed part of François's wing and the nave of the St Calais chapel and built a wing when a new heir was born, the future Louis XIV. Gaston, no longer so dangerous, had his royal funds cut off by Richelieu and the rest of François's building was saved. Gaston lived in what was left of it.

The side of the château from the esplanade has the pointed gable of the thirteenth-century States General Chamber and the attractive Louis XII building with balconies to the bedrooms of Louis and his Minister Cardinal d'Amboise. A fine round arched portal, with a life-sized figure of Louis on horseback, leads to the inner courtyard. Only the chancel remains of St Calais chapel but it has some fine modern glass by Max Ingrand.

As in the François wing, you will find some fine old fire-places in the big rooms of the Louis wing by climbing to the first storey to the Beaux Arts Museum. This has interesting portraits, including those of Marie de' Medici by Rubens, Gaston d'Orléans and Louis XIV by Mignard, a series showing Adam and Eve in Paradise (Flemish sixteenth century) and an amusing 'proud moment' picture of all the VIPs of Blois as the Duchess of Angoulême passed through the town in 1823!

The château fell into disrepair in Louis XIV's reign, became a barracks, then was much restored last century, but damaged in 1944. More restoration has taken place since 1980. (Château visits daily unguided or with English-speaking guides. At the bottom of the staircase is shown in French a 'diaporama' – audio-visual history of the château.)

North-west, off ave Jean Laigret, is Pavillon d'Anne de Bretagne, Anne's elegant summer house, once in big gardens. It is now the Blois tourist office.

Westward from St Nicolas Church is the big Poulain chocolate factory, opened in 1848. (Visits on weekday mornings. Ask at tourist office or factory itself – tel. 54.78.39.21.)

In place du Château is a museum to Robert Houdin, better known as Houdini – a name stolen later by a US escapologist. Jean-Eugène Robert, born in Blois in 1805, was a clockmaker until he used the new electricity and clever mechanical devices to become a magician. When the Algerians were revolting under warlike leaders, he was sent there to destroy the influence of the marabouts, religious men claiming magic powers. One trick with a gun convinced their leaders that he was invulnerable. He also invented a periscope, electric clock and possibly the first electric motor. Twice he gave shows for Queen Victoria at Buckingham Palace. One exhibit, a glass clock, seems to have no mechanical parts. His grandson, the architect Paul Robert Houdin, put on the first ever son-et-lumière at Chambord in 1952.

Blois's son-et-lumière is called 'Spirits Prefer the Night' (*see* Festivals below).

Blois is an important market town for corn, wine, straw-berries and asparagus. Along the north bank of the Loire, six kilometres by N162, at Ménars is Madame de Pompadour's old château (*see* Ménars, page 206). Nine kilometres south-east by D956 is Château de Beauregard.

TOURIST INFORMATION Pavillon d'Anne de Bretagne,
3 ave Jean Laigret (57.74.06.49 – shut Sunday low
season)
MARKETS Daily (morning Sundays)
FESTIVALS Son-et-lumière nightly July, August, nightly
except Thursday, May, June; some days April,
September. About 45 minutes. First session in French,
second in English most nights (check at tourist office).
Commercial Fair end April–early May

## HOTELS

*L'Horset La Vallière*, 27 ave Maunoury (54.74.19.00). Recent, in town centre; modern rooms; comfortable restaurant with sensible prices. ROOMS E. MEALS B–E.

*Hostellerie de la Loire*, 8 rue Mar. Lattre-Tassigny (54.74.26.60). 17 rooms vary, some very simple. Overlooks Loire. Old style dishes very well cooked. ROOMS C–D. MEALS A–D. Shut Sunday low season.

*Le Médicis*, 2 allée François I (54.43.94.04). Renovated. Near station. Attractive; nice covered terrace. Imaginative cooking. ROOMS D–G. MEALS C–F. Shut 2–30 January; Sunday evening low season.

## RESTAURANTS

*Espérance*, 189 quai Bernard, 2km SW along N152 (54.78.09.01). Lovely Loire views. Best cooking in Blois; good range of menus. MEALS C–F. Shut last week February; 22 August–4 September; Sunday evening, Monday.

*Bocca d'Or*, 15 rue Haute (54.78.04.74). Modern cooking in nineteenth-century cellar. MEALS D–E. Shut February; Monday lunch, Sunday.

*Rendez-vous des Pêcheurs*, 27 rue Foix (54.74.67.48). Fresh fish from Nantes. Good value. MEALS C.

*Orangerie du Château*, 1 ave J. Laigret (54.78.05.36). Opened 1988 in the genuine château orangerie alongside Pavillon d'Anne de Bretagne (tourist office). Both historic monuments. Classic cooking, inevitably popular with tourists. MEALS D–F. Shut February holidays; Sunday evening, Monday in winter.

*La Péniche*, promenade Mail, quai St Jean (54.74.37.23). On a barge on the Loire river. The bearded Germain Bosque cooks lovely classic and regional dishes. MEALS D–F. Shut Sunday.

# *Le Mans*

[SARTHE, MAP 2, page 272]

Almost only businessmen and ardent motor-racing enthusiasts spend much time on their travels in the successful industrial town of Le Mans. The traffic alone is discouraging and the whole place seems totally absorbed in manufacture and business. Trade fairs, exhibitions, trade deals, banking and insurance are a way of life.

Yet the hidden treasures of Le Mans are far greater than those of many tourist towns and the medieval town of Vieux Mans is delightful.

The cathedral of St Julien stands proudly on top of a hill, its glorious architectural eccentricities disdaining the criticism of timid purists who want to file away their churches in pigeon holes marked Romanesque, Flamboyant, Gothic and Renaissance, and who regard any diversion from symmetry as blasphemy. St Julien's breaks the rules almost joyously. It is like an impressive and handsome mongrel dog which ought to be the founder of a new breed. You must see it for yourself. Not only are styles mixed but various builders seem to have stuck on odd bits, not all for the better. Someone put an unlovely porch over the south doorway which has twelfth-century statues similar in themes to those of the Royal Doorway at Chartres. The awesome choir, with a double ambulatory and twelve chapels in a half circle round it, towers above the nave and has thirteenth-century windows in vivid blues and reds almost equal to those of Chartres. See, too, the sixteenth-century tapestries over the choir. The Renaissance tomb in the Baptistery of Charles d'Anjou (1472) is by the Venetian sculptor Francesco Laurana.

From the outside, St Julien's is one of the most impressive cathedrals in Europe. Many of its idiosyncrasies can be blamed on history. The Romanesque part had been completed with transept towers when in 1063 William the Bastard of Normandy seized Le Mans from the Count of Maine and, true to character, infuriated the locals by taking away all their trade and citizen privileges. Then he went off to conquer England and the people of Le Mans revolted. Three times, William had to take the city back from its own people. Then his granddaughter Matilda married Geoffroy Plantagenet, Count of Anjou, who thus added Normandy and this area of Maine to his lands. He often lived in Le Mans and was buried in the Cathedral in 1151. His son Henry Plantagenet, later Henry II of England, was born in Le Mans and gave the town back its privileges. He loved it and intended to spend his old age there but his rebellious son Richard Coeur de Lion, in alliance with Philippe-Auguste of France, captured it. Philippe-Auguste held it until the new King of England, John, took it back. But he lost it again and Philippe-Auguste gave it to Richard's widow, Queen Berengaria, who did a great deal for it. She founded nearby Epau Abbey. The cathedral is floodlit inside and special organ music is played on Saturday evenings, 15 June to 31 August.

The winding streets and stepped alleys of the old town have restaurants and little shops of craftsmen and antique dealers between half-timbered fifteenth-century houses, Renaissance façades and fine eighteenth-century houses with wrought-iron balconies.

At No 1 place St Michel in the cathedral precincts lived the poet and satirist Paul Scarron (1610–66). An abbé, he was also a wit and a fast-liver until he had a bad illness. He joined the chapter at Le Mans cathedral but his illness became worse and he went to Paris to write for a living. His satires influenced Defoe, Fielding, Le Sage and Smollett. Although becoming increasingly paralysed, he lived well and ran a Bohemian household, visited by many writers, politicians and leaders of fashion.

Rather cynically, as he became more paralysed, he married a lovely but penniless seventeen-year-old orphan, Françoise d'Aubigné, granddaughter of the Protestant soldier poet and friend of Henri IV. She was almost a prude and put a stop to his Bohemian life. He died in 1660 leaving her in poverty, but her friend Madame de Montespan, mistress of Louis XIV, gave her a job looking after her two children, whose father was the King. Louis loved these children and Françoise looked after them so well that the King showered gifts on her and she was able to buy the estate of Maintenon, so she became a Marquise. She became very useful to the King and her prudery did not discourage her from pushing her friend Madame de Montespan from the Royal bed to become the Royal mistress. And when the Queen died she persuaded the king to marry her in secret. When Louis finally died, she retired to a home she had set up for poor girls of aristocratic families.

Just off place St Michel is a house called Maison de la Reine Bérengère in a street of that name. It was not really Queen Berengaria's house. It was built by a rich alderman in 1490 and contains a museum of Maine art, including glazed pottery from Malicorne and folklore (shut Mondays, Tuesdays).

The town hall by place St Pierre is in the former palace of the Count of Maine (1760). East of the cathedral is Jardin Horticulture, a fine garden with rocks and cascading streams, and a walk with views over the cathedral. It was laid out in 1851 by Alphand, who designed Paris parks including the Bois de Boulogne.

The tourist office is in a timbered house with a death's head on a post on a corner of rue Wilbur Wright – named after the US airman who made the first flight in France on 8 August 1908 from the racecourse inside the Le Mans car race circuit. He was brought over by Léon Bollée, one of the motor-car pioneering family. Long before the Le Mans 24-Hour Race for sports cars was started in 1923, Le Mans was a pioneer city for designing

*A street in Le Mans*

and making cars. The Bollée family produced cars from 1873, when Amédée Bollée built his first steam car, to 1924, when their factory was sold to William Morris (later Lord Nuffield) to produce his first 'bull-nose' Morrises in France. In 1878 the family pioneered independent suspension on their Mancelle car, then continued to produce advanced designs, including the first shaft-driven car with spiral-bevel gearing and then the futuristic streamlined torpedo-shaped racing cars in 1899 with a 20-hp 'monobloc four' engine with twin carburettors in a chassis with rear independent suspension. These cars approached 100 kph (60 mph) – incredibly fast at the time. One Bollée brother produced big production cars, the other a few expensive cars.

You can see their steam and petrol cars in the Automobile Museum of the Le Mans racing circuit, just across from the Automobile Club at the north end of the stands. Drive through a tunnel off D139 south of the town just before you reach the stands. The museum is inside the Bugatti Circuit, which is used as a school for racing drivers. The museum has about two hundred vintage cars from early days to recent times, including steam and electric, and an 1885 De Dion, but exhibits are shown in rotation (shut Tuesdays low season).

The twenty-four-hour race circuit at Le Mans has changed over the years to take faster cars. It once ran into the city and was much longer. Now its two side-legs are D138 and D139, joined at the bottom by D140 which runs from the exciting Mulsanne corner to Arnage corner. Along D139 at Porsche bend it joins private roads past the karting track, motor-cycle track and the famous S-bends (les Esses) with side road to the pits and stands. It is 13.64 kilometres long.

The list of notable runners includes some nostalgic names of cars no longer made – Chenard Walcker (which won the first race in 1923), Bugatti, Delahaye, Lea-Francis, Alvis, Sunbeam, Talbot, Stutz, Healey, MG, Singer, Darracq, Riley. The huge Bentleys dominated at first, winning in 1924, then four times in 1927–30, prompting a sour comment from Ettore Bugatti himself: 'The British always did make good lorries.'

Jaguars have won seven times, Alfa Romeo four times, and other great winners include Mercedes, Ferrari, Bugatti, Aston-Martin, Lagonda, Delahaye. The first car to average over 100 mph was a Jaguar in 1953 which averaged 105.8 mph. It was using a new invention – Dunlop disc-brakes! Porsche dominated almost completely until recently, with the ex-Grand Prix formula Belgian driver Jacky Ickx as the most successful Le Mans driver ever. But regulations now allow cars that are virtually racing cars with bodies totally unrecognizable from the cars in showroom windows. No longer can a man step into his highly tuned road sports car and motor it round consistently for twenty-four hours to finish third behind two Mercedes as my friend Tom Wisdom, the London motoring journalist, did in the 1950s. Once people all over Europe listened to the race on radio and wanted their favourite cars to win. Now interest is confined to motor-racing enthusiasts. But there is still a carnival at the circuit with fairgrounds, bars, picnics, restaurants, dancing and all-night parties. The horse racing course of Les Hunaudières is inside the circuit.

The Cistercian abbey, which Queen Berengaria of England founded in 1229, is in a country park on the banks of the river Huisne four kilometres south-east of Le Mans by D4. It is used for exhibitions and concerts (shut Thursday). The Queen's recumbent figure on her tomb is in the church. The present building is from the fourteenth to fifteenth centuries. The original was destroyed in 1365, either by a brigand band or by local people to stop the English fortifying it.

TOURIST INFORMATION 38 place République
(43.28.17.22)
MARKET daily except Monday. Friday is the most
important.
FESTIVALS April (early) – 24hr motor-cycle race. Mid-
June – 24hr car race. Early July – Medieval Festival 'Les
Cénomanies'. Late September – Formula 3000 car race

## HOTELS

*Concorde*, 16 ave Gén-Leclerc (43.24.12.30). Elegant, re-decorated hotel in centre. Good regional cooking. ROOMS E–G. MEALS C–E.

*Chantecler*, 50 rue Pelouse (43.24.58.53). Good value, near station. ROOMS D. Feuillantine restaurant run separately. MEALS A–F. Restaurant shut 1–7 April; middle July–early August; 21 December–2 January; Sunday and Monday evenings. (Tel. restaurant 43.28.00.38.)

*Closerie*, Restaurant Auberge Foresterie, 4km on N157 route Laval (43.28.69.92). Excellent value meals; newly opened 3–star hotel. ROOMS E–F. MEALS B.

## RESTAURANTS

*Grenier à Sel*, 26 place Éperon (43.23.26.30). Inventive cooking without fashionable nonsenses; good portions. MEALS C–F. Shut part February; Sunday, Monday.

*Ciboulette*, 14 rue de la Vieille Porte (43.24.65.67). In old town. Fresh ingredients from the market. MEALS D–F. Shut first 3 weeks August; Saturday, Sunday.

# *Nantes*

[LOIRE-ATLANTIQUE, MAP 4, page 274]

To keep its important position as a port and industrial centre, Nantes has sacrificed much of its heritage. Like Liverpool, it grew on cotton, sugar, rum and the slave trade, and it was the gateway of waterborne trade right through the Loire valley. It has kept up with the needs of modern ship-borne trade more successfully than Liverpool.

After Second World War damage it was completely transformed. Though some of the old was saved, the rest was torn apart to make way for massive factories, high rise offices and apartments and wide, straight roads. It is a memorial now to

France's aggressive post-war bid for technological 'progress' and industrialization. Three Loire tributaries which flowed through it have been covered with concrete, two islands have been swallowed and the little trains which used to move goods from the quays and send impatient drivers mad have gone. But there are still terrible parking problems. Gone, too, are its old narrow streets with dark dubious bars and cafés.

The port at the mouth of the Loire, together with its former outer port of St Nazaire, still builds naval and commercial ships, especially dredgers.

Nantes still has sugar refineries and canneries, its old specialities, but now also produces oil-boring equipment, refrigeration plants, electronics, telecommunication equipment, ships' boilers and chemical products. The first ships' engine using nuclear energy was produced there. They still distribute and export Loire wines, especially Muscadet.

Nantes was once capital of the Duchy of Brittany and played a very important part in history. After the Revolution it was made capital of a new non-Breton département called Loire-Atlantique, which it still is. It is also now capital of the new Pays-de-la-Loire region, entirely separate from Brittany. Loire-Atlantique also includes places such as La Baule, which are still regarded as Breton resorts, but you cannot leave out Nantes and the Muscadet wine country from a true guide to the Loire Valley. So I have put the whole of Loire-Atlantique, including Nantes, in my guide to Brittany and in this book included Nantes and the places bordering the river.

Through the Middle Ages Nantes and Rennes argued over which was capital of Brittany. The Dukes stayed in both almost alternately and fought with the French over Nantes until Anne, Duchess of Brittany, married two French kings and her daughter married another and bequeathed Brittany to France.

In the eighteenth century Nantes became very prosperous, big shipowners and traders lived like aristocrats and built themselves mansions. Slave boats sailed to the Guinea coast of Africa laden with brandy and goods to exchange for slaves. They then sailed to the West Indies where the wretched slaves who had survived were sold. The boats returned to Nantes with sugar, spices, cotton and rum. It was called the Ebony Trade.

The Revolution brought an end to it. Most Nantais were strongly religious Catholics (the Protestants had fled after the Edict of Nantes had been revoked), were Royalist and against the Revolution. A terrible revenge was taken against them. Paris sent the notorious Jean-Baptisite Carrier to purge Nantes of Royalists. He arrested everyone slightly suspect and when he ran out of prison space he put them into barges which were scuttled in the Loire opposite Chantenay. One of his tricks was called 'les mariages républicains'. A man and woman were stripped naked, tied together and thrown in the Loire to drown. He killed 16,000 people in four months. Even the Revolutionary Tribunal which had started the Terror condemned him. He himself was guillotined.

The Revolutionary Convention then banned the Slave Trade and under Napoleon home-grown French sugar beet was substituted for sugar from the Antilles (French West Indies), originally because of a British Navy blockade. Furthermore, ships became too big to reach Nantes, which suffered a great depression and turned away from the sea to metal industries and food canning. Then in 1856 Nantes founded an outer port at St Nazaire and in 1892 dug a lateral canal to the river. By 1911 new techniques were used to dredge the estuary to take bigger ships. The canal was abandoned. Cargo ships up to 8¼ metres' draught can dock at high tides, but the really big ships such as supertankers, battleships and aircraft-carriers use St Nazaire.

The Château des Ducs in Nantes is a severe fortress with a few softer touches, such as the Tour de la Couronne d'Or with Italianate loggias, began in 1466 by Duke François II and finished by his daughter Duchess Anne.

The court of the Duke's palace, part of the château, was used for jousting and for performing plays – from religious mystery plays to farces. The Governor's Palace, rebuilt after a fire in 1684, contained the prisons. Among people held there was Cardinal de Retz, the Archbishop of Paris, who plotted against Louis XIV's chief minister Mazarin and was a leader in 1648 of the Fronde, an uprising of aristocrats. He escaped from Nantes to Spain, then England, but returned to become Abbot of St Denis in Paris. Another, earlier, prisoner was the Breton

Baron Gilles de Rais, who fought beside Joan of Arc and became Marshal of France. He retired to his estates and was alleged to have indulged in appalling orgies. He was accused of kidnapping a hundred and fifty children, using them for his lusts and sorceries, then killing them.

Nicolas Fouquet, Louis XIV's finance minister, was also imprisoned there. His free spending made Louis suspicious that he had his hand in the royal purse, and when he built a château at Vaux-le-Vicomte more than fit for a king and threw one of France's most lavish parties, that was too much. He was arrested and Louis never forgave him.

Louis XII married Anne of Brittany in the château, and there the newly crowned Henri IV issued his Edict of Nantes, giving rights of religious worship to the previously banned Protestants. He went to Nantes at the request of the ordinary people, who had been suffering sorely from the extremist Catholic League and its leader and Governor of Nantes, the Duke of Mercoeur, who had separatist ambitions for Brittany and area.

Musée d'Art Populaire Régional in the château shows some pleasing interiors of old peasant houses, furniture, costumes and *coiffes* (headdresses). Musée des Salorges is a maritime museum showing eighteenth- to nineteenth-century figureheads, models of seventeenth- to eighteenth-century boats, especially slavers, and little models of Loire river boats. Also on show are the earliest preserving jars, a hundred and fifty years old, still containing vegetables, and a large model of the famous Petit Beurre biscuit factory. (Château and museums shut on Tuesday except in July, August.)

The cathedral of St Pierre, started in 1434, was not actually completed until 1893, was badly damaged in 1944 and by fire in 1972. It is impressive inside. The clean, effective lines of its Flamboyant nave soar to 37½ metres, compared with 33½ metres for the vaulting of Notre Dame in Paris and 30½ metres for Westminster Abbey. The height is safe because it is built of limestone, not heavy granite. The Renaissance tomb of Duke François II and his wife is beautiful. They lie on a white marble slab.

The Jules Verne museum (3 rue de l'Hermitage – shut Tuesday) in a nineteenth-century mansion is devoted to the

*The cathedral of St Pierre*

great imaginative writer (*Around the World in Eighty Days* and *Journey to the Centre of the Earth*). Verne was born in Nantes in 1828 and died in 1905.

The Beaux Arts museum contains some interesting paintings by good artists rather than great masters, including Georges de la Tour (1593–1652) who has been recently 'discovered' after being forgotten for three centuries. There is one Rubens taken from Tournai cathedral.

At Maison de Guigny, 3 rue Mathelin-Rodier, uphill from the castle, a crazy comedy scene took place in 1832. The Duchess of Berry, an attractive, lively widow, was daughter-in-law of the deposed Bourbon King Charles X and her infant son the Duke of Chambord was heir to the French throne, which had been stolen by his uncle Louis-Philippe when he had been appointed Regent for the infant. The Duchess, exiled in Holyrood, Scotland, arrived in Nantes to raise a rebellion. She hid in this house for six months, with a staff of two men and a printing press sending out propaganda for her son.

A million francs was offered for information leading to her arrest. A clerk betrayed her. Her secretary spotted troops filling the streets and she, with her maid and two men, hid behind the attic fireplace. Unable to find her, the police left a guard in the house. Two of them lit a fire and the four behind the chimney became so hot that the women's dresses caught alight. The men put out the flames 'dispensing with ceremony', as the Duchess wrote afterwards. But the policemen awoke cold and relit the fire. This time the gentlemen failed in their duty. They were being asphyxiated and had to come out. The Duchess was sent to prison. When her son grew up, he did not really want the throne as Henri V, though he had three chances. He 'passed forty years of blameless inertia', dying in 1883 at sixty-three years of age.

TOURIST INFORMATION place du Commerce
(40.47.04.51)
WINE INFORMATION Interprofessional des Vins du
Pays Nantais, 17 rue des États (40.47.15.58) across rue
des États from Pont Levis of the château – includes
tastings
MARKETS daily; bigger market Saturdays
FESTIVALS June – Concours Hippique (Horse Trials);
End June–early July – Jazz Festival; First fortnight
September – Nantes Carnival

## HOTELS

*Pullman Beaulieu*, Île Beaulieu (40.41.30.00). Beside Loire river. Well equipped functional rooms, good taste. *Restaurant Tillac* now very good – regional and classic cooking. ROOMS F–G. MEALS B–E.

*L'Hôtel*, 8 rue Henri IV, facing château (40.29.30.31). No restaurant. Pretty rooms. Reasonably quiet. ROOMS E.

*La Lande-St Martin*, at Haute-Goulaine, 10km E on N149 (40.06.20.06). Reliable, comfortable, pleasant gardens away from Nantes industry. ROOMS C–D. MEALS B–E. Restaurant shut Sunday evening.

*Abbaye de Villeneuve*, at Les Sorinières, 10km S by D178 (40.04.40.25). Eighteenth-century abbey in peaceful park. One of the excellent Savry family hotels. Pricey. ROOMS G. MEALS F–G.

## RESTAURANTS

*La Cigale*, 4 place Graslin (40.69.79.41). Authentic 1900 brasserie, very popular with Nantais, young and old. Terrace in pedestrian street. Simple dishes, good choice. MEALS A–C.

*Maraîchers*, 21 rue Fouré (40.47.06.51): Super cooking in bistro atmosphere. Pricey. MEALS C–G. Shut Sunday.

# Orléans

[LOIRET, MAP 5, page 276]

Some patriotic Frenchmen still say that Paris is the head of France and Orléans is the heart. If so, then it is a hard heart these days, with its maze of concrete flyovers, motorway feed-roads, spaghetti junctions, and its new tall buildings. But see it from the south bank of the Loire looking over the bridge Pont George V across roof tops to St Donatien and, beyond it, the great cathedral of Ste Croix, and you can see that the old warm heart of Orléans has somehow survived through the city's violent history, including terrible damage in 1940. One of the three bridges is still the key to the city. Though Pont George V was named after the English king after the First World War, it was built when a medieval bridge collapsed in 1751 and called Pont-Royal. Madame de Pompadour crossed it when it was scarcely finished on her way to her château at Ménars in 1760. She opened the new bridge, and a local wit said that it must be safe, for it had borne France's greatest burden. It became Pont National, then Pont George V after the First World War. It led to the old town. In June 1940, German bombing started terrible fires which destroyed a quarter of the old town. To stop the German forces chasing them southward, the French blew up one arch. When the Germans had repaired it, they changed its name to Pont Adolf Hitler!

Alas, Orléans had to be rebuilt in a hurry, and there was much bickering between conflicting interests of industrialists, bombed-out people needing new homes, traditionalists wanting to preserve and restore the old town, and 'greens' trying to preserve open spaces. Mostly, concrete and bulldozers won. The ancient quarter of La Charpenterie was replaced with a multi-storey car park and a plasticky-looking market. But rue Royale was rebuilt from the George V bridge to the place du Martroi, where the old pavilions have been rebuilt. Rue Royale was started in Louis XV's reign but never finished. The arcades were never built. The new one is wide, elegant, animated and has arcades. The new suburb of La Source, south of the river, is modernly pleasant and has good facilities although built in a green belt area. The Floral Park started in 1967 is a beautiful masterpiece.

Place du Martroi, now blessedly kept for pedestrians, is the centre of Orléans and in the centre of the square is a statue of Joan of Arc on a horse, designed by Denis Foyatier in 1855, with scenes from her life in bas-relief around the pedestal. It is not surprising that Orléans makes so much of Joan of Arc as a tourist attraction. She *did* save the city by slipping in with a

*Joan of Arc*

supply cart and rousing the dispirited French garrison to break
the English siege. Joan's feast day has been celebrated almost
without interruption in early May since 1430, the year after she
entered Orléans. But no girl was allowed to represent the Maid.
'She' was a boy dressed in city colours. In the nineteenth century
even the boy was dropped. She was represented by a standard.
In 1912 the cathedral bells were rung to welcome a girl representing Joan, but not until 1945 was a girl chosen every year.

A road made last century but called rue Jeanne d'Arc runs
from rue Royale to the Cathedral of Sainte Croix. Here in the
chancel she gave thanks for her first victory over the English.
And here is a marble statue of Cardinal Touchet kneeling
before St Joan's altar. He fought for years to have her canonized. It was 1920 before she became a saint but soon she
became patron saint of France. The chapel is dedicated to her
and has a marble statue of her by the sculptor André Césare
Vermare.

The cathedral was started in the thirteenth century,
extended until the sixteenth century but was partly destroyed by
Protestants in 1568. They took away the base stones of four
pillars, replaced them with hollow logs filled with gunpowder,
then lit fuses – just as Philippe-Auguste's *sapeurs* had done to
English medieval castles.

When the Protestant leader Henri of Navarre announced he
was a Catholic to become Henri IV, he tried to show his sincerity
by promising to rebuild the cathedral in Gothic style. Starting in
1601, rebuilding continued through several reigns, always in
Gothic style, avoiding the dangers of a style hotch-potch but
bringing criticism that it was anachronistic. Gothic was supposed
to end with the Renaissance. In Louis XIV's reign the argument
between supporters of the two styles became so heated that the
King stepped in as referee, deciding in favour of Gothic. Later
Marcel Proust described it as the ugliest church in France. Its
two towers do look rather strange and it is cold-looking inside.
Spires were added, then removed. The present ones were added
under the Empire of Napoleon III. They rise to 113 metres.
The towers had to be restored after damage from German
incendiary bombs.

At the other end of rue Jeanne d'Arc in place de Gaulle is
Maison Jeanne d'Arc where her friend Dunois lodged her when
she got into the city. It belonged to Jacques Bourgeois, treasurer
of Charles, Duke of Orléans, who was still a prisoner in England
from his capture at Agincourt. In fact, the house where Joan
stayed was knocked down by the Germans in 1940. This is a
1965 copy, with the story of her raising of the siege, including an
audio-visual presentation (open daily except Mondays, 1 May
–31 October, afternoons only for rest of year).

Just north-west of the cathedral in place d'Étape opposite the town hall is Hôtel Groslot, built in 1530, enlarged in 1790 with two matching wings. There is a statue of St Joan looking more feminine than usual at the foot of the steps, a replica of the one in marble at Versailles by Princess Marie d'Orléans, given to Orléans by her father King Louis-Philippe last century.

Hôtel Groslot, built by a merchant, received kings when they were in the city. In 1560, the seventeen-year-old King François II, his girl bride Mary, Queen of Scots, his mother, Catherine de' Medici, the Duke of Guise, his brother the Cardinal of Lorraine and their court came to Orléans. At Guise's suggestion the young king called an Estates General in Hôtel Groslot, demanding the presence of the two Protestant leaders, the Prince of Condé and his elder brother Antoine de Bourbon, King of Navarre. They were promised safe conduct. Condé fell into the trap, was arrested and sentenced to death. The King of Navarre was to be goaded into anger and killed by Guise's men under the excuse of guarding the King of France. But Catherine de' Medici warned him, he refused to lose his temper and they had no excuse to kill a king, however minor. Suddenly François died, in the house, from a brain infection. Condé was saved.

Condé returned later with a Protestant army and occupied the house. The son of its original owner, Jérôme Groslot, now a city magistrate, got his revenge with a Guise-like reign of terror on Catholics, hanging them for past misdeeds. He was killed in Paris in 1572 at the Guise-inspired massacres of St Bartholomew's Night and Condé was captured and shot by the Catholic Leaguers.

Alongside the Town Hall opposite is the new Musée des Beaux Arts, of which Orléans is proud. Its range of pictures from the fifteenth century to the twentieth is unusually wide and interesting. Among those particularly worth a long look are a fifteenth-century *Virgin and Child with Angels* by Matteo di Giovanni, a fine early Velasquez of *St Thomas, Bacchus and Ariadne* by Louis Le Nain (1593–1648), an artist known for his peasant scenes, a charming portrait of *Pompadour* by François Hubert Drouais, court painter during her time as the Royal mistress, and a superb *Fête Gloanec* painted by Gauguin when in Brittany. A whole room is devoted to Max Jacob, the poet and painter arrested at nearby St-Benoît-sur-Loire by the Gestapo (*see* page 46).

Orléans' Parc Floral in La Source on D14 south of the Loire river is superb for nearly all the time it is open, from April to mid-November. It blazes with one group of magnificent colours after another amid old trees, lakes, fountains and modern sculptures. It covers 30 hectares and if you cannot manage a long walk, you can go round in a train of covered but open-sided carriages.

In April tens of thousands of daffodils, tulips, hyacinths and other bulbs and stocks are in bloom. Azaleas, rhododendrons and a collection of irises of unusual colours are massed in May. In June and July 200,000 roses bloom and in July and August hundreds of thousands of plants of many types and colours. The dahlias which bloom in August and September are truly superb, and roses are still in bloom. In early November there are still chrysanthemums of many sizes and colours.

The park is named after what is called La Source du Loiret, the attractive little river which flows a mere 13 kilometres into the Loire just beyond St Hilaire-St Mesmin. In fact, the river's source may be at St Benoît about 17 kilometres away. La Source is where the river emerges after going underground. Or the Loiret could be an arm of the Loire, going underground at St Benoît. It comes up at La Source to form a pool where the temperature never varies from 12 to 15°C all the year. So it never freezes, and flamingos, cranes, ducks and other web-footed birds winter there. The water bubbles up at forty cubic metres a minute and its temperature is a great help to the flower growers. Deer and emus roam the park, which is shut in the mornings during winter.

The new university has been built around here and, in the new suburb of La Source built among the greenery, live many of the scientists, intellectuals and students. It is calm by day, dead by night. Alas, the university offices are in Château de la Source, a classical and elegant seventeenth-century house, so that you cannot go inside it. Between 1720 and 1725 Henry St John, Viscount Bolingbroke, lived there and formed a circle of French philosophers, literary men and revolutionary politicians. Voltaire read the manuscript of *Henriade* to them. Bolingbroke had been England's Tory Foreign Secretary under Queen Anne and had negotiated brilliantly the Treaty of Utrecht which had ended the War of the Spanish Succession to the disadvantage of England's allies.

When Queen Anne died and George I came to the throne, it was revealed that Bolingbroke was a secret Jacobite and had been planning the restoration of the Stuarts to the throne. He

*Orléans*

fled to France. Allowed to return to England, he looked after the exiled Voltaire and introduced him to leading writers and philosophers. There Voltaire was attracted to the philosophy of Locke. It was a strange friendship – the English Jacobean Tory and the French rebellious philosopher whose writings did much to foster the French Revolution.

Olivet, the little town on the banks of the Loiret, is now virtually a suburb of Orléans and not so fashionable as in the last century, but remains the haven to which many Orléans people escape on weekends and where some of them live. Families still take a day trip to its riverbanks for picnics, fishing and boating. The old windmills on the riverbank paths have long since become houses, some of the expensive old houses have become restaurants and hotels, some are divided into apartments, some have almost decayed, but are now being rescued and restored. Riverside terraces of restaurants could still be the setting for Renoir's *The Boating Party*. Most elegant is the covered terrace of Les Quatre Saisons, with its pink and white cloths over white tables, pink napkins, and usually pink flowers in the overhanging baskets. Even the white plastic stackable chairs have a certain style. And Le Rivage, which I have known for more than forty years, has boats tied up below its terrace for fishing or rowing to work up an appetite for old Loire dishes like grilled sandre, friture of small river fish, and river eels in feuillete of puff pastry.

TOURIST INFORMATION place Albert Ier (38.53.05.95)
MARKETS Tuesday, Wednesday, Thursday, Saturday
FESTIVALS around 8 May Festival of Joan of Arc; At
Olivet – 2nd week June – Watersports Festival

## HOTELS

*Cèdres*, 17 rue Mar. Foch (38.62.22.92). No restuarant. Modern. Convenient for centre; rooms very peaceful opening onto garden. ROOMS C–E.

*Orléans Parc* at La Chapelle-St Mesmin, 5km W by N152; 55 route d'Orléans (38.43.26.26). Nineteenth-century house in gardens by river Loire. Restaurant separately run. ROOMS D–E. MEALS D–G. Restaurant shut mid-August–1 September; Sunday, Saturday lunch.

*St Pierre*, 3 rue St Pierre du Martroi (38.53.38.77). Only seven rooms, near cathedral. Excellent value meals; wine bar for snacks. ROOMS C–E. MEALS B–D. Shut July, New Year; Sunday evening, Monday.

## RESTAURANTS

*Crémaillère*, 34 rue Notre-Dame-de-Recouvrance (38.53.49.17). Basically classic cooking with imaginative touches. Very good. Pricey. MEALS E–G. Shut Sunday evening.

*Antiquaires*, 2 rue au Lin (38.53.52.35). Old restaurant with period décor near Pont George V. Classic cooking with flair. MEALS C (weekdays), E–F. Shut Easter, 3 weeks August; Sunday, Monday.

*La Loire*, 6 rue Jean Hupeau (38.62.76.48). Good value, friendly. MEALS C–E. Shut mid–end August; Saturday lunch, Sunday.

# *Tours*

[INDRE-ET-LOIRE, MAP 3, page 273]

To visit Tours after the Second World War and right into the middle 1960s was a painful experience. Tours entered the war in 1939 as a historic, beautiful but faded and crumbling provincial city, proud to have been the Loire's centre for transport and industry for centuries. Most of it was contained between the Loire and Cher rivers. The wartime destruction was appalling. Nine thousand people were killed and many acres of buildings were ruined. Bulldozers took over for years.

Tours was not so much restored as almost totally changed. Far more even than Orléans, it became part of modern industrial France. Its industries spread north to swallow the little town of St Symphorien and southwards into big residential suburbs to house the new workers. Beyond the Cher is the huge university 'cité' where the students live. Industry brought ugly concrete expressways, traffic jams and concrete apartment blocks. But parts of the old city have been carefully and sympathetically restored at enormous cost.

The Gauls built originally on the right bank of the river and the Romans on the opposite bank. Their town was Urbs Turonum, the town of the Turons, hence Tours.

Prosperity came to the town through the spread of Christianity and the cult of St Martin, the Roman officer who gave half his cloak to a beggar, became a Christian, and changed his uniform, sword and charger for a rough gown, staff and a donkey. He became so renowned for his faith and charity that he was begged to become Bishop of Tours. He took the job and with burning zeal systematically destroyed all the old temples, statues and shrines, replacing them with churches and chapels. He set up the great teaching monastery of Marmoutier, just outside Tours. He died at Candes in AD397 and when his body was rowed by monks to Tours it was said that trees grew green, birds sang and plants burst into flower – in November. So our Indian Summer becomes in France St Martin's Summer.

So many pilgrims went to St Martin's tomb that a huge basilica was erected round it. Tours became rich from the pilgrim tourist trade. Alcuin, the great teacher from York Minster school, became Abbot of St Martin at the end of the eighth century, and set up his school for copying books.

The invading Norsemen burned down the basilica, abbeys and twenty-eight churches. A new basilica, built during the eleventh to thirteenth centuries, was abandoned during the Revolution and pulled down in 1802. Two Romanesque towers, Tour d'Horloge and the much-restored Tour Charlemagne, remain. The way to reach this old part of the city from the north bank is to cross the lovely eighteenth-century Pont Wilson, a bridge of fifteen arches, 420 metres long, which was partly blown up by the French in 1940 to stop the Germans chasing the retreating French government and by the Germans in 1944 to escape the Allied forces. It was not reopened to traffic until 1982. Locals still call it Pont Pierre (stone bridge). It leads to rue Nationale, originally called rue Royale, then, when Balzac lived there and called it 'The Queen of Streets', it was called rue Napoleon. Most of the old part of the city lies within 300 metres either side of the street, so that you can walk, which is the best thing to do in narrow old streets and Tours' heavy traffic. Westward along rue des Halles are the two towers, the site of the old basilica, and also the new Basilica of St Martin built between 1887 and 1924 – a rather odd building with a dome suggesting St Paul's in London. The street continues to the covered market. North from the new basilica is a charming square well worth seeing. Now called place Plumereau, it was carroi aux Chapeaux (the hat market) and is still lined with fifteenth-century wood-framed and stone-gabled houses. A vaulted passage leads into place St-Pierre-le-Puellier, a delightful little square with gardens. A Gallo-Roman and medieval cemetery has been excavated and the foundations of an ancient church uncovered. Go under a porch and there are some fine façades in rue de la Paix.

The west end of place St-Pierre leads to a very charming street with houses covering a wide range of styles from twelfth-century to eighteenth-century mansions. On the right is an unusual brick and stone house with fifteenth-century gable called Maison de Tristan, now the language centre. Several university faculties are around here. There are restaurants and cafés and the area is fairly lively especially in the evenings. On the opposite side of rue Nationale in the north-east quarter is the Cathedral, a masterpiece with some of the finest stained glass in France. I must admit that I didn't see *all* of it for years. It is made of delicate tufa stone, which crumbles, so that there is often scaffolding hiding part of it. It took a long time to build, from 1239 until the middle of the sixteenth century, and shows the whole development of Gothic style. The apse is thirteenth-century, the façade, built between 1427 and 1484, has adorned gables over the doorway and rich Flamboyant decoration. The north tower, completed around 1507 by the architect and sculptor Pierre de Valence, who also worked on Rouen Cathedral, is crowned with an early Renaissance dome with a little

lantern turret. The tower represents the Father, the south tower, from around 1550, represents the Son, so it is deliberately two metres shorter.

The glory of the narrow interior is the gorgeous stained glass, especially when the sun shines through the windows, reflecting the colours into the church. The tall windows showing the legends of the saints, the Passion and the Tree of Jesse in the chancel are more than seven hundred years old and are very similar to those in Sainte-Chapelle in Paris. The rose windows are even more beautiful.

Outside the north door of the cathedral is a charming cloister, Cloître de la Psalette, with an attractive sixteenth-century open staircase. It was the close of the 'Psalette', the choir school. In Balzac's *Curé de Tours*, Madame Garnard lived there, while the curé lived at 8 rue de la Psalette. Since Balzac's day nearby buildings have gone, showing the Flamboyant and Renaissance architecture. The former library on the ground floor was one of the greatest in France. Its windows now have modern glass by Max Ingrand. Balzac, who was born in Tours in 1799, loved the city.

The old Archbishop's Palace, on the other side of the cathedral, is elegant and especially attractive from its flower gardens. It houses the Beaux Arts museum which contains delightful silks and panelling from the time of Louis XIII to Louis XVI. Louis XI introduced the making of silk and cloth of gold to Tours to save costly imports. He moved it from Lyons, whose people he thought to be too lazy. In the sixteenth century, twenty thousand artisans were employed at two thousand looms. The museum also shows Rembrandt's *Flight into Egypt*, painted on wood, and pictures by Rubens, Dégas, and the local artist Jean Fouquet, the leading French painter of the fifteenth century, especially for miniatures and panel-paintings.

In the twelfth-century part of the mostly seventeenth- to eighteenth-century palace is the old Ecclesiastical Tribunal, the very place where the church judges decided that poor Jeanne de France, the Queen of France, had never consummated her marriage with Louis XII and that he was free to marry Anne of Brittany. Jeanne's interrogation by these churchmen was vicious, with constant reference to her deformities. The girl had a hunched back and diseased hip, and their marriage had been forced on them when Louis was fourteen and Jeanne was twelve by her father, Louis XI, who wanted the direct family line to continue. While Jeanne was being interrogated at Tours, at Amboise Louis piously perjured himself at the church altar, with one hand on the bible, swearing that he had never slept with Jeanne and adding coarse insults.

The people, who loved Jeanne, gave the church judges a few

coarse insults, too, when they left the Court in Tours. Jeanne founded a religious order and was canonized as Sainte Jeanne de Valois in 1952. The Church was making it up to her, albeit somewhat late.

Old crafts and life of the medieval journeymen-craftsmen are shown in the Musée du Compagnonnage in a sixteenth-century monks' dormitory of a former abbey at 8 rue Nationale. In the old cellar is a very good and enjoyable museum of wine, from vine-growing to production, from Noah's tipple to the current vintages (closed Tuesdays).

North of the cathedral near the river quais is the twelfth-century tower that was part of the old city gates built by Henry II of England. It is now called Tour de Guise. When the Duke of Guise was killed by Henri III of France, his fifteen-year-old son was imprisoned on the top floor of this tower, and the new King Henri IV kept him there to prevent him escaping to revive the Catholic League. He came down only for Mass in the chapel and was then heavily guarded. After three years he made love to the laundress brought in to clean his linen and she smuggled a rope to him. Coming out of chapel, he challenged the guards to a race up the spiral stairs, hopping on one leg. Being young, he got well ahead, sprinted to the top on both legs and bolted himself in his room. While the guards banged on the door, he let himself down on the rope outside to the ground, ran down the quay chased by shouting crowds, stole a baker's horse and rode away.

At the end of rue Nationale, by the town hall, is place Jean-Jaurès, the hub of Tours where people as well as traffic meet. Rue Nationale has most of the big shops. Beyond the square, rue Nationale becomes avenue de Grammont, which is lined with chairs and tables of cafés. West of the square is boulevard Béranger where they hold the great flower market.

Three kilometres along the south bank of the Loire by quai Pont Neuf and avenue Proudhon are the ruins of the Priory of St Cosme where the poet Ronsard was buried in 1585. He was prior for twenty years and lived in the charming little Prior's lodging, still there, but altered in the seventeenth century when the outside staircase was moved inside.

Nearby are the modest remains of the Château de Plessis-lès-Tours, including the room where Louis XI died in 1483, having built the château in 1463. It is worth reading Walter Scott's *Quentin Durward* to discover what a dreary life he led there. Cruel and bad-tempered, he had spent much of his life making enemies, imprisoning many in the terrible swinging cages at Loches like suspended bird cages not big enough for the victim to stand and rocking each time he moved. In his old age he became frightened of revenge and he hid at Plessis. He had a trellis of iron bars round the whole château, spikes on the walls and mobile sentry boxes in the grounds with firing slits. Crossbowmen patrolled the park, ordered to shoot anyone who looked at all suspicious. When younger he had used a leopard for hunting in the forest. Now he kept it in the courtyard and had boar, rabbits and foxes brought in for it to chase and tear to pieces. He was very pious and when dying called in the severe priest of the Minim Order, Francis of Paolo, to give him last rites. Francis performed his duty but refused to pray for Louis' recovery. But Louis had done something for the ordinary people of France. He had improved their lives by developing trade and industry and he was called King of Merchants. (Château closed Tuesdays and January.)

TOURIST INFORMATION place Mar. Leclerc (possible move to boul. Heurteloup) (47.05.58.08). Guided tours round old quarter
MARKETS Daily in Food Hall; Flowers Wednesday, Saturday in boulevard Béranger; Craft and secondhand market 1st and 3rd Sundays of the month in place Grand-Marché
FESTIVALS Early May trade fair; May Flower Pageant; July Garlic and Basil Fair; Wines of Touraine 2nd Saturday February

## HOTELS

*Univers, Restaurant Touraine,* 5 boul. Heurteloup (47.05.37.12). In centre but charming; quiet, opening onto courtyard. Napoleon, Churchill and Hemingway stayed here. So did Henry James, one hundred years ago, and said that the staff were so unnaturally polite that you could suspect they had some hidden vice and that they were pacifying you in advance. The chef came from 'Barrier'. ROOMS E–G. MEALS E. Restaurant shut Saturday.

*Groison, Restaurant Jardin du Castel*, 10 rue Groison (47.41.94.40). Restored eighteenth-century house, quiet. Attractive meals. ROOMS F–G. MEALS E–G. Shut early January–early February. Restaurant shut Saturday lunch, Wednesday.

*Bardet*, 57 rue Groison (47.41.41.11). Very pricey, but in charming Napoleon III house, quiet, lovely restaurant and Jean Bardet's cooking now rivals the great Charles Barrier. Swimming pool. ROOMS G. MEALS F–G. Restaurant shut Monday and Sunday evening in winter.

*Central*, 21 rue Berthelot (47.05.46.44). Pleasant, in city centre, garden. No restaurant. ROOMS D–E.

At Joué-lès-Tours (5km SW on D86 route Chinon).

*Château de Beaulieu* (47.53.20.26). Pricey; very attractive eighteenth-century manor in park. Classic cooking. ROOMS E–G. MEALS E–G.

*Théâtre*, 57 rue Scellerie (opposite Grand Théâtre) (47.05.31.29). Old house restored. No restaurant. ROOMS C–D.

## RESTAURANTS

*Barrier*, 101 ave Tranchée (47.54.20.39). Charles Barrier closed after tax problems, returned to continue his superb, personalized regional cooking, his two Michelin stars, and his huge fan club. MEALS E–G. Shut Sunday evening.

*La Roche Le Roy*, 55 rte St Avertin (47.27.22.00). Very good cooking, some classical dishes, some individual, some regional by Alain Couturier, formerly at La Poivrière in southern suburb. MEALS E–F. Shut 2 weeks August; Sunday.

*Le Relais*, place Mar. Leclerc (47.05.46.12). Inspired station buffet with garden décor and ex-Barrier chef. Eat cheaply or dearer more ambitious meals. MEALS A(weekdays), C–D. Shut Friday evening, Saturday.

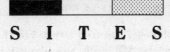
# *Azay-le-Rideau*

[INDRE-ET-LOIRE, MAP 3, page 273]

So many chateaux of the Loire are beautiful, attractive or dignified, but few tempt you to covet them as a place to live. Château
d'Azay-le-Rideau makes me dream of being extremely rich, of
refurnishing it in beautiful but comfortable Renaissance furniture and tapestries, and moving in, asking my friends to magnificent banquets with my choice of Loire wines, awaking to a
view of the Indre river below my window, watching the beautiful
women guests being rowed away on little river promenades
from the waters of the arm of the river diverted to make a moat,
taking a final stroll at night over the wooden moat bridge and
round the charming little park, to see the whole truly beautiful
Gothic and early Renaissance dream house with its pointed
towers, high chimneys, tall roofs, dormer windows and parapet.
It looks like a very beautiful fortress, but it was built essentially
as a home. The turrets, moats, and cobbled sentry walk are
token defences. Like Chenonceau, it was planned by a woman,
and although she employed an architect, Philippa Lesbahy
directed the building from 1518–29 while her husband, Gilles
Berthelot, one of the most important financiers in Europe, was
away, busily doing deals, especially for his king, François I. He
was a Treasurer-General of the Finances of France and Mayor
of Tours.

Alas, Philippa never lived in her dream house, which must
have saddened her until her death. She was cousin to the de
Semblançay family, and eighty-two-year-old Jacques de
Semblançay was the King's trusted treasurer, a man famous for
his personal integrity. François ordered Jacques to send a large
sum of money to Marshal Lautrec, who was campaigning for

France in the Milanese. Lautrec never got the money, lost his
campaign and lost the Milanese. Semblançay swore that he had
sent the money. He and Lautrec virtually accused the King's
mother, Louise of Savoy, of embezzling it. Semblançay was
hanged for corruption. Gilles Berthelot fled to Italy. He could
see the writing on the wall. François needed money and loved
beautiful châteaux. He took Berthelot's departure as a sign of
guilt and confiscated the château. The house was not really
finished. François handed it to the captain of his Archers who
had no money to complete Philippa's plans. But it is good
enough – a work of genius. Balzac, who loved it, called it 'a
polished diamond framed by the Indre'.

You enter by the wooden bridge over the moat into the main
courtyard. You will see various initials and emblems at the
entrance to the staircase, including an 'F' for François and his
Salamander – a piece of flattery which did no good. The staircase is elegant and was remarkable for its day. It was neither
spiral nor in ladder form, but went straight up from landing to
landing with the direction reversing on each floor. Furthermore,
it was *inside*. A woman's touch of comfort! There is an impressive
vaulted kitchen with a large fireplace, and many rooms are
furnished with fine Renaissance furniture and hung with tapestries. Among the paintings is a splendid picture of Gabrielle
d'Estrées, looking elegantly handsome, with her breasts bared
and beautiful.

The son-et-lumière has a Renaissance theme.

These days, Azay-le-Rideau relies heavily on the château
and its visitors, so there are some traffic and parking problems
in season. It is a pleasant little town with narrow streets and good
river views from roads around it. A medieval fortress stood on
the same site, built on piles in the river like the present château.
Joan of Arc's *gentil Dauphin* Charles passed this way with an
army when he was only fifteen. The fortress was held by Burgundians who jeered at the French and at Charles himself. As he
proved when he was Charles VII, he was vicious and brutal
when he had the upper hand and his men far outnumbered the
Burgundians. He took the castle, butchered all 350 of their
soldiers and officers, and burned down the town. It was known
as Azay-le-Brûlé – Azay the Burnt. Of that town there remains

*Azay-le-Rideau*

St Symphorien church, eleventh and twelfth century with a double-gabled façade.

Azay-le-Rideau produces a very nice little-known white wine from the usual Loire grape, Chenin. It is called by the Appellation Contrôlée of Touraine Azay-le-Rideau.

TOURIST INFORMATION Syndicat d'Initiative,
rue Nationale
(47.45.44.40)
MARKET Wednesday
FESTIVALS Wine Fair – last weekend in February; Apple
Fair – last weekend in November
SON-ET-LUMIÈRE – Easter and last weekend May–last
weekend September

## HOTELS

*Grand Monarque*, place République (47.45.40.08). In the Jacquet family since 1900. Slumped a little through family illness, now revitalized but the same splendid traditional regional dishes. Bedrooms much improved. ROOMS D–F. MEALS D–G. Shut mid-December–mid-January. Restaurant open mid March–early November.

*Biencourt*, 7 rue Balzac (47.45.20.75). Good value, clean. No restaurant. ROOMS C–D. Shut mid-November–1 March.

## RESTAURANTS

*Aigle d'Or*, 10 rue Adelaide Richer (47.45.24.58). Good value; fresh local products; good choice of menus. Run by ex-maître d'hotel from luxury Château d'Artigny. MEALS D–E. Shut 10–20 December; mid-January–mid-February; Sunday evening, Wednesday.

*Automate Gourmand*, 11 rue du Parc, Chapelle-St-Blaise, 1km. (47.45.39.07). Just a bistro; automate refers to the décor of old toys. Amusing; good value. MEALS B–D. Shut 1–21 March; 24–30 December; Tuesday.

# Chenonceau Château

[INDRE-ET-LOIRE, MAP 3, page 273]

Chenonceau is possibly the most beautiful house in the world. It was the first château to be designed as a comfortable home with no thought for defence and it has the most amusing history of all the châteaux of the Loire. It was the work of three women. Catherine Briconnet, wife of Thomas Bohier, Collector of Taxes for Charles VII, Louis XII and then François I, designed it in

*Chenonceau*

1512 and at the time it was completely revolutionary. It was built over the waters of the river Cher on piles which had once supported a water mill, and it was designed for comfort and convenience. Gone were the draughty outside spiral staircases and the long draughty corridors which joined strings of rooms and anterooms. There was one central straight-up staircase and on each floor a central vestibule room with all other rooms opening off it. Even the servants must have blessed Catherine for making their hard lives a little easier. The château that she left was a small, stunningly graceful white building with Italian symmetry, flanked by pretty little corbelled towers, sharply pointed, and beautifully ornamented balustrades and roof windows, all standing in the Cher river.

Bohier and his wife had obtained the estate of Chenonceau

in the first place by dubious methods. He had bought up land bit by bit all round an original château until the owner, Pierre de Marques, had no right of way to it and after a long legal battle he sold out. Bohier held a long string of important jobs under four kings. He was sent to Italy by the king while the château was being built. Three years later he died in Italy and two years later Catherine died. When his financial dealings were investigated by order of François I, it was found that he had been using Royal money for his deals and owed the King a fortune. François took the castle from his son.

Later the attractive and very intelligent mistress of Henri II, Diane de Poitiers, added to Chenonceau a lovely formal garden, which is still there, and hired one of the architects of Fontaine-bleau, Philibert Delorme, to build a bridge across the Cher 60 metres long. It was to be a beautiful new entrance to the château. Henri II paid for it by putting a tax on church bells.

When Henri was killed in the jousting lists by Montgomery, the commander of his Scots guard, his widow Catherine de' Medici kicked out Diane and took over the château. These two women, different in every way and hated enemies, both adored Chenonceau. Catherine may have been despised as a trades-man's daughter by French courtiers but she was, of course, from one of the richest and most powerful families in Florence, lovers of beauty and patrons of the arts. She, too, had a garden and a lovely park laid out. She built two storeys onto the bridge and buildings beyond. The long gallery of the enclosed bridge is very beautiful to this day. In the First World War it was used as a hospital, with long rows of beds. In the Second World War it was on the very border of Occupied and Unoccupied France, and through the gallery passed escaped prisoners-of-war, Resistance men, and Frenchmen on the run from the Gestapo.

Two other women were involved deeply in its history. One was Louise-Marie-Madeleine Guillaume Dupin, second wife of the Farmer-General of Taxes, who bought the château in 1733. Madame Dupin was delightful, intelligent and good-hearted. She invited Jean-Jacques Rousseau to be her secretary and to teach the children of her husband's first marriage. 'We were very gay in this lovely place,' he wrote, 'and we ate very well. I became as fat as a monk.' He also composed several pieces of music for three voices and a three-act play for the family to perform. Madame Dupin lived to be ninety-three and her local kindness and charity saved the château from destruction in the Revolution.

Then in 1864 the château was bought by Madame Pelouze, an expert on Renaissance architecture, who restored it as nearly as possible to its original design. The Menier chocolate family bought it in 1909 and spent a fortune keeping it up.

Catherine de' Medici was a strange woman. She was plain, it seems, and became fat early in life. Her meddling in politics was disastrous. Inevitably, she was desperately jealous of her husband Henri II's intelligent and beautiful mistress, Diane de Poitiers. Pierre de Bourdeilles, abbot, wit, diplomat and Royal Chamberlain, wrote under the pseudonym of 'Brantôme' witty, sometimes scurrilous, stories of Court intrigues, junketings and scandals. He told how Queen Catherine had a hole cut in her rival's bedroom ceiling to spy on her. One balmy night that was tempting for love-making she saw what she admitted to be a 'beautiful, white-skinned woman, delicate and fresh, half-naked, caressing her lover, and the lover returned her caresses until they left the bed and disported themselves on the rug'.

The lover was, of course, Catherine's husband, King Henri. Diane was twenty years older than him.

After Henri was killed, Catherine threw Diane out of Chenonceau, but, in a strangely generous gesture, gave her the Château of Chaumont. After Chenonceau, Diane found it far too gloomy, and retired to her old home at Château d'Anet, near Dreux.

Catherine loved show and held some spectacular parties at Chenonceau. Visitors were greeted by girls disguised as mermaids rising from the moats along the great avenue leading to the castle. Singing nymphs ran from the thickets, then satyrs rushed out to chase them. The satyrs were driven off by mounted knights. Banquets, dances, masquerades and fireworks followed. Once there was a naval battle of scaled-down ships on the Cher river, with ships catching fire and sinking. She threw the greatest party for her son, Henri III, whose sexual interests were ambiguous. At masques and parties he appeared with painted lips and cheeks, pearls in his ears, a pearl necklace around his throat. His 'mignons' were painted, too, hair curled and rising above a little velvet cap like fashionable women wore and their heads sticking out of starched ruffles. The guests were served at tables by the younger ladies of the Court, duchesses and countesses, naked to the waist and wearing men's pantaloons. They were called Maîtrices de l'Hôtel – appropriately, for most of them, married or not, were mistresses of at least one of the men at Court. One of them was Charlotte de Beaune, now Madame de Sauve and later Marquise de Noirmoutier, who showed great religious tolerance. She slept alternate nights with a Protestant and a Catholic. The Catholic Duc de Guise spent his last night in her bed before being murdered on the orders of Henri III.

Despite his odd behaviour, Henri's wife, Louise of Lorraine, a devout girl, was devoted to him. She was at the party. He wrote a last affectionate letter to her when he was lying wounded telling her to stay at Chenonceau. He was dead when she got it, and she obeyed his order completely. She dressed in Royal mourning white until her death, hung all his rooms in the château in black, covered his bed, chairs and even his prayer stool in black, ornamented with silver tear-drops, and she prayed for him day and night. In the village they used to say that her ghost was seen at the windows on moonlit nights, feeling her rosary. La Bonne Reine Blanche, they called her.

Especially in summer, when the crowds pour in by car and coach from all over Europe, the arrival at Chenonceau lacks atmosphere. There is a snack bar, a souvenir stall selling Château Chenonceau wine, a restaurant in the old stables, an open train, and streams of tourists hurrying back and forth along the drive, cameras ready as if they must photograph it immediately before it collapses. I love it in spring or autumn when you can wander in peace along the long approach drive under plane trees beside the canals, rest in the gardens and dally beside the Cher where Diane de Poitiers liked to take a morning bathe. But whenever you see it, Chenonceau looks delicious – serene, bright and happy.

You enter the château through the guardroom, hung with lovely sixteenth-century tapestries. The chapel alongside has two bays. Its five-sided choir has a sixteenth-century bas-relief of

Madonna and Child and two centuries of graffiti on the walls. Scots Guards serving Mary Stuart left contributions dated 1543 and 1546. The modern stained glass replaced sixteenth-century glass destroyed in a 1944 bombardment.

The bedroom of Diane is almost bare, but has a good sixteenth-century fireplace by Jean Goujon and Flemish wall tapestries. The Henri Sauvage painting of Catherine de' Medici on the mantelpiece must be a puckish joke. Catherine de' Medici's Cabinet Vert, a neighbouring room, has a beamed ceiling, fine furnishings, paintings and an Oudenarde Flemish tapestry. Although he only stayed twice, François I's bedroom has some of the greatest treasures, including a magnificent fireplace, lovely Italian furnishings and two interesting paintings – Diane de Poitiers as the *Huntress Diana*, almost certainly by Francesco Primaticcio, one of the two Italian artists who decorated Fontainebleau, and the *Three Graces* by one of the Van Loo family. His models were the three Mailly-Nesle sisters, two countesses and a duchess, all shown nude. All three were mistresses of Louis XV, who liked to go from sister to sister. He took two of them on his Flanders campaign in 1744 but the Flemings were so scandalized that he had to send them home. As they left, the people of Metz emptied chamber-pots over their carriages.

In the Grand Salon, called Louis XIII's chamber, is a dramatic painting of *Christ and St John* attributed to Rubens, a portrait of *Louis XIV* by Hyacinthe Rigaud which Louis sent after a visit, and a picture of a most attractive young lady with big brown eyes – Madame Lupin, eighteenth-century mistress of the house.

Upstairs rooms have been recreated effectively in sixteenth-century style with magnificent Gobelin tapestries. In the vestibule are Oudenarde tapestries showing scenes and sculptures in Carrara marble of Roman Emperors, brought by Catherine de' Medici from Florence.

Most Frenchmen love Gabrielle d'Estrées, favourite mistress of their favourite King Henri IV, and it is no surprise that the bedroom she used when she stayed at the château has been completely restored. She came with Henri to see Louise of Lorraine, widow of Henri III. Her brother, the Duke of Mercoeur, was last leader of the Catholic League, Henri's enemies. Henri wanted him to give up and give France some peace. A deal was made under which the Duke's daughter Françoise should marry César of Vendôme, son of Henri and Gabrielle. As a nice wedding present César inherited Chenonceau in 1624. Although his room is very attractive, he preferred his estate at Anet.

Catherine's long gallery is still the great jewel of Chenonceau. Its black and white chequered floor contrasts with the soporific flow of the quietly flowing Cher which you see from its windows – a view bringing thoughts of all the people, the great and the sinister, the happy and sad, who have stood watching the water through the centuries. There are lifeless models of many of them, authentically costumed, in the waxworks museum in the building called Les Dômes which you can see to your left of the entrance drive as you leave the château.

The village, which is spelt with an 'x' on the end, Chenonceaux, is basically an old agricultural village but most of it has been turned over to tourism – a handful of restaurants, little hotels, snack-bars with antique shops. The old 'Relais Bon Laboureur' has been promoted. It has added 'et du Château' to its name since my youth when it was a fairly simple Logis with excellent value meals. A hundred years ago, when it was already a hundred years old, Henry James was praising its food. 'Where else but France, at a village inn, would we have fared so well?' Now it is bigger, much more luxurious, serves modern cuisine, and is much pricier.

A son-et-lumière is held in summer in the illuminated gardens of the château.

TOURIST INFORMATION 1 bis rue du Château (Easter–
September 47.23.94.45)
FESTIVALS 2nd week in July – Boudin Sausage Fair;
Son-et-lumière nightly end June–mid September

## HOTELS

*Bon Laboureur et du Château*, 6 rue Dr Bretonneau (47.23.90.02). See text. You must book in season. ROOMS D–F. MEALS E–F. Open mid-March–end November.

*Renaudière* (47.23.90.04). Looks faded but has a pleasant garden and restaurant; eat outside in summer. Good value meals. Attracts younger visitors. ROOMS C–D. MEALS B–E. Open early March–mid-November; shut Sunday evening, Monday lunch.

## RESTAURANT

*Gâteau Breton* (47.23.90.14). Very good value cheap meals. Old style bourgeois dishes. Garden for summer eating. MEALS A–C. Shut 15 November–15 February.

# Fontevraud-l'Abbaye

[MAINE-ET-LOIRE, MAP 2, page 272]

Here at least *some* of the prickly, quarrelsome Plantagenets lie at peace together. In the abbey church are the tombs of Henry II of England, his wife the beautiful, wayward Eleanor of Aquitaine, her favourite son, Richard Coeur de Lion, and Isabella, wife of the unreliable King John of England, Eleanor and Henry's youngest son. They lie together in stone effigy despite efforts by the English to have them moved to Westminster Abbey. Napoleon III agreed to this, but so many Frenchmen protested that he asked Queen Victoria to let him change his mind.

Situated on the borders of Anjou, 21 kilometres from Chinon, and 16 kilometres from Saumur, the abbey was founded in the twelfth century with a monastery for men and a convent for women. The Abbess ruled both, to the intense annoyance of the monks, and in the fourteenth century the monks actually dared to revolt against feminine domination.

It was governed by thirty-six abbesses in succession, all aristocrats, several of Royal blood, and most of the nuns were high-born. It was richly endowed by the Plantagenets, and Eleanor of Aquitaine retired there after the death of her husband and of her son Richard Coeur de Lion, who were both buried there. She continued to give 'advice' to her youngest son John until she died there in 1204, aged eighty-two.

In 1686, after Madame de Maintenon had displaced her from the Royal bed, the beautiful Marquise de Montespan also retired to the abbey.

It became a high-class finishing school for the daughters of the powerful. Louis XV sent his daughters there in 1739. In 1791, the abbey was closed, and Napoleon made the buildings into a prison. They remained so until 1963. Then bulldozers knocked down the nineteenth-century prison buildings and workshops where prisoners made buttons, and restoration was largely finished by 1975. It has since been used for conferences, seminars, exhibitions and concerts as well as being open to the public (closed on Tuesdays).

The church, finished around 1150, is a majestic building. It has a single nave with broad cupolas which were restored this century, having been demolished to make way for more prisoners' beds in the nave.

The cloisters in the nuns' convent, Ste Marie cloisters, are mostly Renaissance, partly Gothic. Through a richly sculptured doorway is the chapter house, decorated with sixteenth-century mural paintings representing abbesses.

The Romanesque kitchen is so unusual that it was once believed to be a vault. It has a remarkable system for taking out the smoke, which then smoked meat and fish on its way out. Smoking was the way meat and fish was preserved in medieval kitchens.

St Michel's church nearby still contains an arcade with small columns and Plantagenet-style vaulting. It has some interesting works of art. In a *Crucifixion* painted on wood by Etienne Dumonstier, the artist tries to show the futility of the war between Catholics and Protestants. Catherine de' Medici is

shown as Mary Magdalene, Henri II as the soldier piercing the heart of Christ and Mary Stuart with a crown is presumably meant to be the Virgin Mary.

TOURIST INFORMATION Chapelle Ste Catherine
(June–September 41.51.79.45)
MARKET Wednesday, Saturday morning

## HOTELS

*Croix Blanche*, 7 place Plantagenets (41.51.71.11). Cheerful, friendly; regional cooking. ROOMS C–E. MEALS B–D. Shut 12–22 November; mid-January–early February.

## RESTAURANTS

*La Licorne*, allée Ste Catherine (near St Michel's church) (41.51.72.49). In pretty eighteenth-century house. Really good classical cooking. Pricey. Book in season. MEALS F–G. Shut 1–10 September; end January–mid-February; Sunday evening, Monday.

*Abbaye*, 8 ave Roches (41.51.71.04). Very good value; bourgeois cooking. MEALS A–C. Shut 1–25 October; 2–end February; Tuesday evening, Wednesday.

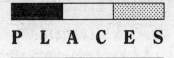

# PLACES

## AMBOISE
### [INDRE-ET-LOIRE – *see* Major Towns, page 47]

## ANCENIS
### [LOIRE-ATLANTIQUE]

Very attractive town with houses rising in tiers above the Loire, which is crossed by a great suspension bridge considered to be the gateway to the Muscadet wine country further south. In fact, in a big building on the ring road, Les Vignerons de Noëlle, a group of producers from all over the Loire valley, make wines by the most modern methods. They export around 400,000 bottles a year to Britain alone.

Ancenis is an old river port where sailcloth was made for centuries. It was known as the Key to Brittany. Now it is known for wine and for its pig market. What is left of its old château is a school.

You can taste wines at the Noëlle caves. The local Coteaux d'Ancenis wines (red, dry white and rosé) are not much known outside the Loire Valley. Labels tell you the grape names – Gamay or Cabernet Franc for reds, Pineau de la Loire (Chenin), Pinot Beurot or Malvoisie (slightly sweeter) for whites. The whites are light, dry and fruity. The north side of the river is on the edge of the Muscadet country, Coteaux de la Loire, which stretches to Nantes. Muscadet wine from Sèvre et Maine, south-east of Nantes, is usually better.

TOURIST INFORMATION place Pont (40.83.07.44)

#### HOTELS

*Val de Loire*, at Jarier d'Ancenis, 2km E by N23 (40.96.00.03). Fairly new, comfortable. ROOMS C–D. MEALS A–E. Restaurant shut Saturday.

# ANGERS
[MAINE-ET-LOIRE – *see* Major Towns, page 57]

## AREINES
[LOIR-ET-CHER]

Village in the Loir plain 3km NE of Vendôme, it has a twelfth-century church with fourteenth-century frescos which have kept freshness of colour, and other interesting decorations. Areines was an important Roman market town.

## ARTIGNY – Château
[INDRE-ET-LOIRE]

Superb eighteenth-century-style château built in 1912. Standing above the D17 west from Montbazon, it was built for the perfume magnate René Coty. It is now a sumptuous hotel, with magnificent furnishings, a round dining-room, the inevitable heli-pad and appropriate prices.

### HOTEL
*Château d'Artigny*, route d'Azay-le-Rideau–Montbazon (47.26.24. 24). Expensive but magnificent rooms half the price of some British country hotels. Relais et Châteaux. ROOMS F–G. MEALS F–G. Shut end November–5 January.

## ARTINS
[LOIR-ET-CHER]

Vieux-Bourg d'Artins is a village on the banks of the Loir with a Romanesque church with Flamboyant windows.

# ARVILLE
## [LOIR-ET-CHER]

Hamlet 11km NE of Mondoubleau on D921 with an interesting Templars' Commandery. The military–religious order of Knights Templars founded in 1119 were not very popular with the ordinary people because of their arrogant behaviour and licentious life. They were recruited from younger sons of aristocratic families. On their way to join the Order fighting the Saracens in the Holy Land, they stayed in a series of forts called Commanderies where they could get safe board and lodging. These also served as sort of international banks. The Order was rich and independent, two reasons why it was disbanded and most of the knights arrested by Philippe the Fair of France in 1307. The twelfth-century chapel is joined to a defence tower, part of the old ramparts.

# ASNIÈRES – Abbey
## [MAINE-ET-LOIRE]

Once a very important monastery, now what the French call a romantic ruin. It is 8km NW of Montreuil-Bellay on D761 and SW of Saumur. It was founded in the twelfth century and if you are nearby is worth visiting for the abbot's chapel of the fourteenth century, with very ancient carved flagstones and tomb statues.

# ASNIÈRES-SUR-VÈGRE
## [SARTHE]

One of the oldest and most attractive villages in the valley of the Vègre, a river running into the Sarthe east of Sablé. From the D190 you get a fine view of the high-pitched roofs of the old houses and Cours d'Asnières, a long Gothic mansion where the canons of Le Mans held their Court for the area.

From the medieval humped bridge is a delightful view of the river, an old mill still in working order among fine trees, and a charming manor house with turrets. Nearby is a seventeenth- to eighteenth-century small château called Moulin Vieux. The church has a Romanesque tower and some interesting thirteenth- to fifteenth-century murals. There is a picture of Hell with Christ releasing souls in Limbo by attacking Cerberus, the three-headed dog, and the unfortunate Damned are being swallowed by Leviathan, the whale. The other scenes are from the Bible.

Along D190 2½km towards Poillé is a late-fifteenth-century château, Verdelles, with four towers closely grouped round the centre. It is virtually unchanged since 1490. You can see inside by making an appointment (tel. 43.71.53.59).

# AUBIGNY-SUR-NÈRE
[CHER]

A Scottish town in France! Well, it was, in the fifteenth century. Charles VII, Joan of Arc's Dauphin, had called upon Scots to help him fight the English, their common enemy. John Stuart of Darnley gave him such brilliant service as the first Captain of the Scots Guards that Charles presented him in 1423 with Aubigny, a little town now on the D940 SW of Gien in the Sologne, and its surrounding country. Stuart brought in his own veterans and craftsmen from Scotland to set up weaving and glass-making. Gentlemen from Scotland settled there, too, with their retinues.

His successor, Berold Stuart, was not only Captain of the Scots Guards but commanded French forces in Italy. He was also responsible for the reconciliation between Louis XI and his cousin, the future Louis XII. The next Stuart, Robert, became a marshal, fought in Italy under François I, and was an ambassador.

Edmé Stuart, made Duke of Lennox by James VI, had a strong influence on the Scottish King who became James I of England. He had conspired to free Mary, Queen of Scots and to put her on the throne – one of the reasons why Queen Elizabeth was moved to have her beheaded for rebellion.

Ludovic Stuart of Aubigny, son of the Duke of Lennox and Richmond, became Canon of Notre Dame in Paris and Royal Grand Almoner.

When the male line of Stuarts of Aubigny died out, Louis XIV grabbed it back and gave it to Louise de Penancoët de Kéroual, known variously as Louise de Kéroualle, Madame Carwell or Duchess of Portsmouth. This attractive baby-faced Breton went to England, after Charles II had returned to take the throne, as a lady-in-waiting to Henrietta, Charles' much-cherished sister. In fact, she had been planted by Louis XIV to influence Charles into an alliance with France. She failed as a political force but became Charles' mistress, and he made her Duchess of Portsmouth. Her son Charles Lennox became Duke of Richmond. She was haughty and rapacious, and much disliked in England. When Charles died she retired to Aubigny, which she improved considerably.

Aubigny is a delightful little town with the river Nère running through it. It makes lingerie and is known for its lively fairs. Half-timbered sixteenth-century houses were built from the oaks of nearby Ivoy forest.

The house on the corner of rue de l'Église and rue Bourg-Coutant, called François I's house, is especially attractive. Across from it is Maison du Bailli, with carved beams and the initials of Berold Stuart and his wife Anne. It was used once by Charles VII himself. Part of the ramparts and three round towers built by King Philippe-Auguste still remain. So does the Stuart château, with a courtyard and turreted staircases. That is now the town hall.

The Stuarts' country mansion Château de la Verrerie is 10km SE at Oizon in a photogenic position on a lake formed by the Nère. Built for John Stuart, it has a Renaissance gallery and a chapel with sixteenth-century paintings. The château is believed to have inspired one of the episodes in *Le Grand Meaulnes* by Alain-Fournier, who was born at La Chapelle-d'Angillon, 14km S of Aubigny (see page 151) and wrote hauntingly about the Sologne.

TOURIST INFORMATION Syndicat d'Initiative, La Mairie (48.58.00.09)

FESTIVALS mid-April–early June – Rural Poetry Festival

HOTELS

*Chaumière*, place Paul-Losnier (48.58.04.01). Cosy restaurants. Regional Berry dishes. ROOMS DEMI-PENSION E. MEALS C–F.

*Fontaine*, 27 ave Charles-de-Gaulle (48.58.02.59). Logis. Good individual-style cooking. ROOMS C–D. MEALS C–F. Shut Sunday evening, Monday lunch.

*La Maison Hélène*, at La Verrerie-Oizon, 10km SE by D89 (48.58.31.01). Seventeenth-century Renaissance house and farm (historic monument) in grounds of Stuart château. Charming. Cooking now more elaborate. Expensive. ROOMS G. MEALS C–F. Shut 1 January–1 March; Tuesday.

# AUVERS-LE-HAMON
## [SARTHE]

Eight kilometres N of Sablé-sur-Sarthe. The village church has some strange wall paintings of local saints. St Luke is riding a bull. St Mémès is holding his intestines, and so on. Also a macabre dance.

# AVRILLÉ
## [MAINE-ET-LOIRE]

Five kilometres NW of Angers. Here they are restoring classic Anjou windmills – *moulins caviers*. Unlike smock mills with wooden roofs turning towards the wind, and post mills, where the whole mill turns, cavier mills are mounted on a masonry base, making cellars for storage. A conical tower points upwards, carrying the mechanism and four great sails. Two beams, which also serve as a ladder, are used to turn the main body of the mill.

# AZAY-LE-RIDEAU
[INDRE-ET-LOIRE – *see* Sites, page 101]


# AZAY-SUR-INDRE
[INDRE-ET-LOIRE]

A hamlet in a delightful position where the Indrois river meets the Indre. The fifteenth-century château, heavily restored, once belonged to the Marquis de La Fayette, the French soldier who became a hero in America when he went to fight in the War of Independence, defending Virginia and fighting at Yorktown. Back in France he became a Revolutionary, supported the abolition of all titles but upset the Jacobins by his reforming zeal and had to flee to Liège, where the Austrians put him in prison. Napoleon got him released in 1797 and he sat in the Chamber of Deputies on the extreme left and became leader of the Opposition. He formed and commanded the National Guard. The US Government voted him a pension.


# BAGNEUX
[MAINE-ET-LOIRE]

Saumur has caught up with it, so that it really is a suburb now (2km S). It has a dolmen (prehistoric tomb) which is one of the most important on the Loire. It is like a gallery with sixteen upright stones holding up a roof of four stone slabs sloping to 3 metres from the ground. It is 20 metres long by 7 metres wide. Another smaller dolmen is 200 metres away.

# BAILLOU
## [Loire-et-Cer]

A pleasant hamlet on D86 SW of Mondoubleau, it stands beneath a sixteenth- to seventeenth-century château. The early-sixteenth-century church on a mound is very attractive.

# BAUGÉ
## [Maine-et-Loire]

A delightful, peaceful town 33km N of Saumur on D938 beside the tiny Couasnon river, with fine old mansions in its still-quiet streets, it is the centre of pleasant scenery of forests, big clearings and heaths. The château was the favourite house of the good King René, last Duke of Anjou, and his mother Yolande of Aragon, and he personally supervised much of its building in 1455. He always preferred his smaller châteaux or manor houses to his great castles at Angers and Saumur and the life of a country gentleman to ruling, and gave up his dukedom to retire to his lands around Aix-en-Provence to hold court with poets and writers. His château at Baugé is now the town hall. An arched doorway leads to a fine spiral staircase. The St Joseph Hospital, founded in 1643, is run by nuns and its Spital (dispensary), with fine wall panelling and wooden floor, has a good collection of pans for herbs, earthenware pots and glass and pewter vessels.

In the eighteenth-century chapel of Les Filles du Coeur de Marie is an historic thirteenth-century relic, said to have been made from the True Cross. It has two cross-arms. It was brought from Constantinople in 1241 to the now-vanished La Boissière abbey and in the fourteenth century had two crucified figures in gold and precious stones. It was taken to Baugé for safe-keeping and the double-armed cross was adopted as the heraldic emblem of the Dukes of Anjou. René became also Count of Lorraine and it was adopted as Lorraine's emblem, too. So it became the Cross of Lorraine, chosen by Charles de Gaulle as the emblem of the Free French Forces in Britain in 1940. While de Gaulle lived, it was a sort of national emblem for France.

There are sixteenth-, seventeenth- and eighteenth-century town houses in the town and at le Vieil-Baugé, 1½km SW, is an ancient church with a strange twisted-helm roof. Here in 1421 an English force was beaten by a local army helped by Scots led by John, Earl of Buchan, who was made a High Constable of France by a grateful Dauphin, who became Charles VII next year.

Three kilometres NW is Château d'Islette, built about the same time as Azay-le-Rideau. It resembles that superb château in some ways, including its round corner towers, parapet walk with battlements and tall roof. It is also enfolded by arms of the Indre river. Inevitably, tradition says that the same workers built both.

Baugé means 'a marshy place' and once the country around it (the Baugeois) was so poor that 'to use your Baugé income' meant to make empty promises. Fruit growing, dairy farming and, especially asparagus growing have made the farms more prosperous but it is still sparsely populated. Incidentally, they play *boules* here with bias-balls much like those used for bowls.

TOURIST INFORMATION Syndicat d'Initiative
(15 June–15 September – 41.89.18.07) and Mairie
(all year – 41.89.12.12)

### HOTELS

*Boule d'Or*, 4 rue des Cygnes (41.89.82.12). Simple, pleasant Logis. ROOMS B–C. MEALS B–E. Shut Sunday evening, Monday except July, August.

*Grand Turc*, 9 ave Jeanne d'Arc (41.89.10.36). Simple, cheap Logis. ROOMS A–C. MEALS A–D. Shut mid-June–early July; mid-December–early January; Saturday.

# BAZOUGES-SUR-LE-LOIR
## [SARTHE]

Delightful little town 7km from La Flèche along N23, it has a twelfth-century church whose wooden vault is decorated with late-fifteenth-century paintings, and a delicious little castle on the Loir river bank, home of a king's chamberlain in the early sixteenth century. Two huge machicolated towers with pepper-pot roofs flank the entrance. One contains the fifteenth-century chapel. The eighteenth-century upstairs salons are pleasant, so is the French-style park. The château looks down the village with old wash-houses along the river, seen well from the bridge. (Château open Easter–September on Saturday afternoon, other-wise 1 July–15 September on Tuesday morning, Thursday afternoon).

# BEAUFORT-EN-VALLÉE
### [Maine-et-Loire]

This peaceful centre of flower and seed growing in the fertile, attractive valley of Anjou on the N147 east of Angers, was once a great defensive post. All that remains is a polygonal tower rebuilt under King René in 1455 and two square towers from the château built in 1346 by the Count of Beaufort, father of the French Pope Gregory XI. The charming little town has several lovely old houses, including a Renaissance house with a beautiful doorway, and its fifteenth-century church has an enormous bell tower. This is a good area for game.

Market Wednesday

# BEAUGENCY
### [Loiret]

Beaugency is a lovable, sprightly little town which would be even more attractive if it did not lure so many summer visitors and summer traffic with which it cannot cope. It is, blessedly, bypassed, but its low bridge over the Loire tempts people to use it to avoid nearby Orléans and its traffic. It is still one of the most pleasant places on the river, looking its best when you drive in from the south across the bridge.

Its little narrow streets have many one-ways, so park down

by the river bridge and walk, although it is built on a hill. It has many treasures from the Middle Ages, many flower-decked old houses, and its setting is delightful. It is a summer holiday town, with several nice older hotels, including one in the old abbey, and a big camp site over the river beside a bathing beach.

Even the Devil himself loves Beaugency. He built the bridge. Judging by the number he built in France, he is a great bridge engineer. This one, 440 metres long with twenty-two arches, he built in one night, in return for the soul of the first creature to cross. As happened elsewhere, the devilish locals welshed on payment. The Mayor pulled the old trick of bringing along a cat and a bucket of water on opening day and frightening the poor puss to run across. The Devil laughed so much that the top fell off the Tour de César and that formidable keep is still topless. The Devil still lives along the river quai at Tour de Diable, and Beaugency people are still nicknamed *chats* (cats).

That bridge was the best over the Loire between Blois and Orléans for centuries and was a natural magnet for armies, so the people had a lively time. Beaugency was taken four times by the English in the Hundred Years War until Joan of Arc retook it in 1429. Then in the Wars of Religion between 1562 and 1598, Protestants and Catholic Leaguers took it in turns. The Protestant Prince of Condé sacked it, then it was set on fire by more Protestants in 1567, the abbey badly burned, and the roof of the twelfth-century Romanesque church of Notre-Dame knocked down. Alas, repairs were a botch-up, with the Romanesque vaulting replaced by an imitation Gothic ceiling in wood painted to look like stone. In 1940 the retreating French blew up part of the bridge and German bombs did more damage, wrecking the stained glass windows of Notre-Dame, which are now replaced with bright and attractive new ones. More bombs fell on the town in 1944.

Considering its violent history, Beaugency has kept a wealth of old buildings, especially in place Dunois opposite the church and keep, and place St-Firmin, attractively lit at night by old street lamps.

Tour de Diable is right next to the Augustine Abbey of Notre-Dame, rebuilt in the eighteenth century. Having the Devil as a neighbour must have kept the monks in line. Now the abbey

is an hotel. The church is elegant, with light columns and radi-
ating chapels. Here in 1152 three archbishops, forty bishops and
many barons piled into the church to judge one of the great
scandals of the Middle Ages. King Louis VII, pious and dull,
accused his wife, Eleanor of Aquitaine, of adultery in Antioch
while she was accompanying him in a Crusade and wanted his
marriage annulled. She wanted to get rid of him, too, so she did
not defend the suit. She settled for a very dubious compromise –
consanguinity, which means that their blood relationship was
too close for a legal marriage. It wasn't, but the facts were
fiddled and they both got their annulment. Her love affairs
seemed of no consequence to the church judges. It was a bad day
for France. She married a young man she already had in view,
Henry Plantagenet, soon Henry II of England, and he got his
hands on Aquitaine and most of south-west France. It took the
French until 1453 to get the English out. And a man who did a
lot towards their final defeat, the Count of Dunois, bastard son
of the Duke of Orléans, and companion in arms to Joan of Arc,
owned the château at Beaugency right behind the church, a
medieval fortress, now partly ruined, which he made into a
home. After Joan's death, he took Chartres from the English,
chased them from Paris and Normandy, and took Bordeaux and
Bayonne. In Château Dunois, where a son-et-lumière show is
given, is an attractive and interesting Folk Art museum in the
arcade-ringed courtyard, including furniture, clothing, games,
old toys and dolls.

Facing the château is the eleventh-century Tour de César,
33½ metres high without the top which Satan laughed off, and
3½ metres thick, so strong that a few Englishmen held off
attacks by Dunois and Joan for a day and a night, and were then
allowed to walk out with their weapons if they agreed not to fight
for ten days!

The tree-shaded Grand Mail runs from N152 above the
town, with beautiful views over the valley down to an attractive
shaded square Petit Mail. A mail is a mallet used in medieval
games, like croquet, played on these avenues. We corrupted it to
Mall, as in London's Pall Mall. Local people now play boules in
Petit Mail.

TOURIST INFORMATION 28 place du Martroi
(38.44.54.42)
MARKET Saturday
FESTIVALS Son-et-Lumière June–September. End June –
Drama Festival at Château

### HOTELS

*Abbaye*, 2 quai de l'Abbaye (38.44.67.35). Impressive; big bed-rooms, very comfortable, smaller rooms rather sombre. ROOMS F. MEALS E–F.

*Écu de Bretagne*, place du Martroi (38.44.67.60). Our old favour-ite. Old post-house on main market square with outside terrace to view the scene. Also modern annexe. Classic and regional dishes. ROOMS B–E. MEALS C–F.

*Sologne*, 6 place St Firmin (38.44.50.27). Simple, very friendly, no restaurant. ROOMS B–D. Shut 20 December–1 February.

# BEAULIEU-LÈS-LOCHES
## [INDRE-ET-LORE]

One kilometre from Loches (*see* page 199) on the opposite bank of the Indre river where Foulques Nera, the bellicose Count of Anjou, founded an abbey in 1004 after he came back from a pilgrimage to Jerusalem, and was buried there, at his own request.

Beaulieu once rivalled Loches but is now a small manufac-turing town that still has the abbey church with a magnificent square twelfth-century steeple, topped by an octagonal spire. The church nave was rebuilt in the fifteenth century after the English had burned it down. Foulques was buried in the church but by 1870 everyone had forgotten where. Then local arch-aeologists followed directions of an old manuscript, took up flagstones, and three feet below found a coffin with a single slab of tufa as a roof. They found primitive coins, rings and other ornaments and a skull which they photographed and put back. It was Foulques' grandfather who had driven the Normans from Anjou in the ninth century. Nobody knew exactly where this race of warriors had come from, and the skull did not help.

# BEAULIEU-SUR-LAYON
## [MAINE-ET-LOIRE]

Winegrowers' village of attractive houses with high-pitched Mansard roofs. The lower slope is steeper than the upper (named after the great French architect François Mansard, who built the château at Blois and whose great-nephew Jules, chief architect to Louis XIV, designed much of Versailles). The village is surrounded by the Layon vineyards where semi-sweet and sweet Coteaux de Layon wines are made from the Chenin (Pineau de la Loire) grape – a lighter wine than Sauternes or Barsac but with 12 per cent minimum alcohol. They have a delicate flavour and are drunk cold but not iced. Their colour is greeny-golden and they have a rich, flowery smell. The Layon river runs from here NW to join the Loire at Chalonnes on the Corniche Angevine.

# BEAUPRÉAU
## [MAINE-ET-LOIRE]

Small town in green countryside south of the Loire, east of the Layon and stretching to Cholet in the south, called Les Mauges. Here on rich pastures cattle are bred. In 1793 a civil war broke out here, a revolt by the people who still believed in God and King against the Republican Revolutionaries, called the Vendean War after the Vendée area further south than Les Mauges. It was a sad, bloody war lasting three years and the result was inevitable, for it was often the musket and cannon against the scythe and pike. It was put down with dreadful cruelty, but to be fair, the Royalist peasants, many from Brittany, committed atrocities, too. The little town of Beaupréau and its old winding streets was Royalist headquarters. The fifteenth-century château on the river Evre, seen splendidly from the south bank, was set on fire by the Revolutionaries but restored in the early nineteenth century when the monarchy was restored. Two large towers flank a seventeenth-century pavilion, with two slate-covered cupolas on the roof.

Tourist Information in season, Office de Tourisme
(41.63.06.49); out of season, Mairie (41.63.00.47)
Market Monday

#### HOTEL

*France*, 4 place Gén.Leclerc (41.63.00.26), Logis with pleasant,
good value meals. Rooms C. Meals A–D. Restaurant shut Saturday evening, Sunday.

# BEAUREGARD
[Château]

Off D956, 9km S of Blois on the edge of Russy forest. An
attractive house, full of delightful things. It was one of many
lodges of that dedicated hunter, François I, who gave it to his
uncle, the Bastard of Savoy. A highly cultured man, Jean du
Thier, secretary to Henri II and a friend of the poet Ronsard,
built the present château, bringing in Italian painters and wood
carvers from Fontainebleau to decorate the interior. Though
unassuming, it is more interesting and attractive inside than
many of the more famous châteaux. A financier, Paul Ardier,
bought it in 1631 and put in the collection of 363 portraits, real
or imaginary, of France's famous people, all the same size, lined
side-by-side around the gallery walls. Kings from the first Valois,
Philippe VI to Louis XIII are there with their queens, well-
known courtiers and some famous foreigners, such as the
Florentine navigator Amerigo Vespucci, who gave America its
name, seen here being received by Louis XII. The ceiling and
wainscoting have paintings by Jean Mosnier, and the floor is of
seventeenth-century Delft tiles showing an army on the march in
authentic uniforms of Louis XIII – infantry, musketeers,
cavalry, artillery. (Château open daily 1 April–end September;
shut Wednesday October–end December. Shut January, February, March.)

# BÉHUARD
## [MAINE-ET-LOIRE]

Charming island in Loire river SW of Angers by D111, reached by a bridge. The wine village of Savennières is on the north bank, Rochefort-sur-Loire on the south bank. Four kilometres long and very thin, the island has about a hundred inhabitants, living in a village of fifteenth- to sixteenth-century houses among rich pastures and cattle and towering poplars. On a rock at the end of the village is a tiny church with worn steps. Part of the nave uses the rock as floor and walls. Inside is a statue of the Virgin, highly venerated, especially by Louis XI. The story of the church is muddled. Some say that it was built by Louis XI, following a vow made when he was in danger of drowning, others that it was built by the monks of the abbey of St-Nicolas-d'Angers, and that Louis went there to worship, staying in the chaplain's house, which is still there. Either way, Louis appears in the late fifteenth-century stained glass window of the Crucifixion.

The island is named after Buhardus, a Breton in the service of Geoffroi Martel, Count of Anjou (1040–1060) who, on the death of his patron, retired to this island with his wife and a monk as his chaplain. He left the island to the monks of St-Nicolas-d'Angers abbey. The inside of the church has some quaint statues.

A path near a wayside cross takes you to a sandy river beach and there is a lovely walk to the end of the island, where the Loire divides. The islanders have one fear – river flooding. The worst in recent times was in 1910, when the ground floors of their houses were right underwater. Some of the old houses are raised above flood level. There are three little café-restaurants serving cheap meals, including the local speciality, friture of river fish and eels, and another, Le Grand Pont, actually on the bridge, with river views from its terrace.

# BELLEGARDE
[LOIRET]

The N60 from Châteauneuf-sur-Loire through the Orléans
forest leads on to this little town among market gardens and
rose nurseries. It is dedicated to roses. Its charming
fourteenth-century château, with a massive square keep flanked by turrets, is surrounded by a moat in which a rose garden
has been planted. Seventeenth-century paintings in the church
include *St John the Baptist* by Nicolas Mignard with the infant
Louis XIV as St John.

# BLÉRÉ
[INDRE-ET-LOIRE]

On the river Cher where D31 crosses it south of Amboise, it
has a twin-town, La Croix, across the river, first linked by a
bridge built by Henry II of England. The river has a barrage
near the bridge, leaving a good stretch of calm water upstream
used for boating, fishing and swimming. The Château of
Chenonceau is 6km E. In the Bléré Château, which has now
gone, was born one of the most important Deputies of the
Revolutionary Convention – Jean Lambert-Tallien. Son of a
servant of the Seigneur of Bléré, he was so intelligent that he
was educated with the Seigneur's own son. He was very much a
moderate in the Revolution 'doing a lot of good because he did
the least possible harm'. At twenty-four he was put in charge of
Bordeaux, where he promptly fell in love with one of his aristocratic prisoners: Thérèse de Cabarrus, nineteen years old,
pretty, wayward and recently divorced from the Marquis of
Fontenay. Robespierre hated him. In the debate in Convention,
which included an argument on whether Thérèse should go to
the guillotine, Tallien led an attack on Robespierre which
brought about Robespierre's overthrow. Tallien married
Thérèse and helped to suppress the Revolutionary Tribunal
carrying out the Terror.

TOURIST INFORMATION Syndicat d'Initiative, rue J.-J.
Rousseau (in season 47.57.93.00)
MARKET Friday, Tuesday
FESTIVALS Melon Fair, 2nd Friday in September

HOTELS
*Cheval Blanç*, place l'Église (47.30.30.14). Outstanding Logis,
very French, with three chimneys for superb bourgeoise cuisine.
Seventeenth-century building, courtyard with fountain for fair
weather eating. ROOMS C–D. MEALS B–F. Restaurant shut Sunday evening, Monday. ·

# BLOIS
[LOIR-ET-CHER – *see* Major Towns, page 65]

# BOISCOMMUN
[LOIRET]

Village 7km NW of Bellegarde on D44 with two towers and
ruins of its castle and an ancient church containing a twelfth-
century stained glass window and interesting paintings in the
organ loft of sixteenth-century people.

# BOIS-MAUBOUCHER – Château
[MAINE-ET-LOIRE]

Just off N162 Laval–Angers road, south of Château-Gontier, a
spectacular château, beautifully situated on a near-island of a big
lake, with an approach drive flanked by fine trees. It is a mysterious building, obviously built over a number of centuries. Two
towers by the water's edge suggest a fifteenth-century fortress.
One wing seems to be unconnected with the rest of the building.

# LA BORNE
## [CHER]

Little village SE of Henrichemont by D22 among Sancerre hills, almost lost in woodland. Its local clays were used for pottery for three hundred years, and there is still an exhibition of it in the local school (afternoons in school holidays, Sundays only in term). The potters have nearly all given way to wood and other crafts.

# BOUCARD – Château
## [CHER]

Take D956 S from Sancerre, turn right onto D7 with magnificent views, then take D74 NW and you reach Château Boucard on the Sauldre river – an attractive moated castle of the fourteenth to sixteenth centuries. Canals by the north wing once surrounded a famous formal garden. There are many interesting features inside, including good Louis XIV furniture, beautiful pewter ware and a slanting hole in the ancient chapel so that the Princesse de la Trémoille could attend services without leaving her bedroom.

# BOULOIRE
## [SARTHE]

On N157 road from Le Mans to Orléans, 22km SE of Le Mans with a castle dominating its market square. Interesting.

# BOUMOIS – Château
## [(MAINE-ET-LOIRE]

Drivers hurrying along the D952 from Saumur towards Angers are too busy traffic-watching to notice Château de Boumois hidden in the trees where the little D229 meets the main road. It is a two-faced castle. From the road it is a jolly-looking château in bright white stone, with a moat and fat towers. The other side facing the countryside has a grimmer, more serious look. Like many Loire châteaux, the feudal exterior hides an inner house of grace and elegance, and shows how people lived.

Boumois was a main seat of the powerful and interesting Dupetit-Thouars family, who managed to survive even the Revolution by keeping out of politics. The best known was Admiral Aristide-Aubert Dupetit-Thouars, whose distinguished career ended fighting against Nelson at Aboukir in 1798. His leg was shot off, so he ordered his men to stand him up in a barrel of sawdust so that he could continue the battle. He also hoped that it would stop him bleeding to death. But he did die, shouting 'Don't lower the flag!' Alas for France, the flag was lowered. Ten years earlier he had organized a massive search in the Pacific for survivors from two lost ships when the explorer the Count of Lapérouse lost his life. Three years before his death he visited Canada, half of which had recently been lost by France to the English. He loved the country but left in his book of travels some poignant and sad conversations with French Canadians and thoughts on seeing the ships on the great Canadian lakes, where 'the French first launched ships worthy of their size', carrying English flags. His elder brother was a distinguished botanist. His nephew, also an Admiral, took over Tahiti in 1842 and made it a French Protectorate.

Inside, the château is very light and has a turret staircase which leads to the living rooms. In the great hall on the first floor is a collection of fifteenth- to sixteenth-century arms. You can walk the parapets. The beautiful Flamboyant chapel has a pointed roof. The dovecote has 1800 nesting holes with a revolving ladder for collecting eggs and cleaning. Built in the seventeenth century, it shows the wealth and power of the family who obviously owned vast estates. The right to own doves and pigeons (fuyé) was limited strictly to the nobility. One nesting hole was allowed for each artent (about half a hectare) of land they owned. The birds were used for meat for the Lord's table and for shooting practice. Clay-pigeon shooting (la Trappe) did not take the place of live pigeons until quite recently.

What infuriated the peasant farmers was that the lords did not feed their birds and the peasants were not allowed to shoot them. So they fed on the peasants' crops. At Boumois there must have been 3600 of these hungry gobblers devastating the countryside. This was one of the major grievances that led to support for the Revolution.

# BOURGES
## [Cher]

Bourges, on the southern edge of the Sologne, has grown rapidly in population and industrial importance, with chemical, aeronautic and metallurgic industries, as well as being a military base. But industry is in the suburbs and the centre, which is extremely interesting, keeps mementoes of the days when Joan of Arc's Dauphin hid there and was scathingly called King of Bourges because he held sway over little parts of the Loire.

Park by the cathedral, if you can, and walk the narrow streets, many of which are still cobbled. From whichever way you approach, the Gothic cathedral of St Étienne on a low hill is the great landmark. Built between 1192 and 1224, it is beautiful and unusual. Enormously wide, with five great doorways, it keeps its absolute Gothic uniformity, with matching repair work during later centuries except for mistakes in the nineteenth century when restorers felt compelled to try to alter things. It was said to have been based originally on Notre Dame in Paris but altered as it was built.

Inside, the size and exact unity is impressive and startling. It is 110 metres long, 40 metres wide and 40 metres high. There are no transepts, so you can see straight down the nave and choir past an unbroken line of columns placed with exact precision to the far end. It has 141 stained glass windows from the twelfth to seventeenth centuries and thirty of these are rose windows. The result is light and colour worthy of Chartres. In the side chapels are legions of treasures. Look for the Gobelin tapestries in the third chapel, woven in 1845 from Raphael's drawings of the sixteenth century; also superb windows of 1215–25 on the choir chapels.

The enormous twelfth-century crypt with fifteenth-century glass is used for an audio-visual show 'Trésors d'Art du Cher' daily in season except Sunday. Outside you can climb the 396 steps of the 65-metre-high Tour de Beurre for views over the city. A Tour de Beurre was not a storage tower for a butter mountain but was built with money paid by the rich for forgiveness for eating butter in Lent.

The old archbishop's palace alongside the cathedral, now the town hall, has a quiet, beautiful garden designed originally by Le Nôtre.

Bourges still has several old mansions, called hôtels, including Hôtel Lallemont in rue Bourbonnoux north of the cathedral, the Renaissance house of a cloth-merchant, now used as a museum of decorative art.

The great mansion really worth seeing is Palais Jacques Coeur, built for the fifteenth-century merchant and financier Jacques Coeur who paid for the campaigns of Joan of Arc, saved France from financial ruin, made jealous enemies who accused him of poisoning the King's beautiful mistress Agnès Sorel, and was banished by the miserable, ungrateful Charles VII who never made a move to save Joan, either. Poor Coeur never lived in the house. He joined the Papal service, was given a fleet to try to free Greek isles from the Saracens and died in the isle of Chios.

He had an impish sense of humour. The house has little jokes such as blank windows with a stone man and woman looking out, a carving of a comic tournament on a gallery chimney piece and unusual decoration in the courtyard showing his commercial interests. The kitchens have an ingenious water-heating system. Beautiful gardens overlooking the river Yèvre, Prés Fichaud, have superb roses.

The University of Bourges was already world famous when students from Heidelberg brought to it the teachings of Martin Luther and the Reformation. One student who absorbed those beliefs was John Calvin.

TOURIST INFORMATION 21 rue Victor Hugo
(48.24.75.33 – Closed Sunday in low season)
MARKETS Daily

FESTIVALS Spring Fête before and after Easter; Vieille Ville en Fête end May; Festival of Experimental Music end May–early June; fair of Bourges and Jacques Coeur end June.

## HOTELS

*Angleterre*, 1 place Piliers (48.24.68.51). Pretty rooms; good value meals. ROOMS D–F. MEALS B–E. Restaurant shut 23 June–7 July; 20 December–20 January; Monday lunch, Sunday.

*Hostellerie Grand Argentier*, 9 rue Parerie (48.70.84.31). No restaurant. ROOMS B–E. Shut 22 December–31 January; Sunday evening, Saturday.

## RESTAURANTS

*Jacques Coeur*, 3 place Jacques-Coeur (48.70.12.72). Local institution. Very good cooking of regional dishes. MEALS D–E. Shut 19 July–19 August; 25 December–2 January; Sunday evening, Saturday.

*D'Anton Sancerrois*, 50 rue Bourbonnoux (48.65.96.26). Regional dishes; good value. MEALS C–E. Shut 24 December–mid-January; Monday, Tuesday lunch.

# BOURGUEIL
### [INDRE-ET-LOIRE]

François Rabelais, the wise wit and satirist whose love of food and wine ('the Divine Bottle') pioneered gourmandise as a French way of life, was singing praises of the full-bodied, deep-red wines of Bourgueil in the sixteenth century, but it took Paris until the 1970s to find them. Even now the Parisians go for the lighter wines from the gravelly vineyards, drunk at cellar temperature a year old or so, not the deep ruby, robust wines of the chalky-clay tuffeau, which can improve for ten years and have the refreshing clean taste of Médoc with a touch of oak. Cabernet Franc is the main grape, though some Cabernet Sauvignon is grown, too, on the vine-covered hillsides above the Loire between Saumur and Tours. The monks of the tenth-century

Benedictine abbey first made the wine and the sale of it made the abbey one of the richest in Anjou in the thirteenth to four- teenth centuries. You can still visit the thirteenth-century cellars in an abbey building with turrets capped by octagonal spires.

Across from the old parish church is an elegant market place with stone arcades. The Tuesday market takes over much of the town and is fun. Go at Easter – there is a wine exhibition, or in September for wine tasting.

The poet Ronsard fell in love in Bourgueil with a gentle shepherdess, Marie, whose name he rearranged to read Aimer – to love. 'The fierceness of two lovely eyes rent my poor head asunder,' he wrote, when she died young.

Four kilometres westward is the wine village of St-Nicolas- de-Bourgueil, where similar wines are made. I was told many years ago by a Bourgueil expert that the best wines come from St Nicolas and Paris-produced guides told me the same. Then I discovered that my 'expert' owned a vineyard in St Nicolas. Most St Nicolas is drunk young and cold (not iced) and five years is considered to be the limit for keeping it.

Restigné, 5km E on D35, another wine-growers' village, has a delightful eleventh- to twelfth-century church with a side entrance doorway carved above with fantasy animals. Four kilo- metres S of Bourgueil is Les Réaux, a black and white checked château in brick and stone, similar to some in Normandy. It was built by Guillaume Briconnet at the end of the fifteenth century, from the same family as Catherine Briconnet who was respons- ible for Chenonceau. Guillaume called it Plessis-Rideau but was made Archbishop of Reims before he could live in it. It was renamed by the new owners in the seventeenth century. There remains a fine gatehouse flanked by round towers. Three kilo- metres W of it on N152 is Chouze-sur-Loire, once an active river port, with an attractive fifteenth-century manor.

Tourist Information place Halles (season only – 47.97.91.39)
Market Tuesday
Festivals Wine Exhibition – Easter; Wine Tasting 2nd Tuesday September; Chestnut Fair – 4th Tuesday October

HOTEL

*Thouarsais*, place Hublin (47.97.72.05). Friendly little hotel, quiet, comfortable. Some rooms simple. No restaurant. ROOMS A–D. Shut 6–15 April; part February; Sunday in winter.

RESTAURANT

*Germain*, rue A. Chartier (47.97.72.22). Local favourite. Owned by pâtissière next door. MEALS B–F. Shut 1st 3 weeks October; Sunday evening, Monday.

# BRACIEUX
## [LOIR-ET-CHER]

Delightful little market town on the edge of the Sologne, equal distance from Chambord and Cheverny châteaux, with two small rivers running through it, the Beuvron and the Bonneure, both rich in fish. Its old covered market is a masterpiece of rustic architecture and very handsome. Wood columns support a sixteenth-century granary with pinnacle turret, now used often as an exhibition hall.

Bracieux was one of the towns that grew up over the years that François I was having his great château at Chambord built. Men were working on it for years and settled around here.

In the little Bonneure valley amidst a magnificent forest are old farms and manor houses, including the enchanting Renaissance Château of Herbault, a private house in a lovely setting. On the edge of the forest, 3km N of Bracieux, is a little château few tourists visit but well worth the short time it takes. Villesavin was built by François I's works superintendent at Chambord, Jean de Breton, for himself and whether with François's permission or not, he seems to have used 'surplus' materials from Chambord and certainly used Chambord's Florentine sculptors, as you can see from the adornment of the Renaissance windows in the steeply sloping roof. The result, finished in 1537, was a ravishing Renaissance house with neo-classical touches. François must have thought a great deal of Le Breton because when he died the King gave his wife a job at the château and his daughter was made administrator. His château is beautifully proportioned while Chambord is a muddle. The Carrara marble fountain in the middle of the courtyard is a beautiful example of ornate Renaissance sculpture.

The restoration work is nearly finished. The original kitchen has interesting pewter ware. There is a small chapel with dilapidated frescos, used as kennels for a while, a dovecote with 1500 perches and a rotating ladder, as at Boumois, and in an old barn are old horse-drawn carriages, a nineteenth-century tricycle, a children's goat-cart and a horse-drawn bus (Château closed 21 December–end February).

#### HOTEL
*Bonneheure*, Bracieux (54.46.41.57). No restaurant. ROOMS D.

#### RESTAURANT
*Bernard Robin*, 1 ave Chambord (54.46.41.22). Formerly Le Relais de Bracieux. Bernard Robin is one of the best 'modern' chefs in France. Lovely garden. You must book. MEALS F–G. Shut 23 December–30 January; Tuesday evening, Wednesday.

# BRÉHEMONT
## [INDRE-ET-LOIRE]

Peaceful village on the sandy south bank of the Loire 6km SW of busy Langeais on the little riverside road D16 which leads to the Château of Ussé (see page 259). A port with fishing boats when the river was the main road; now its fishermen use lines from the old slipway.

#### HOTEL
*Castel de Bray et Monts*, place Église (47.96.70.47). Converted from an eighteenth-century manor six years ago by a chef once at the Ritz. Comfortable, individualistic rooms, some in a former de Valois family chapel in the hundred-year-old garden. ROOMS D–G. MEALS E–F. Shut 20 December–1 February; Wednesday in winter.

# BRIARE
### [Loiret]

Little town on the Loire 10km upstream from Gien, has a
famous bridge across the river built by Eiffel who designed the
Eiffel Tower in Paris. The bridge is more beautiful and more
useful. Six hundred and forty metres long, it carries the Canal
de Briare. You can walk across it on a wide pavement with
balustrade, giving good views up and down the river and to the
woods and countryside which is especially pleasant to the north.
From below it is strange to see a boat floating over your head.

The Duke of Sully, Henri IV's brilliant soldier and states-
man who made France solvent, ordered the building of the
Briare-Loing canal to join the Seine and Loire. It is 104km long
and joins the Seine at Saint-Mammes, thus in effect joining the
Canal Lateral to the Channel, North Sea and many waterways of
North Europe.

TOURIST INFORMATION, place Église (in season –
38.31.24.51)

#### HOTEL

*Hostellerie Canal*, 19 quai Pont-Canal (38.31.22.54). Alongside
canal, shady terrace. Quiet. ROOMS C–D. MEALS B–E. Shut
mid-December–mid-January; Restuarant shut Sunday evening,
Monday in winter.

# BRIDORÉ
### [Indre-et-Loire]

Small village nine kilometres NW of Châtillon-sur-Indre, which
has a fine fifteenth-century church and imposing fourteenth- to
fifteenth-century castle, with deep dry moats on three sides, a
fine gatehouse and rectangular keep with pepper-pot roofs.

# BRISSAC – Château
## [MAINE-ET-LOIRE]

At Brissac-Quincé, 18km SE of Angers, it is one of the most rewarding and awe-inspiring châteaux because the present Duc de Brissac still lives in it and the furnishings are so superb. He has written a book on it and if you are very rich you can arrange to stay for dinner, bed and breakfast. Charles de Cossé, Count of Brissac, was the Governor of Paris who handed the city keys to Henri IV in 1494 after he announced his conversion to Catholicism. Henri made him a Duke. In 1502 he bought the fortress which had been badly damaged in the Wars of Religion and started to build the new part, but work stopped in 1621 when the money ran out, leaving the château incomplete, as it still is. His attempts to pull down two round towers failed completely. The present Duke called it 'a new château not completed in an old castle only half destroyed'.

It stands in a nice park running down to the Aubance river. On a hillside opposite is the family mausoleum with statues and a black marble obelisk. The château has two hundred rooms and reaches seven storeys in the Renaissance section. The Duke and Duchess have had seven hundred guests at receptions and concerts. The magnificently furnished rooms have superbly painted and gilded ceilings. One suite has a ceiling showing butterflies becoming women. The rooms are hung with seventeenth-century paintings and with tapestries. The Royal Hunt Suite has sixteenth-century tapestries of hunting scenes. The Louis XIII Suite, where he slept in 1620 after reconciliation with his mother, Marie de' Medici, is hung with Aubusson tapestries. That reconciliation lasted only a few weeks. The glorious dining-room displays superb silverware. Among the family portraits peering down from the walls is the Widow Cliquot herself – the 'Veuve-Cliquot' of Champagne. She was related to the ancient Cossé family.

The most surprising room is on the second floor. Behind a door surmounted with a lyre is a delightful theatre, seating two hundred people, built by the Duke's great-grandmother last century but in eighteenth-century style. It still has some original scenery and *belle époque* décor. (Château open daily 1 April–

1 November, but closed Tuesday except 1 July–15 August –
telephone 41.91.23.43).

TOURIST INFORMATION – Brissac-Quincé, place du
Tertre (41.91.21.50)


HOTEL

*Castel* (41.91.24.74): no restaurant. ROOMS C–D. Shut 11–end
February.


# CANDES-ST-MARTIN
## [INDRE-ET-LOIRE]

It stands at the foot of a lovely green hill looking down on the
meeting of the Loire and Vienne, and it runs so suddenly into
Montsoreau that an old saying grew up 'You can sleep with your
head in Montsoreau and your feet in Candes'.

Candes rises in tiers up cobbled alleys past old stone houses,
clad in roses, to a signposted spot from which you can see over
the village rooftops to the meeting of the waters among little
islands.

There are many traces of the old town walls and moats, but
the treasure of Candes is the wonderful St Martin's Church,
built in the eleventh and twelfth centuries, fortified in the
fifteenth, and now happily being restored. It stands on the site
of the cell where Martin, the Roman soldier turned Christian
missionary, died in 397, eighty years old. He had come there
from his great monastery at Marmoutier to settle a long-
standing dispute between monks of Poitou and Touraine. They
then quarrelled over his body until the monks of Marmoutier
removed it secretly to his own abbey.


# CANDÉ-SUR-BEUVRON
## [LOIR-ET-CHER]

Fourteen kilometres S of Blois where the peaceful little Beuvron
river runs into the Loire after its journey through the Sologne

and under the hill at Celletes below the Château of Beauregard. A pleasant little town in a nice setting, with Chaumont only 6½km SW on D751, and a good place to stay quietly while you explore nearby châteaux or the Beuvron valley, with its old windmills.

### HOTELS

*Lion d'Or* (54.44.04.66): rustic inn popular with my *Complete Travellers' France* readers for traditional cooking, cheap prices and good value. Rooms vary. ROOMS A–C. MEALS A–D. Shut 4–12 June; 10 December–10 January. Restaurant shut Tuesday.

*Hostellerie de la Caillère*, route Montils (54.44.03.08): pretty old farm cottages, creeper clad, in old garden. Jacky Guindon's cooking causes arguments among French guide gastronomes. One accused him of 'outdated *nouvelle cuisine* of ten years ago'. Ancient-modern! Good local ingredients – wild mushrooms, carp and pike from the river, wood pigeons. ROOMS C–E. MEALS B–F. Shut mid-January–end March. Restaurant shut Sunday evening and Wednesday in winter.

# CHALONNES-SUR-LOIRE
## [MAINE-ET-LOIRE]

As you come down the Corniche Angevine going west from Angers you reach the old port of Chalonnes, where the Louet rejoins the Loire on the eastern outskirts and the Layon flows into it a little further along. You see the church, with a graceful, slender spire, right on the water's edge and the tree-lined quays where punts, launches and motor-cruisers are tied up. The town's bridge leads out over a string of islands which spread upstream for 2km and downstream another 5km. In 7km you reach St-Georges-sur-Loire which has not been on the river for a long time. The quayside views at Chalonnes are delightful.

MARKETS Tuesday, Friday

### HOTEL

*France, 5 rue Nationale* (41.78.00.12): Logis. ROOMS C. MEALS A–E.

# CHAMBORD – Château
## [Loir-et-Cher]

Why François I built this dazzling, awesome, flamboyant folly of 440 rooms in what was then an almost-uninhabited wilderness of the Sologne, damp and inaccessible, completely mystified his contemporaries – especially as he was even more broke than usual. Of course, he was addicted to hunting and this was some of the greatest hunting country in France. But there was a hunting lodge there already, which he could have extended and made more comfortable. He was also addicted to flamboyance and show, but if he wanted to outshine the other great Loire châteaux, he would logically have put it in a place where the world could admire it. But when François had an obsession, he followed it regardless. Even when the Royal treasury was empty and he could not find the money to ransom his two sons held prisoner by Spain, he continued to build, which was monumentally selfish, because he himself had been captured by Spanish troops and he had given his sons as prisoners to take his place because he could not afford his own ransom!

If he was to use the château as his main residence in the Loire he would have needed all those rooms. There were no other lodgings around and the *whole* Court always travelled with him. All had to be housed and the twelve thousand horses which carried them, their servants, furniture, crockery and baggage had to be fed and watered. He received artists, writers and scientists, too.

The resulting château is a huge oblong palace, 156 metres long and 117 metres deep in 14,000 acres of park and forest, which is now a game reserve, surrounded by the longest wall in France – 34km (20 miles). Visitors are only allowed into a section to the west of the park. The rest is a hunting ground for VIPs invited by the President of France, including foreign government guests. The château has six massive towers, fourteen main staircases, seventy secondary ones, and 365 chimneys. Inside, nearly all those chimney pieces are sculpted. One staircase is possibly the most famous in France. It is a double spiral, rising right up to the lantern which stands way above the top floor of the château. It is built so that a person on one spiral can see and talk to one on the other but the two can meet only at the bottom or the top. It is beautifully decorated. When Louis XIII gave Chambord to his half-brother Gaston d'Orléans to discourage him from conspiring against the King, his daughter, the notorious Grande Mademoiselle's favourite game was to make her father chase up and down to try and catch her.

The château was finished in time for François I to receive Charles V there in 1539. François had a group of young women dressed up as Greek goddesses go to meet Charles and spread flowers in front of his horse. Charles was duly impressed by them and the château, but still went away without coming to an agreement about the Milanese, about which they had argued so long.

The odd thing is that in the eighteen years which Chambord was habitable before his death, he is said to have stayed there only forty nights. Henri II continued the building. François II and Charles IX went often and their young courtiers had a fine time. This is not surprising. The château was uncomfortable and difficult for servants but with its staircases and secretive landings and towers it must have been a splendid place for a party. Charles IX, though sick, was so devoted to hunting that he stayed ten hours in the saddle and tired five horses. Three hundred falcons were kept at Chambord. Louis XIII must have been quite glad to pass it over to his brother Gaston d'Orléans. The cost of keeping it up was stretching the Royal purse almost as much as building it did.

Young Louis XIV loved Chambord. He too was a flamboyant young man. It may well have influenced him to plan Versailles and build it in another inaccessible forest. He brought Molière and his theatrical troupe to Chambord, converting the big guard room into a theatre for them. Their first performance in 1669 was a comedy with ballet *Monsieur de Pourceaugnac*. Lully was composer. Louis and his courtiers were obviously bored with it. Then Lully tried a slapstick gag fit for pantomime. The royal mistress Madame de Maintenon reported that Lully got up on the stage, broke into a run and jumped off, landing on the harpsichord in the orchestra, shattering it. The King laughed. So did the court.

Next year Molière staged his *Le Bourgeois Gentilhomme*. The

King sat poker-faced and hardly laughed. So the courtiers did the same. But at supper he told Molière in a loud voice how much he had liked it. So the courtiers decided that they, too, had enjoyed it, and the second performance was a huge success.

Louis XV lent the château to his father-in-law, Stanislas Leczinski, deposed King of Poland, who filled in the moat which François had fed with water by diverting the river Cosson. Then he presented it to Marshal Maurice Saxe, bastard son of the King of Poland who had deposed Stanislas. He gave Saxe 40,000 livres too, to help him keep up the estate – a thanks offering for having won France's few victories against Austria, including the battle of Fontenoy. Saxe was a violent, courageous soldier, conceited and luxury loving. He kept an extraordinary private army at Chambord – two cavalry regiments composed of tartars, Cossacks, Wallachians and negroes from Martinique. They had six cannon captured in battle and rode Ukrainian ponies which ran free and fed themselves in the forest but came to a trumpet call. If any soldier disobeyed the simplest order, he was hanged from a forest tree.

Saxe treated women abominally – surprising in the age of Pompadour and Du Barry. He arranged for his mistress, Adrienne Lecouvreur, star of the Comédie Française, to be poisoned. Then he fancied another actress, Le Favart, whose husband was a well-known actor-manager in Paris. Saxe, who had great influence in the capital, made certain that Le Favart could no longer get work there and brought him and his wife to Chambord to produce and act for his guests on the stage where Molière had played. Saxe bedded the wife.

Two years later, it was announced that Saxe had died from a chill. The court believed that he died from wounds received in a secret duel with the Prince of Conti, whose wife he had seduced. Saxe had arranged a great send-off for himself. The six cannon were fired in Chambord courtyard every hour for sixteen days.

Chambord was too big and expensive to keep up. No one wanted it. During the Revolution it was looted and virtually stripped of furniture. In 1809 Napoleon gave it to Marshal Berthier, who did not stay in it but stripped the forest of its beautiful hardwood and sold it. He had fought with Lafayette in the American War of Independence, and become chief of staff to Napoleon. When in 1815 he saw a Russian army crossing into France, he threw himself from a window.

In 1821 Chambord was bought by public subscription for the Duc de Bordeaux, grandson of Charles X and heir to the French throne. When Charles was driven out of France, his uncle Louis-Philippe, Duc d'Orléans, undertook to be Regent for the young Duke, but stole the crown. When he, too, was thrown out, the Duc de Bordeaux could have been King Henri V but showed little interest. As Duc de Chambord he stayed at Chambord 'passing forty years of blameless inertia'. After his death no one even had the money to pull Chambord down and the State was forced in 1930 to buy it.

Ground floor rooms have been partly refurnished. There are many fine tapestries in these rooms and on the second floor. The last Duke's suite has his collection of miniature soldiers, including miniature artillery which could pierce a brick wall, and his manifesto of 5 July 1871 which was an excuse for not taking the throne: 'Henri V will not abandon the white flag of Henri IV'. In other words, he would not pay allegiance to the Tricolor, only to the flag of Joan of Arc (Château open daily).

The first son-et-lumière was presented at Chambord in 1952 by M.P. Robert Houdin, descendant of the great scientific illusionist (see Blois page 65).

FESTIVALS Son-et-Lumière – Easter; Friday, Saturday, Sunday in April, May; daily 1 June–30 September

## HOTELS

*Grand St-Michel* (54.20.31.31): opposite the castle. Booked early in season. Presidents Giscard d'Estaing and Mitterand have stayed there for hunting parties. Front-seat view of Son-et-Lumière. ROOMS C–E. MEALS C–E. Shut mid-November–20 December. Restaurant shut Sunday.

*Manoir Bel Air* at St Dyé-sur-Loire, 4km (54.81.60.10): very pleasant, with park and views of the Loire. ROOMS C–F. MEALS C–E. Shut 20 January–21 February.

# CHAMPIGNY-SUR-VEUDE
## [INDRE-ET-LOIRE]

Even if you are not interested in old churches, do not miss the Renaissance gem here, Sainte-Chapelle, with its magnificent sixteenth-century Renaissance stained glass windows. It is north of Richelieu in the pleasant green valley of the Veude, and was the chapel of a château built by Louis I of Bourbon in the early sixteenth century. He accompanied Charles VII to Naples and came back with the same love of Italian architecture.

Cardinal Richelieu bought the château from Gaston d'Or-léans and, as with several others, had it knocked down because he wanted no competition with the magnificent château he was building for himself at his new town Richelieu. Pope Urban VIII stopped him knocking down the chapel. The farm of the château still remains, transformed into a lovely classical house by Gaston's daughter, La Grande Mademoiselle.

The stained glass windows are in superb glowing colours, gorgeously and delicately elegant. The crucifixion is the centrepiece with St Louis below. He reigned as Louis IX from 1226 to 1270 and died in Tunis on his way to one of his Crusades. He was patron saint of France until St Joan took over in 1920. A series of the windows show his life and death. They include vividly coloured groups of Crusaders and tents decorated with family arms.

# CHAMPTOCEAUX
## [MAINE-ET-LOIRE]

On the borders of Anjou and Loire-Atlantique, the D751 south of the Loire swings up a rocky hill to a corniche through steep wooded hills, with the Loire in a gorge below. Strung along a ridge is Champtoceaux, with superb views from a balcony behind the church of the Loire dividing to encircle islands. There is a sleepy little old port by the river, and remains of a castle above, illuminated in season.

An Anjou Coteaux de la Loire white wine is produced here.

HOTEL

*Voyageurs* (40.83.50.09): simple. ROOMS B–C. MEALS A–E. Shut mid-December–end January. Restaurant shut Wednesday.

RESTAURANT

*Jardins de la Forge* (40.83.56.23): simple auberge café-restaurant until a pupil of the great chef Paul Bocuse took over. Now it has a Michelin star. Superb river fish. MEALS D–G. Shut 8–23 October; part February; Sunday evening, Tuesday evening, Wednesday.

# LA CHAPELLE D'ANGILLON
## [CHER]

A Sologne village in a hollow on the banks of the Petite Sauldre river on D940 north of Bourges, it was the birthplace in 1886 of Alain-Fournier (Henri Alban Fournier) author of a sort of modern fairy tale *Le Grand Meaulnes*. It is woven around a girl whom the author had only seen once when he was twenty. It was the only novel he wrote. It was published in 1913 and next year he was killed fighting near Verdun. He left behind a few short stories and a lot of correspondence. Yet he made a deep mark in French literature and the book set a fashion in the 1920s. His published correspondence fills four volumes!

The Fournier house is on the left side of the D940 leading to Gien, 100 metres from the crossroads, and most guides identify Chapelle d'Angillon with Fournier's Ferté d'Angillon. Souvenirs of Fournier are sold. Château de Béthune has an audio-visual presentation about him. In the church of St Jacques his name is on the First World War memorial and his parents are buried in the adjoining churchyard. There is no mistaking the descriptions of Sologne countryside, either. But John Ardagh, who has made a deep study of Fournier's life and work, points out in his delightful book *Writers' France* (Hamish Hamilton) that he moved when he was five to Epineul-le-Fleuriel, 60 miles further south by the Cher, where his father was headmaster and this was the all-important Sainte-Agathe of the book, where

Fournier's hero went to school. My friend Vivian Rowe wrote in a book on the Loire in 1969: 'Perfectly recognizable still are the school, the Café Daniel, the place de l'Eglise, the quartier des Petits Coins'.

Truth is, Fournier fused the two areas into one. But La Chapelle has the last word – its main street is now called 'rue Alain-Fournier'.

Château de Béthune is a feudal castle with towers and a keep surrounded by a moat. In the seventeenth century it belonged to Maximilien de Béthune, Duc de Sully. He led the Protestant forces of Henri of Navarre (Henry IV) to victory at Coutras and Ivry, and later when Henri was King, achieved the remarkable feat of making the French pay their taxes. In 1590 when he took over there was nothing in the national chest. In 1609 there were twenty million. (Open Palm Sunday to 31 October except Sunday morning).

# LA CHAPELLE-HEULIN
## [Loire-Atlantique]

Wine village on a Muscadet wine-road from Nantes along which dozens of growers offer 'Dégustations et Vente Directe' (Tastings and Direct Sales). Take the old N149 (not N249) from Nantes, then D756. Turn left at Chapelle-Heulin to Domaine des Gautronnières where the Fleurance family, vignerons since the seventeenth century, produce old-style Muscadet in oak casks, concentrated and fresh on the palate.

Just past Chapelle-Heulin is a drive to the left leading to Château de la Noë de Bel Air, marked on the yellow Michelin map. Here le Comte de Malestroit's family have lived and made good wine sine 1741. Their château was burned down in the Revolution, so the family built the elegant Palladian-stye house you see now. In 1960 the present Count put his wines on the market and they became known around the world. To taste and buy you must telephone 40.33.92.72.

# LA CHARTRE-SUR-LE-LOIR
## [SARTHE]

On the Loir river 43km W of Vendôme, this village is a delightful holiday or weekend spot for sailing, fishing and swimming (a fine outdoor pool). A little known, rare white wine, Jasnières, is made nearby. In good years it has great delicacy and finesse. In great years it has a little natural sweetness. In poor years it is rather acidic. Climatic conditions are difficult. Chartre has several small hotels and restaurants.

TOURIST INFORMATION Syndicat d'Initiative
(15 June–15 September – 43.44.40.04)

HOTEL

*France* (43.44.40.16): good traditional country inn. Fishing in private pool. Very good cooking – 3-chimney Logis. ROOMS A–D. MEALS A–F. Shut 15 November–15 December.

# CHÂTEAU-DU-LOIR
## [SARTHE]

Small town spread along a valley of the river Yre, a tributary of the Loir, on the La Flèche–Vendôme road. The old part of the town is clustered round an interesting church, once part of a priory of which the poet Ronsard was prior. All that is left of the medieval castle from the Hundred Years War is a keep in gardens near the town hall. Good views from the top of the keep. The fourteenth-century Manoir du Riablay is now an hotel. Lovely countryside along Loir river.

TOURIST INFORMATION 2 ave J. Jaurès (June–
mid-September – 43.44.56.68)

HOTEL

*Manoir du Riablay* (43.79.45.86): opened in 1988 in fourteenth-century manor, with sixteenth-century dining-room. Beautiful and peaceful. In a park. Charming rooms very pricey. ROOMS G. MEALS C–G.

# CHÂTEAU-GONTIER
### [MAYENNE]

A fine old town of narrow, winding streets founded by Foulques Nerra in the eleventh century, it has one of the biggest cattle markets in France, with up to five thousand head sold every Thursday. It is on the N62 N of Angers. Once it was an important port on the canalized Mayenne river, which runs through it and it still has big quays with fine trees for shade.

Foulques Nerra gave the Benedictines land for building the eleventh-century church of St Jean. It is in flint and sandstone and has a pure Romanesque interior, though the stained glass windows are modern. The old ones were destroyed in 1940. The twelfth-century frescos include the story of Adam and Eve and of Noah's Ark. The Promenade du Bout du Monde in the old priory gardens has pleasant river views and a little zoo.

TOURIST INFORMATION Syndicat, Hôtel-de-Ville
(43.07.07.10)
MARKETS Thursday and Saturday morning
FESTIVALS Fair of St Fiacre – mid-August

### HOTELS

*Jardin des Arts*, 5 rue Abel-Cahour (43.70.12.12): ancient house but modern-style bedrooms. River views. ROOMS D–F. MEALS B–E. Shut 10–30 December; Sunday evening. Restaurant shut Saturday lunch, Sunday evening, Monday lunch.

*Hostellerie Mirwault*, 2km N by rue Basse-du-Rocher (43.07.13.17): nice position among gardens and terraces by the river. ROOMS C–D. MEALS C–E. Shut 28 December–15 January. Restaurant shut Sunday evening, Monday.

### RESTAURANT

*Prieuré*, at Azé, 2km SE by D22 (43.70.31.16) : old presbytery; terrace facing river; good country dishes. MEALS A–E. Shut Monday except July, August.

# CHÂTEAU-LA-VALLIÈRE
## [Indre-et-Loire]

A happy little country town 33km NW of Tours by the very attractive D959, which runs through fertile fields and fine woods and copses, with glimpses of the huge, shallow pools dotted around the pleasant countryside. Or take D34, a smaller road, just upstream from Langeais – a quieter road which runs alongside some of the pools. This little known countryside has been one of our most successful areas for picking gîtes. Knowledgeable French people hide here for weekends or quiet holidays. Château-la-Vallière is in the little river Fare valley and has the biggest of the étangs – a reed-edged pool a mile wide in one place. To the south is a forest of oaks and pines, with clearings of heathland. Called Étang du Val Joyeux, the pool is in an attractive woodland setting and is a lovely spot for sailing, bathing and fishing. There is a camp site.

Once called Château-en-Anjou, the town changed its name through a royal love affair. Louise de la Baume le Blanc had been born in La Vallière manor NW of Tours. She was a gentle good-looking girl with a slight limp. She became lady-in-waiting to Charles I of England's strong-minded widow, Henrietta Maria, in 1662 and at Fontainebleau she had the misfortune to catch the eye of Louis XIV. She was nineteen years old. She remained the chief royal mistress for five years. Louis gave her Château-en-Anjou, changed its name and made her Duchesse de la Vallière. She bore Louis four children. She was toppled out of the Royal bed by a far more worldly-wise woman, Madame de Montespan. Louise was persuaded to retire to a Carmelite nunnery in rue St Jacques in Paris where she eventually took vows. She was there thirty-six years.

Three and a half kilometres along D34 are the 'romantic' ruins of Château de Vaujours, with a fortified barbican and rampart walls with round towers at intervals. One tower is complete. Louise was also Duchesse de Vaujours, but only visited the château once.

# CHÂTEAUNEUF-SUR-LOIRE
[LOIRET]

A small, pleasant market town has arisen from the 1940 bombardment – inevitable, because it is an important bridgehead over the Loire. It is 25km E of Orléans. The few old remains are attractive. One of Louis XIV's Secretaries of State with the impressive name of Phélypeaux de la Vrillière built himself a miniature Versailles. His superb Italian-style tomb is still in the church but only the rotunda remains from his château and part of his gardens which are now a public park known for azaleas and giant rhododendrons. A formal French garden is bordered by a moat with a bridge, ducks and swans, and there are lovely shady riverside walks, a bathing beach and swimming pool. The picturesque covered market looks old but was built in 1854.

In the basement of the rotunda is Musée de la Marine de la Loire, a fascinating museum showing the three-thousand year history of Loire boats and the men who sailed them. You can see a model here of the boats which carried the most traffic, *Chalands* (sometimes called *gabares*). Chalands were flat-bottomed, and had no keel and a draught of less than a metre when fully laden. Their bows were flat and raised like a landing craft so that they slid onto obstructions instead of ramming them. But if the water was low, they might have to stay aground until the rains came. Most were 15 metres long but the biggest were 30 metres long, with a 5-metre beam and could carry 60 tonnes. They had a single mast, lowered by winch at bridges and carrying usually one long rectangular sail. There was no rudder. They were steered with a sort of oar and a huge pole that was attached to the bow and used by a very strong man like a pole on a punt. To tack, the crew would throw out a big anchor, pole the ship's head round, then haul in the anchor. They carried to Nantes wine, Orléans vinegar, wool, timber, grain and coal and returned with fruit, fish, salt and various imports, mostly sugar, spices, tobacco and rum.

Other boats included sapines, poled with the current to carry wine to Nantes, then sold there and broken up for the wood, and large light *coches d'eau* which carried passengers and were rowed both ways. From Orléans to Nantes took about eight days, the journey back about a fortnight – not much slower than using the appalling roads, more comfortable and probably safer. King and courtiers often went by boat. But the railways must have come as a relief to merchants. There were so many rackets, tolls, and backhanders involved in river transport that the cost of a cargo could multiply by four between Nevers and Nantes.

TOURIST INFORMATION 1 place A. Briand
(38.58.44.79)

HOTEL

*Parc et Restaurant La Capitainerie*, Grande Rue (38.58.42.16): overlooks château grounds. Rare 3-chimney Logis restaurant. Very good. ROOMS C–D. MEALS C–F. Shut February; Sunday evening, Monday.

# CHÂTEAUNEUF-SUR-SARTHE
[SARTHE]

Between Angers and Sablé-sur-Sarthe, Châteauneuf is a good place for hiring boats or picking up a river cruise. There are lovely riverside walks watching the fast-running clear river which passes under the arches of the bridge. Old mills and a big church make the riverside attractive. The old Hôtel de la Sarthe by the bridge has a nice wide riverside terrace. Cruises on the Sarthe by modern panoramic boats run from March to December with lunch on board (Anjou Croisiers, quai Savette, Angers tel. 41.88.37.47).

TOURIST INFORMATION quai de la Sarthe (shut
mornings low season – 41.69.82.89)

HOTEL

*Sarthe* (41.69.85.29): regional dishes. ROOMS C. MEALS A–E. Shut 7–28 October; part February; Sunday evening; Monday except July, August.

# CHÂTEAU-RENAULT
## [INDRE-ET-LOIRE]

Founded in 1066 by Renault, son of Geoffroi de Château-
Gontier, it stands on a hill with streets curving down to the
meeting place of the Brenne and Gault rivers (26km SW of
Vendôme on N10). Traditionally a leather-work town, it has
added electronics and chemicals to its industries.

Through a fourteenth-century gateway you reach terraces
with shading limes and views to the rivers. The seventeenth-
century château, now the hotel, was owned by two renowned
sailors – the Marquis de Château-Renault, who served Louis
XIV, and the Comte d'Estaing, beheaded in the Revolution.
This d'Estaing family was very distinguished. Pierre d'Estaing
saved the life of King Philippe-Auguste at the battle of Bourines
in 1214. In 1790 a girl of the family married the Comte de la
Tour. Her daughter married a man called Giscard and his son
Théophile started a court action to add his grandmother's name
d'Estaing to his own. The original d'Estaing family opposed it,
the action went on for around fifty years and surprisingly Théophile won – in 1922 when he was dead! Valéry Giscard
d'Estaing, ex-President of France, is Théophile's great-
grandson.

TOURIST INFORMATION Parc de Vauchevrier (Easter–
end September – 47.29.54.43)

### HOTEL
*Écu de france*, 37 place Jean-Jaurès (47.29.50.72): 3-chimney
Logis. Good value. ROOMS D–E. MEALS B–D. Shut 24 Dec-
ember–1 February; Sunday evening; Monday lunch except July,
August.


# CHAUMONT-SUR-LOIRE
## [LOIR-ET-CHER]

A small town of one street on the banks of the Loire with its
well-known château up a long hill which is hard work to climb. A

powerful pile, built over fifty years by the Counts of Anjou for defence. In a land of so many impressive or beautiful castles, it is not outstanding except for its remarkable stables, which are fun. In the fifteenth century the owner of Chaumont, Pierre d'Amboise, joined rebellious barons against Louis XI and was made to pull down his castle. Then the King relented and he started to build the present castle in 1465. His son and grandson finished it and his grandson was so popular with Louis XII that he became a Marshal of France, admiral, lieutenant-general in Italy and royal steward. The castle, with its huge round towers, looks bellicose.

When Henry II was killed in a jousting accident, his widow Catherine de' Medici bought it. She may not have lived there much but a room connected by a staircase to the top of the tower is said to have been the study of her astrologer, Ruggien, and the tower was his observatory from which they studied the stars together. Furthermore, it is said that he was able to foretell the fate awaiting her three sons – François II, Charles IX and Henri III, who all met violent ends. If so, she obviously did not warn anyone. What Catherine did was to turn her husband's mistress, Diane de Poitiers, out of the beautiful Chenonceau, which Catherine took, and give her the rather dreary Chaumont in exchange. She also made Diane return all the jewels that Henri had given her. Catherine had kept a careful list.

Diane found Chaumont far too gloomy and draughty, despite lovely views over river and woodland, and soon retired to her old home at Château d'Anet near Dreux. Her retirement was a loss to France. Older than Henri, she had been not only his mistress but also a wise organizer and manager, and things went terribly wrong after she left the scene of government.

Madame de Staël, the volatile and brilliant writer, thought the château gloomy, too, when she was banished there by Napoleon, whose police had destroyed her half-written book *De L'Allemagne*. But she loved only Paris, and the limelight of her fashionable salon which lured the most powerful politicians and best writers. Her tragedy was that she spent much of her life in enforced exile because she never pulled any punches in what she said or wrote. She was even an emigré in 1792 to Mickleham in Surrey with Talleyrand, the cynical and ruthless politician.

The owner when she was at Chaumont was Le Ray, Governor of Les Invalides. He had turned part of the castle into a successful factory, producing medallions of famous people, designed by Nini, an Italian artist-engraver who had his baking oven in a former dovecote. There, Benjamin Franklin sat for his medallion portrait.

Chaumont's period of ostentation and luxury began in 1875 when a spoilt sixteen-year-old called Marie Say told her father, as they passed by, that she wanted it. So he bought it for her. She married a young prince, Amadée de Broglie, a truly luxury-loving young man. The superb Renaissance majolica Sicilian tiles of hunting scenes in Catherine's conical room they bought from a palace in Salerno. they brought in electricity for heating and lighting, taking it as well to the village down the hill, so that it was one of the first in France to have electric street lamps. To improve and extend their park, they bought two hamlets and knocked them down, and knocked down and rebuilt the church because they did not like it. They also knocked down a wing of the château to improve the view.

To entertain guests, they hired trains to bring the whole cast of the Comédie Française and the Paris Opéra to Chaumont for the weekend. One guest, a delighted Maharajah, gave Marie an elephant and she had a stable built for it. The stables are still splendid. There are miniature stables for the children's ponies and stables lined with velvet for the family steeds. In the saddle room are English prints and vastly expensive whips and harnesses from Hermès designer shop.

They had to sell their beloved horses in 1917. The sugar-beet factory providing their wealth went bankrupt, the manager shot himself, but the Prince went on spending and became nearly bankrupt. The State has owned the château since 1938. Although not fully furnished, it has some fine Renaissance furniture and tapestries and although the Prince broke up big rooms to make more smaller ones and knocked down that wing, so that the fine courtyard has only three sides, it is still impressive and worth seeing (shut on Tuesdays). The Prince was truly the black sheep of the Broglie family. From 1671 they produced a line of distinguished and talented men – great soldiers, statesmen, two prime ministers, foreign secretaries, an Ambassador to

London, and more latterly, very distinguished scientists, including one who won the Nobel Prize for pioneering work on the undulatory theory of matter.

### HOTEL

*Le Château*, 2 rue du Mar. de Lattre-de-Tassigny (54.20.98.04): lovely house, pretty individually furnished bedrooms. Swimming pool. Friendly. Bourgeois cooking. ROOMS D–F. MEALS B–E. Shut 1 December–1 March.

# CHÊNEHUTTE-LES-TUFFEAUX
## [MAINE-ET-LOIRE]

Leaving Saumur to go to Angers on the less crowded and more attractive left bank road along the Loire D751, you come to the quarries of Chênehutte which were dug to provide the tufa stone to build a lot of the Loire châteaux. Now they are are used to grow mushrooms. The sixteenth-century priory which commands the river with splendid views, is now an excellent Relais et Châteaux luxury hotel in wooded grounds of fifteen hectares.

### HOTEL

*Prieuré* (41.67.90.14): same group as Mas d'Artigny at St Paul-de-Vence and Château d'Artigny (page 116) but more relaxed and friendly. High above the river; attractive wooded garden; modern cooking; bedrooms in bungalows not so good as in main building. Very pricey. ROOMS G. MEALS F–G. Shut 5 January–1 March.

# CHENILLE-CHANGÉ
## [SARTHE]

Twenty-five kilometres north of Angers on the Mayenne river, here canalized but winding and attractive, splendid for pleasure craft. Chenille and Château-Gontier (page 154) are good places to hire boats (Maine-Anjou- Rivières tel 41.95.10.83).

# CHENONCEAU
[*See* Sites page 104]

## CHEVERNY – Château
[LOIR-ET-CHER]

Charming, less famous than nearby Chaumont or Blois (which is 7km N) but I find it very likeable and interesting, partly because it is still lived in. It is a magnificently decorated and furnished home, not a museum. In fact, some of the decoration is almost *too* rich, but it is authentic.

It is an elegant house in white tufa stone with slate roofs and perfect symmetry without losing its beauty, and it stands in a fine park with superb trees – limes, cedars, horse chestnuts and Wellingtonia.

This château, finished in 1634, was built by Henri Hurault, Count of Cheverny, who had owned the previous one. He wanted to start a new life with a new wife. Hurault was a soldier in Henri IV's army, away much of the time campaigning. His young wife Françoise became bored. Back in Paris, he saw in a mirror King Henri making signs to courtiers that he was being cuckolded. Without telling the Court, Hurault called for his horse, rode home to Cheverny and found his wife in bed with a page. The page jumped from a window but broke his ankle. Hurault ran round and killed him, then went back to the bedroom and killed his wife. The King banished him for three years – to his own château at Cheverny. There he married the pretty daughter of his bailiff and rebuilt the château. They had seven children.

The male line of the Huraults died out in 1755 and the château passed to others until in 1825 a member of the cadet branch of the family, Marquis Hurault de Vibraye, bought it back and it is still owned by the present Marquis de Vibraye.

Cheverny is still waiting for the King of France to come. When Henri IV gave permission for the new château to be built he claimed 'droit de gîte' which meant that a bedroom must always be kept furnished and waiting in case the King wanted to drop in after hunting – or even to chase one of the women of the house – the very favourite sport of the Kings of France. The room is still there, the superb bed has a canopy of fifteenth-century white Persian silk, embroidered with now-faded flowers. It is hardly a room to *sleep* in – there is too much to look at. It is almost overpowering. A series of seventeenth-century tapestries follow the dramas of Ulysses' travels. On the ceiling Perseus meets the Medusa, the girl with wings, long teeth, serpents for hair and a terrifying look whose head Perseus cut off. Just the thing for a bedtime story.

Another thirty painted panels tell a melodramatic story fit for classical ballet or opera. It's about an Ethiopian princess abandoned at birth who becomes a priestess at Delphi, then falls in love with a handsome Thessalonian. They flee aboard a ship, get captured by pirates, enslaved and separated. She gets involved in a war and becomes the slave of the king of Ethiopia at his court. Her real identity as a princess is revealed. Whom should she meet there but her Thessalonian lover who turns out to be a prince in disguise. They marry and make merry.

The staircase is carved in white stone fruit and flowers; ceilings, window shutters and pillars are all elaborately painted. The Gobelin tapestry of the Abduction of Helen of Troy is in the guard room and is delightful. The fireplace is carved, gilded and decorated with the story of Adonis, by Jean Mosnier, who worked here for eighteen years. He painted most of the remarkable ceilings and the humorous Don Quixote scenes in the dining room. Mosnier, son of a glassblower, was born in Blois in 1600. When he was sixteen he made a Madonna painting which so impressed Marie de' Medici that she sent him to Italy to be taught. He stayed nine years, then returned to work for Marie at the Luxembourg Palace in Paris. Then he returned to Blois and stayed in the area until he died.

The grand salon of Cheverny is covered with paintings from wall panels to ceiling, the small salon has fine seventeenth-century Flanders tapestries, and both rooms are superbly furnished in Louis XIV and Louis XV furniture.

The stables and kennels, left from the previous château, are remarkable. One stable is a museum of hunting with two thousand antlers on walls, ceilings, rafters and pillars. From

November to Easter the hunt meets twice a week, and you can see them ride off with the jostling, wagging hounds and hear the celebrated 'Trompes de Cheverny' coiled horns. (Château and stables open daily). A son-et-lumière 2nd fortnight of July, 1st fortnight of August.

Three kilometres SW of Cour-Cheverny village is a charming little Renaissance manor house, Château de Troussay, with furnishings, carvings and sculptures saved from vanished local houses and an interesting collection of farming tools.

### HOTEL

*St Hubert*, Cour-Cheverny (54.79.96.60): old house comfortably extended. Excellent regional cooking. Some coaches stop for meals but plenty of space for the passengers. ROOMS C–D. MEALS B–F. Shut 20 December–1 February; Sunday evening; Wednesday in winter.

### RESTAURANT

*Pousse Rapière* at Cheverny rue Nationale (54.79.94.23): building a good reputation. MEALS B–F. Shut 15 December–1 January; Monday; Sunday evening in winter.

# CHINON
## [INDRE-ET-LOIRE]

I love Chinon. It is such a happy place. Perhaps the spirit of Rabelais still haunts it. (*See* Artists and Writers, page 44.) Though a prosperous wine town, with a lovely twelfth-century bridge over the Vienne, it seems to move at a leisurely pace and that is how it deserves to be explored. Luckily in modern times a bridge was built downstream and Route Nationale D751 by-passes it by 3 or 4 kilometres. Its old houses and shops rise steeply from the river in narrow streets to the remains of a medieval Gothic fortress with not so many happy memories. Chinon has a rich history.

It is only 16km from the meeting of the Loire and the

Vienne, which, like the Loire, is a river of many moods. Most visitors see it in mid-summer when sometimes its waters hardly moisten the piles of the old bridge. In spring and autumn it becomes a bubbling, fast-running torrent and you know that the solid walls defending the quays and attractive riverside road lined with shops and restaurants are very necessary.

The charms of Chinon seduce you immediately. Park your car at the end of the riverside road at place Jeanne d'Arc or near the town hall in place Général de Gaulle. From place Jeanne d'Arc stroll along rue Rabelais, turn into place Général de Gaulle and left at the end turn into rue Voltaire. In a side turning (rue Dr Gendron) is a little wine museum (open 1 April –30 September except Thursday). A little further along is rue Caves Peintes, which has views of vine-covered slopes and at the end of the street are cellars made from Roman quarries, called Caves Peintes because they had wall paintings when Rabelais' character Pantagruel used to sink a few glasses of cold dry white wine there. The Chinon wine syndicate still keeps wine in its 1½km-long cellars and you can hire the big gallery for a party of up to four hundred friends. Rabelais was a local lad and the name of his greatest hero Gargantua is kept alive in a hotel in a fifteenth-century mansion in rue Haute St Maurice (*see* Hotels).

There are some lovely beamed houses in rue Voltaire and in Grand Carroi, centre of the medieval town. Here is the wood and brick Maison Rouge where Joan of Arc dismounted when she came here on her first mission to meet the Dauphin. She is said to have stepped on the kerb of a well which is still there. Just beyond is the Maison des États Généraux, a big fifteenth-century mansion where Joan of Arc's Dauphin, later Charles VII, called meetings of the Estates General in 1428 when he had fled here because the English had taken much of France, including Paris, and were besieging Orléans. It was to the castle up the hill that Joan went to tell him of the mysterious voices calling her to lead an army to save France. The Maison is now Chinon's museum, with collections of furniture, *objets d'art*, relics of Joan and a portrait of Rabelais by Delacroix. If they tell you that Richard Coeur de Lion died here, don't believe it! But much of the castle was built in the twelfth century by Henry II of England and he

*Vineyards near Chinon*

died here. When Henry II had hypocritically imprisoned his wife, Eleanor of Aquitaine, for the same weakness that had brought her divorce from Louis of France – her tendency to slip into bed with other men – she turned their sons against him and Richard even joined with the new stronger French King Philippe-Auguste to fight against him. Defeated, very ill and dispirited, this once-great King retired here to his favourite castle. Then he heard that even his favourite son John had turned against him, so he gave up and died. His servants stripped him of his jewellery and rich clothes and disappeared.

Once he was King, Richard fought Louis-Philippe. He strengthened the castle and the French failed to take it. But when he died and the weaker John became King of England, Philippe beseiged it for a year and finally took it by his customary method of getting his sappers to undermine the walls until they split.

Cardinal Richelieu bought it in the seventeenth century and had much of the castle broken up for the stone, which he used for his new town and Château of Richelieu, 19km SE. He even dismantled the great hall where Joan had recognized the Dauphin even though he was dressed as a courtier to fool her. You can imagine the laughter and scoffing of the courtiers when the peasant girl from Lorraine walked in and told the Dauphin that God had sent her a message that he was to give her an army to defeat the English and save France. That he did is less likely to have been through inspiration than desperation at his plight. She put new heart into the French soldiers at a time when their enemy the English were exhausted, short of troops and many of them were sick.

All that remains of the great hall is the fireplace. The castle was in three parts, separated by dry moats. Fort St George, named after England's patron saint, was dismantled. Across the moat is Château du Milieu (Middle Castle), entered under a fourteenth-century clock tower, tall and thin, with a bell from 1599 which still rings on the hour. From the gardens are views over Chinon, the Vienne and its valley which repay the climb up to the château.

A bridge takes you to Fort de Coudray. You can visit the Logis Royaux, the royal apartments, against the wall of the middle castle only on guided tours. On the restored ground floor is a museum with a fine seventeenth-century tapestry showing Joan recognizing the Dauphin and a model of the château as it was in the fifteenth century. (Shut December, January and Wednesday low season.)

From the château ramparts overlooking the river you can see the mid-river island which supports the bridge, Île de Tours. The island has a sinister past. Here in 1321 the Jews of Chinon, 160 men, women and children were burned alive, accused of poisoning wells. The wells were almost certainly contaminated by typhoid, but the ignorant people of the Middle Ages always believed great evil of Jews.

From Clos de l'Echo on the north side of the château you can see on a hillside Clos de l'Echo vineyards, owned by Rabelais's family. It is called Clos de l'Echo because it produces a distinct echo used traditionally by Chinon men to tease their women with leading questions.

'*Les Femmes de Chinon sont-elles fidèles?*'

'*Elles?*' answers the echo.

'*Oui, les femmes de Chinon.*'

'*Non,*' says the echo.

The vineyards, owned now by the Couly-Dutheil family, produce a full-bodied fruity red wine aged long in cask. In great years a superb wine called Baronnie Madeleine is made. This is old-fashioned Chinon red, made with Cabernet Franc grapes, called locally Le Breton. It was traditionally kept up to ten years. Chinon also produces now lighter wines from the Gamay grape used for Beaujolais, drunk young, cold and fruity. This became fashionable in Paris, to the advantage of producers who do not have to mature and store it, and who can thus keep the cash flowing faster. Chinon also produces quite a lot of dry white Touraine Sauvignon wine and some light rosé.

At Château Ligré, a fine old house just off D749 and marked on the local Michelin map, Gatien Ferrand, dynamic flag carrier for Chinon wines, and his wine-maker son Pierre, produce excellent red wine, vital, full, subtle and ageing superbly. White wines are fruity. You can ask to taste but don't expect the red carpet – they are busy with professional visitors tasting to buy in quantity (tel. 47.93.16.70).

Rabelais himself might well have known Château Marçay, a superb fifteenth-century turreted château 6km S of Chinon, just off D759 and also Michelin-marked. It survived all the wars and troubles to become an hotel and restaurant with excellent cooking and Chinon and Bourgueil wines.

Also just off D759 south of Chinon is La Devinière, a stone house of Rabelais' family. He was probably born there, although a local story claims that he was born in a field on the way there because his mother had eaten too much tripe! He certainly used the house as a background for part of his story *Gargantua*. It is now a Rabelais museum (shut Wednesday out of season and in December, January). The local village of Seuilly has troglodyte houses (cave houses) down its main street.

Boat trips on the river Vienne are offered in April, May, June, September and October. In July and August they depend on the height of the river. (Cruise Chinon–Montsoreau, Saumur 49.93.89.46). There is much pleasure-boat activity on the river.

A steam train ('Train 1900') runs from Chinon to Richelieu (1hr 15 min). Some trains make a food and wine stop at Ligré-Rivière (Saturday, Sunday mid-May–end September).

TOURIST INFORMATION 12 rue Voltaire (47.93.17.85)

MARKETS Thursday, Saturday, Sunday

FESTIVALS Son-et-Lumière – Friday, Saturday evenings in season; Chapitre de Saint-Vincent des Étonneurs Rabelaisions (wine festival) – end January; Chapitre de la Fleur des Étonneurs Rabelaisions (flower, wine, food festival) – early June; Chapitre des Vendanges des Étonneurs Rabelaisions (grape-picking festival) – end September; Wine Fair – 2nd Saturday/Sunday in March; Marché Medieval (traditional medieval market) – early August

### HOTELS

*Gargantua*, 73 rue Haute St-Maurice (47.93.04.71): back to its old form, with bedrooms improved, service good, cooking excellent, although Gargantuan portions have shrunk and become lighter. In a lovely fifteenth-century house where Rabelais's father practised law. Staff in medieval costume on Friday, Saturday. ROOMS C–F. MEALS D. Shut 15 November–1 February; Thursday lunch, Wednesday in winter.

*Chris' Hotel*, 12 place Jeanne d'Arc (47.93.36.92): one of several nice little hotels in old houses, with comfortable bedrooms. Antique furniture. No restaurant. Friendly. ROOMS C–D.

*Diderot*, 4 rue Buffon (47.93.18.87): our old favourite. No restaurant. Eighteenth-century house, antiques, attractive rooms. Garden. ROOMS C–D. Shut 20 December–10 January.

*Château de Marçay*, at Marçay 7km S on D759 and D116 (47.93.03.47): see text. Superb and very pricey. ROOMS G.

MEALS F–G. Shut mid-January–mid-March. Restaurant shut Sunday evening, Monday in winter.

### RESTAURANTS

*Au Plaisir Gourmand*, quai Charles VII, 2 rue Parmentier (47.93.20.48): best restaurant for miles. In an attractive eighteenth-century house on the river quai, Jean-Claude Rigolet cooks superb regional dishes, seeking out original recipes. Cheapest menu called 'La Cuisine du Terroir'. Excellent! Booking essential. MEALS E–G. Shut mid-end November; 3–26 February; Sunday evening, Monday.

*Océanic*, 13 rue Rabelais (47.93.44.55): superb fish. In my favourite Chinon street, an old favourite with local people and my *Travellers' France* readers, so book if possible – or go early. Simple bistro. MEALS C–D. Shut 20 December–5 January; Sunday evening, Monday.

*Orangerie*, 79 bis rue Voltaire (47.98.42.00): old house built into ancient town wall. Simple; stone walls. Good bourgeois cooking. Cheap. MEALS B–C. Shut December, January; Sunday evening, Monday.

# CHOLET
## [MAINE-ET-LOIRE]

Town in the south of Les Mauges, SE of Nantes, SW of Saumur, still renowned for producing cloth, handkerchiefs and table and household linen. Rows of shops in the centre sell them, including small red handkerchiefs with white borders – traditional badge of the Vendeans, the Royalists who tried to reverse the French Revolution. Here they suffered defeat in October 1793. They were executed in thousands in Angers.

Now Cholet also produces footwear, electronics, plastics and agricultural machinery.

Eighteenth-century mansion in a park houses the Beaux Arts museum, with paintings by Toulouse-Lautrec, Braque, Matisse.

TOURIST INFORMATION place Rougé (41.62.22.35)

MARKET daily except Monday, Sunday
FESTIVAL Carnival – third Thursday in Lent
(mi-Carême)

HOTEL
*Belvédère*, Lac Ribou, 4km SE by D20 (41.62.14.02): tranquil, in
countryside; some rooms overlook lake. Excellent delicate cooking. Book. ROOMS D. MEALS C–F. Shut 22 July–21 August;
Sunday evening, Monday lunch.

# CINQ-MARS-LA-PILE
[INDRE-ET-LOIRE]

Along N152, 5km NE of Langeais, it is named after a mysterious
slim tower, thirty metres high, ending in pyramids at each corner. It was possibly built in Gallo-Roman days, but a family
called Saint-Médard had a château here in the eleventh century
and it may be a corruption of their name. Two towers remain
from their castle. Of the manor house to which the family
moved only a wing survives, thanks to the wrath of Richelieu. In
that house Henri, Marquis de Cinq Mars was born in 1620. He
was only twenty-two when he ended his life on the scaffold at
Lyon but his life story did give Alfred de Vigny material for his
great historical novel, *Cinq Mars* (1826). De Vigny was born
nearby at Loches.

Cinq-Mars became a page in Cardinal Richelieu's retinue.
The Cardinal's power was maintained by spying, even on King
Louis XIII. He usually used women as his spies but Louis XIII
was prudish – a reaction, perhaps, to the fun and games he had
seen at the Court of his father, Henri IV, 'le Vert Galant'. So
Richelieu planted young Henri at Louis's court. The King
became almost passionately fond of the handsome boy of
eighteen and they were constant companions, despite some
quarrels which Richelieu patched up.

The King was so jealous when Cinq-Mars had an affair with
a courtesan that Richelieu himself had to seduce the girl to break
up the liaison.

Cinq-Mars became very arrogant. He plotted with Gaston d'Orléans, the King's constantly plotting younger brother, to get rid of Richelieu. He went further. He entered into treasonable negotiations with Spain. When the plot was discovered by Richelieu, Gaston shopped Cinq-Mars, who was hanged. Richelieu ordered that his château be demolished. Richelieu died before this was done but an angry Louis insisted that the order should be obeyed. The ruins have a lovely garden and forest park.

# CLÉRY-ST-ANDRÉ
## [LOIRET]

When he was trying to drive the English from Dieppe while he was still Dauphin, Louis XI made a vow that if he were victorious he would give his weight in silver to the basilica of Notre-Dame-de-Cléry, which had been knocked down by the English Commander the Earl of Salisbury in 1428 on his way to besieging Orléans, 15km to the NE. Louis won at Dieppe and kept his word. When he died in 1483 he was buried there as he had wished. His son, Charles VIII, finished the rebuilding. The square tower was left from the original church. When Salisbury had his head knocked off by a cannon ball at Orléans, the French said that the Virgin herself had directed the shot because he had desecrated her shrine.

Louis used to stay at a house that is still in the town. He had his own secret oratory in the church with access by a spiral stair to an opening above the sacristy door, so that he could hear Mass without being seen by the congregation. He lived in great fear of being assassinated, which he deserved to be for his cruelty, viciousness and double-dealing. He claimed: 'He who has success has honour.' Alas, not many people would contradict that today.

He had his vault dug out in his lifetime and used to go and lie in it. Louis' bones and those of his wife are still in the vault which opens onto the nave near a statue of him. In a glass case are their two skulls, split open for embalming. The original bronze statue was taken and melted down by the Huguenots. It was replaced in 1622 by an excellent marble statue by the Orléans sculptor Michel Bourdin. Louis is kneeling, 'praying forgiveness, I suppose, for his baseness and his murders', as Arthur Young, the English traveller and agriculturist wrote in 1787.

A worthier man is buried in the Dunois Chapel – Jean, Count of Dunois, Joan of Arc's 'gentil Bâtard' (Gentle Bastard), staunch friend and companion in arms, who after her death continued her work of driving out the English. He, too, had given money to help rebuild the church.

The Chapelle Saint-Jacques (St James's Chapel) was used by pilgrims on their way to St James's tomb at Compostella in Spain and is decorated with carvings of pilgrim girdles, wallets and staves.

The heart of Louis XI's son, Charles VIII, is buried near Louis's tomb. Another, King Henri II, presented the oak south door and carved stalls and both are decorated with his initials with those of his mistress, Diane de Poitiers.

# CLISSON
## [LOIRE-ATLANTIQUE]

D149 SE from Nantes leads to the charming little Musçadet wine town of Clisson, with Italian-style arcades, terraces and steps among trees and old houses. It is at the meeting of the Sèvre and Moine rivers both crossed by fourteenth-century humped bridges.

The Italian look was given to it by the sculptor Lemot of Lyon around 1800 after the town had been burned down and abandoned during the Revolution. Somehow the wooden-roofed market hall survived, so did the impressive ruins of the château built between the thirteenth and fourteenth centuries. It belonged first to the Clisson family, then to the Dukes of Brittany. Duchess Anne's father, Duke François II, was married there and virtually rebuilt it around 1470.

Best known of the Clissons was Olivier (1336–1407). When

he was seven his father was beheaded as a traitor by the French during the Breton War of Succession. His mother, Jeanne de Belville, nailed the head to the ramparts of Nantes, then in Brittany, took her children to see it and made them swear revenge. Then with four hundred men she captured six castles that were siding with the French and butchered their garrisons. The French were closing in, so she armed a ship at Nantes and sank every French ship she met at sea. When Olivier grew up, he fought successfully with the English and Jean de Montfort against the French and Du Guesclin. But in the Hundred Years War he fought with the French and Du Guesclin and his brutality got him the name of 'Butcher of the English'. When Du Guesclin died, he became Constable of France in command of all the French Armies. But he was thuggish and arrogant and he was banished finally to the Château at Josselin which he had gained by marriage. His motto was 'I do as I please'.

Clisson has a son-et-lumière in July, August.

### RESTAURANT
*Bonne Auberge*, 1 rue Olivier-de-Clisson (40.54.01.90): outstanding, imaginative cooking. Expensive. MEALS D–G. Shut mid-August–early September; 15–end February; Sunday evening, Monday.


# COMBREUX
## [LOIRET]

A hamlet 8km NE of Châteauneuf-sur-Loire, Combreux is the centre of many ponds rich in water lilies and near to the disused Orléans canal. Nearby is a reservoir, Étang de la Vallée, in a setting of woodland and tall grasses where wild water birds take cover. You can swim, fish, sail, windsurf or just pedal a pedalo. Boats are for hire.

Combreux has a sixteenth–seventeenth-century moated château. The surrounding Forêt d'Orléans is one of the biggest in France, stretching from just NE of Orléans to within 15km of Gien, and has masses of marked routes for walkers and cars.

## HOTELS

*Auberge de Combreux* (38.59.47.63): old creeper-clad house with more bedrooms in modern chalets with little gardens. Small pool, tennis. Half-board only mid-summer. Family cooking. ROOMS D–E. MEALS B–E. Shut 22 December–20 January.

*Croix Blanche* (38.59.47.62): country Logis; pleasant garden. Very good value. ROOMS C. MEALS B–E. Shut 23–end September; Monday evening, Tuesday.

# CORMERY
## [INDRE-ET-LOIRE]

The pretty little D17 road, beautiful in places, starts from the N143 N of Loches and follows the eccentric twists and turns of the delightful Indre river to Cormery, then on to Montbazon. Cormery is a nice little town, famous for macaroons. Here are the remains of the eighth-century abbey to which the Yorkshire-man Alcuin, greatest scholar in France, retired in 796 and died in 804, having in that short time made it into one of the most influential schools in Western Europe. Alcuin was the head-master of York Choir School who was persuaded by the Emperor Charlemagne to become teacher to his whole family, including himself.

## RESTAURANT

*Auberge du Mail*, place Mail (47.43.40.32): simple, old-style restaurant with good value meals. Terrace. MEALS B–E. Shut 27 June–5 July; mid-November–1 December; Thursday evening, Friday.

# CRAON
## [MAYENNE]

Town 19km W of Château-Gontier and 56km NW of Angers, which is little known except to farmers of the surrounding bocage countryside. But it has horse-races in September and a really beautiful château. The château has no historic interest but is built entirely of white tufa stone of Saumur, a stone that grows whiter with age. The Marquis d'Armaillé had it built in 1720 and it has the elegance of that age and the unity of design that fits beautifully into a lovely garden, with a large terrace in front. The river Oudon runs through the park. Inside are several rooms in eighteenth-century style with Louis XVI furnishings. In the park is a nineteenth-century refrigerator – an underground cave in which snow and ice were shovelled in winter to keep food ice-cold in summer.

# CRAVANT-LES-COTEAUX
## [INDRE-ET-LOIRE]

The D21 east from Chinon through the Vienne river valley is a quiet little flat road leading through the Cravant vineyards, sloping away to the horizon. The wine produced is Chinon appellation. The Vieux-Bourg-Cravant, one kilometre N, has a church with a fine tenth-century nave, eleventh-century door, and remains of a fresco representing the church's original donors.

# CUNAULT and TRÈVES
## [MAINE-ET-LOIRE]

You may not be very interested in old churches but if you are passing along D751 near Gennes or Chênehutte-les-Tuffeaux NW of Saumur, alongside the Loire, do stop to look at the twelfth-century Romanesque priory church which is majestically impressive. Its massive eleventh-century bell-tower is one hundred years older than the rest and is handsome with three arcaded storeys. The spire was added in the fifteenth century. Alas, the church is now empty, but is worth seeing for the beautiful pillars and 223 richly carved capitals. It was built to take pilgrims in September and gives an impression of enormous spaciousness. It is so high that some enthusiasts use binoculars to study sculptures on the friezes and arcades.

Trèves is now virtually the same place. It was called Trèves by the bellicose Foulques Nerra because for once in his life he made a truce there with the Count of Blois. A crenellated tower survives from a fifteenth-century castle and at the foot of it a small pretty Romanesque village church.

# DOUÉ-LA-FONTAINE
## [MAINE-ET-LOIRE]

One of the oldest towns in Anjou, it was built over underground galleries and quarries cut out of the rock. Now it is a rose-growing area of lovely nurseries, with a Jardin des Roses open to the public. Journées des Roses, a rose festival, is held in mid-July in the Arena, made from open quarries back in the fifteenth century, with rows of seats cut out of the rock as the Romans did. It is also used for plays and musical performances.

There are three interesting cave sites. Six kilometres N by D69 and D177 is the troglodyte village of Rochemenier. It was a big underground village but a modern village above ground has hidden it. Two troglodyte farms, abandoned in 1930, are open to the public (shut Monday except in July and August).

At La Fosse, 5½km north of Doué by D214, you can see how the troglodyte farmers lived. They carved out ovens, chimneys, vegetable stores, silos and dug holes direct into the ground to store crops. Then they sold the chalk (open 1 July–15 October; mid-March–April; Saturday, Sunday rest of year).

At Dénezé-sous-Doué, 5½km N by D69, a cave discovered in 1956 has sixteenth-century grotesque figures, some playing musical instruments, carved on its side. They appear to be performing initiation ceremonies and it may well have been a secret meeting place of an illegal society of stonemasons. (Open daily 1 April–31 August; afternoons for the rest of year.)

# DURTAL
## [Maine-et-Loire]

The N23 SW from La Flèche to Angers meets the Loir river at Bazouges-sur-le-Loir and crosses it at Durtal, 13km from La Flèche, near the A11 motorway. It is an attractively placed sleepy little town which offers good fishing and bathing, and walking in the nearby Chambiers forest. It has a racecourse, too. There are watermills on the water front and a large, rather dilapidated, restored castle turned into an old peoples' home. To reach it from place du Marché, you pass what is left of the town wall built in the eleventh century by Geoffrey Martel, then you go under a superb deep archway with two round towers, Porte Verron, built in Henri IV's time. From the castle esplanade or from the old bridge are good views of the Loir. Durtal has a three-star camp site. A good place for a gentle holiday.

TOURIST INFORMATION Mairie (41.76.30.24)

RESTAURANT

*Boule d'Or,* 19 ave d'Angers (41.76.30.20): excellent value. MEALS A–E. Shut most of August; 15–end February; Sunday evening, Wednesday.

# EVRON
## [Mayenne]

Twenty kilometres SE of Mayenne by D7, it is in an under-rated region with pleasant walks round lakes and woodlands. In a cattle area, it has a renowned meat festival on the first Sunday of September. Its beautiful church, Basilica of Notre Dame, has a Romanesque tower and nave dating from the twelfth century. Legend says that it was founded because a seventh-century pilgrim brought back from Palestine a phial containing drops of milk reputed to be from the breast of the Virgin. While he had a sleep he hung the phial on a thorn bush which grew so tall that he could not reach it. He tried cutting the bush down but the axe stuck in the wood. So the Bishop of Le Mans was called. When he knelt before the tree it dutifully shrank. The Bishop built a church there and founded a monastery so that the monks could guard the relic. The legend is told in fourteenth-century stained glass in the church, which also has a thirteenth-century statue of the Virgin in silvered wood, murals and four seventeenth-century Aubusson tapestries.

Four kilometres SW is Château Montecler with a drawbridge and vaulted gateway from Henri IV's reign. At Mézangers, 5km NW, is Château du Rocher with one magnificent Renaissance façade. At Étang du Gué, near Mézangers, is a watersports centre, including sailing and windsurfing. Mézangers also has a tenth-century church and the fine fourteenth- to fifteenth-century Château du Rocher.

TOURIST INFORMATION 1 place Basilique, Evron (43.01.63.75)
FESTIVALS Meat Festival – 1st Sunday September

### HOTELS
*Gare*, 13 rue de la Paix (43.01.60.29): Logis. Good value meals. ROOMS C. MEALS A–D.
*Relais du Gué de Selle*, At Mézangers, 7km NW by route Mayenne (43.90.64.05): old farm in peaceful countryside. Cooking a mixture of classic and modern. ROOMS C–D. MEALS B–E. Shut December–2 January; part February; Sunday evening and Monday except 15 June–15 September.

# LA FERTÉ-BERNARD
## [SARTHE]

Town of ten thousand people 49km NE of Le Mans, on the N23 and near the A11, it is in a countryside of lush meadows with many little snaky rivers, including the Huisne which goes through the town. It has some old houses and market buildings, and a famous sixteenth-century Renaissance choir of Notre-Dame-des-Marais. Good fishing around here, including lakes at Vibraye (15km S) and Tuffé (14km SW). Canoeing.

TOURIST INFORMATION Mairie (43.93.04.42)
MARKET Monday
FESTIVALS Folk – July

HOTEL

*Perdrix*, 2 rue Paris (43.93.00.44): well-run Logis with imaginative cooking. ROOMS C–D. MEALS B–E. Shut Tuesday.

RESTAURANT

*Dauphin*, 3 rue Huisne (43.93.00.39): good value, sensible cooking. MEALS B–E. Shut mid-August–mid-September; Sunday evening, Wednesday.

# LA FERTÉ-ST-AUBIN
[LOIRET]

Strung along the N20 S from Orléans, it is known as the gate to the Sologne. A splendid castle, rebuilt in 1635 by François Mansard and in the old quarters typical old squat Sologne houses in brick and half-timbered. The river Cosson flows through the castle moats, which are lined with elegant balustrades. The château is surrounded by a large, pleasant park. 'Ferté' means small fortress. Six kilometres E is Domaine Solognot du Ciran, signposted on D108. The estate is typical of the Sologne – woodland, fields, streams and pool, with a local museum in the house. (Shut Tuesday – telephone 38.65.90.93.)

TOURIST INFORMATION Syndicat d'Initiative
(38.64.67.93)

HOTEL

*Perron*, 9 rue Gén. Leclerc (38.76.53.36): old style hunting inn; beams, open fire. Local dishes wild boar, ham, carp, other game, river fish. ROOMS D. MEALS C–E. Shut part February; Sunday evening, Monday in winter.

RESTAURANT

*Ferme de la Lande*, 2½km NE by route Marcilly (38.76.64.37):

very good cooking in a lovely old Sologne farmhouse. MEALS
D–F. Shut 2nd two weeks August; early March; Sunday evening,
Monday.

# LA-FERTÉ-ST-CYR
## [LOIR-ET-CHER]

Centre for fishing in small lakes and streams including the river
Cosson (13km S of Beaugency on D925). Woodland walks.
Pheasant-rearing area.

### HOTEL

*St Cyr* (54.87.90.51): comfortable modern Logis, family run.
Nice bedrooms. Traditional cooking. ROOMS C–D. MEALS A–E.
Shut mid-January–mid-March; Monday except evening in sum-
mer: Sunday in winter.

# LA FLÈCHE
## [SARTHE]

Very likeable little town between Le Mans and Angers on N23
and a fine place to stop en route for the Loire valley. It lies on a
bend in the Loir river near a dam and two old mills. Its military
academy turned out generations of soldiers but La Flèche itself
is a relaxed, friendly town, warm rather than smart. Down by
the river are pedalos for hire and, reached through arches of
roses, is the Auberge du Moulin. Here are the charming gardens, les Carmes, rather hemmed in now. From the bridge is a
lovely view of the gardens and river.

Henri IV grew up in La Flèche and the ashes of his heart are
in the seventeenth-century St Louis chapel of the military
college.

The town grew around a medieval fortress on the river. A
priory was founded and given as part of a dowry to Charles de
Bourbon, Duke of Vendôme. When he died in 1536 his widow

built herself a Renaissance house there. Fifteen years later her son Antoine de Bourbon and his wife Jeanne d'Albret took it over and their son, Henri of Navarre, was conceived there. He was born at Pau but spent happy years of his childhood at La Flèche. When he became a Catholic and King Henri IV he gave the house to the Jesuits as a college. Descartes, called 'father of modern philosophy', was a pupil. His belief in logical argument based on an undeniable premise has had an effect on French thinking and education for centuries and is the basis of much education today but becomes difficult when others *do* deny the premise. He was also a pioneer of modern analytical geometry.

The Jesuits of La Flèche sent out early missions to the Indians of Canada and three were massacred by the Iroquois and canonized. The first bishop of Quebec was a graduate of La Flèche.

After the Jesuits were expelled from France in 1762, the college became a military school. Napoleon made it a Prytanée for the sons of officers and higher civil servants. It still is, with pupils wearing uniform. In school holidays there are guided tours which include St Louis chapel.

The Château de Carmes is of seventeenth-century buildings on the ruins of the fifteenth-century fortress. Five kilometres away on D104, just off the D306 to Tours, is a small zoo, Le Tertre Rouge.

TOURIST INFORMATION Hôtel de Ville (43.94.02.53)
MARKET Wednesday, Sunday

### HOTELS

*Vert Galant*, 70 Gde Rue (43.94.00.51): simple old inn of real character, used by locals. I love it. Comfortable bedrooms. Good satisfying meals of bourgeois cooking are good value. ROOMS C. MEALS A–D. Shut 20 December–15 January. Restaurant shut Thursday.
*Relais Cicero*, 18 boul. Alger (43.94.14.14): charming seventeenth-century house. Flower garden. No restaurant. ROOMS E–F. Shut 21 December–6 January.

# FONTEVRAUD-L'ABBAYE
### [*See* Sites page 111]


# FOUGÈRES-SUR-BIÈVRE
### [Loir-et-Cher]

In a charming village SW of Cheverny on D52, surrounded by
nursery gardens and fields of tempting asparagus is a text-book
feudal château, unbelievably like a film set with its fearsome
pointed towers with only tiny windows. It has a drawbridge,
machicolations and everything gloomy and fortress-like for
defence. It is surprising, because it was rebuilt like this in 1470,
when many owners were converting their old fortresses into
something more comfortable to live in. Appropriately it was
built by a man called Refuge who was Louis XI's Minister of
Finance. Perhaps he was protecting his money. It would be
gloomier if his brother-in-law had not replaced archery firing
slits with windows. (Shut Tuesday, Wednesday.)


# FRÉTEVAL
### [Loir-et-Cher]

Northwards from Vendôme a very pleasant route follows the
east bank of the Loir river through charming villages. One that
is passes is Fréteval, where the N157 crosses the river. It is a
likeable little village, beloved by fishermen, with a bridge leading
to the Forêt de Fréteval where there are pleasant marked walks
and drives. The ruins of a feudal castle guard the village.

*A traditional interior*

# GALLERANDE – Château
## [Sarthe]

Twelve kilometres E of La Flèche the D13 runs alongside the moats surrounding the park of Château du Gallerande. Cedars, oaks and limes surround ordered lawns on which peacocks strutted happily when I saw it. Flanked by fortified towers, the castle has an unusual octagonal keep.

# GENILLÉ
## [INDRE-ET-LOIRE]

In the valley of the Indrois tributary of the river Indre, the beautiful D10 NW gives lovely views of the lake of Chemillé-sur-Indrois, then continues to the village of Genillé on the river, with houses climbing from the water to its fifteenth-century château. The church, partly from the twelfth century, partly from the Renaissance, has a fine carved wood vault and seventeenth-century pulpit. The belfry dominates the outside.

### HOTEL
*Agnès Sorel* (47.59.50.17): the beautiful mistress of Charles VII doesn't get much recognition these days, but this little village hotel-restaurant is a pleasant tribute, with four comfortable, country-style bedrooms. They are great value. Impressive cooking, not very cheap. Book. ROOMS C. MEALS C–E. Shut February; Sunday evening, Monday low season.

# GENNES
## [MAINE-ET-LOIRE]

A long handsome suspension bridge joins this little town with the attractive little town of Les Rosiers (page 233), 16km NW of Saumur. Gennes is built on the sides of a steep knoll, topped by the ruins of St Eusèbe church, built from the eleventh to fifteenth centuries, with a twelfth-century steeple. The sad graves at the base of the south wall are from June, 1940, and are of cadets from the Saumur Military Academy.

Colonel Mishcon, commandant of the Academy, his staff and cadets were so ashamed of the deal Marshal Pétain had made in capitulating to Hitler that they ignored orders to retreat to Montauban. Their force of twelve hundred men and eight hundred cadets decided to hold three Loire bridges, at Gennes, Montsoreau and Saumur, to cover the escape of other French forces. They had two ancient field guns, First World War machine-guns, practice rifles and hand grenades. At midnight on the 19th June the first German tank tried to cross the Saumur bridge. It got a direct hit from a cannon fired by a cadet. Six more tanks and two lorries got the same reception. The Nazis brought up high-speed armour and rushed the bridge. It blew up. All three bridges had been mined.

The Germans took twenty-four hours to bring up reinforcements and pontoons. Finally they crossed the river. The Academy force had hundreds of casualties and ran out of ammunition before giving up.

Pétain's Vichy French wanted to court-martial the Commandant for wasting young lives in a hopeless cause. But they had held up the Germans while French soldiers reached the South of France so that they could soon join de Gaulle's Free French in Britain, and had set an example for French resistance to the Nazis when their Government had given in and national morale was very low.

I met one of the officers in a German prison camp later. 'We were fighting an evil for France and the world. How could we give in without firing a shot?' he said.

In the hills behind Gennes are four dolmens (prehistoric passage graves).

La Madeleine, on the D69 Doué road, just outside Gennes, was used last century by a farmer as a bakery.

TOURIST INFORMATION Syndicat d'Initiative, square Europe (May–September 41.51.84.14)

#### HOTELS

*Hostellerie de la Loire*, 9 rue des Cadets de Saumur (41.51.81.03): attractive beamed old Relais de Post which has pleased my readers since the first edition of *Travellers' France*. Flowered terrace with river views. Traditional cooking, 3-chimney Logis, very good value. Good local wines. ROOMS C–D. MEALS B–D. Shut 2 January–mid-February; Monday evening, Tuesday.

*Naulets d'Anjou*, 18 rue Croix de Mission (41.51.81.88): modern. New owner. ROOMS C–D. MEALS B–D. Shut 1 November–mid-March. Restaurant shut Monday low season.

# GERMIGNY-DES-PRÉS
[Loiret]

Village with a charming cypress-shaded square 3km SE of Châteauneuf-sur-Loire by the D60, a very pleasant road to Sully, running at times beside the Loire. Germigny has a gem of a church, built by an abbot in 806, restored in 1869. In the apse is a marvellous Italian mosaic fixed to its roof, made of 130,000 glass cubes in gold, silver, azure, purple and green. It represents the Ark of the Covenant, housing the tablets of the law given by God to Moses.

The mosaic was found by accident in 1840, before the restoration. Boys were seen playing with cubes of glass, so archaeologists removed thick plaster and the wonderful coloured glass was found underneath. It seems that this mosaic was already three hundred years old when it was brought from Ravenna by Theodulf, the abbot of nearby St Benoît, who built the church in 806. Charlemagne used to visit Theodulf, so the little boys were probably playing with glass he had admired.

Wooden statues include one of the Virgin as a little girl being taught to read by her mother, St Anne, here dressed like a French peasant.

# GIEN
[Loiret]

Appealing quiet little town, decked in flowers in summer, on the Loire SE of Châteauneuf, and at the SE end of the Forest of Orléans, it is a wonderful example of post-war rebuilding.

The devastation in the Second World War was almost total. In June 1940, to cut off the retreat of the French army, the Germans bombed Gien for three days. It burned for many more days until blessedly heavy rain put out the fires before they reached the château. In 1944 the Allies wanted to cut the railway bridge. Fifty US Flying Fortresses pattern-bombed the target but missed it and knocked down a lot more of Gien. The fourteenth-century road bridge was cut by a lone RAF Mosquito which knocked away just one arch, so that it was easily rebuilt after the war.

A wonderful job of rebuilding the fifteenth-century church was made by André Gélis, chief architect of Historic Monuments. Only one square tower was left. He made a framework of reinforced concrete and built up walls from pink bricks baked in wood-fired kilns. They give a beautiful effect, especially in the nave where the capitals of the narrow pillars are in coloured Gien pottery showing events in the life of Joan of Arc, after whom the church is now named, and the walls are decorated with coloured pottery plaques showing the stations of the cross. The rich modern windows are by the great Max Ingrand. On her way to seek the Dauphin in Chinon, Joan of Arc ('a young boy') rode sodden and weary into Gien with six companions in 1429.

Gien's pottery factory (Faïencerie), started in 1821 using local clay and sand, is on D952 Orléans road west (78 place Victoire) and has a museum showing hundreds of nineteenth-century pieces and production techniques. Dinner services and *objets d'art* are the traditional products, but it also made Gien's attractive street name plates in coloured faïence. Traditional colour is bleu de Gien (deep blue enhanced with yellow-gold). But it produces also an old-style brown glazed pottery called vieux grès, and also bright many-coloured designs with animals and birds. The museum is open 9–11 a.m., 2 p.m.–5.30 p.m. by appointment with the Tourist Office (*see* Information below).

Anne of Beaujeu, strong-willed and clever daughter of Louis XI, built Gien on the site of a Charlemagne fort in 1500. It was her main residence. At twenty-three she became Regent of France for her young brother Charles VIII and it was she who sent him with a large army to besiege Duchess Anne of Brittany and persuade her to marry him. Later she arranged for Anne's daughter Claude to marry the young heir to the French throne, François, ensuring that Brittany became and remained part of France. Brantôme called her 'one of the great Kings of France'. She gave Gien its beautiful bridge and its church. Her château had to be rebuilt after the Flying Fortress bombing.

It houses the Musée International de la Chasse with a big collection of hunting weapons from prehistory to the present, including crossbows, arquebuses, powder-horns, sporting guns. It has an art museum, too, with tapestries, porcelain, old decorated pipes, sculptures and about five thousand ornamented buttons from hunting jackets. In the main hall, with a fine timbered ceiling, is a collection of paintings by François Desportes (1661–1743), painter of the hunt to Louis XIV. Although his paintings are dramatic and lifelike, many show cruel fights set up between dogs and wild animals. There are some attractive bronze sculptures and engravings by the nineteenth-century animal artist Florentin Brigaud and outstanding tapestries by René Perrot, a fine artist of today.

TOURIST INFORMATION rue Anne-de-Beaujeu
(38.67.25.28)
MARKETS Saturday morning, Wednesday morning
(poultry)

HOTELS

*Rivage*, 1 quai Nice (38.67.20.53): much praised restaurant. Dishes classic with inventive touches, plus regional specialities (snails in Sancerre; sandre in Pouilly). Rooms improved. ROOMS D–E. MEALS D–F.

*Beau Site, Restaurant Poularde*, 13 quai Nice (38.67.36.05): old hostelry well renovated. River front. Traditional dishes. ROOMS C–E. MEALS B–F. Shut 1–15 January; Sunday evening low season.

# GOULAINE – Château
## [LOIRE-ATLANTIQUE]

A fine old château still producing fine wine. In the Muscadet country near the village of Haute-Goulaine reached by N149 and little local roads 15km E of Nantes, and marked on yellow Michelin map. The Goulaine family has lived there at least since 1100 when Alphonse de Goulaine arbitrated in an argument between Philippe I of France and Henry I of England, since when the family have been allowed to put the fleur-de-lis of France and the old leopards of England on its coat of arms.

They have been producing wine almost as long and the present Marquis produces my favourite Muscadet, called Marquis de Goulaine, Château de la Grange. The present château, started about 1480 by Christophe de Goulaine, Gentleman of the Chamber to Louis II, had two wings added in the seventeenth century and is a splendid example of flowery Gothic architecture flirting with Renaissance. It is built of Saumur tufa which hardens with time. Inside decorations and chimneys are mostly Louis XIII and there is fine furniture. Louis XIV actually slept in the King's bedroom when attending the States General at Nantes. Most 'King's bedrooms' lay unused for years awaiting monarchs who never came. There is also a conservatory of beautiful exotic butterflies. (Château open June–September except Tuesday; rest of year Saturday, Sunday.)

### RESTAURANT

*Mon Rêve* at Basse-Goulaine on D751 beside Loire (40.03.55.50): in lovely house and lovely setting. Traditional cooking of regional ingredients . MEALS D–E. Shut Tuesday evenings and Wednesday off season. ·

# LE GRAND-PRESSIGNY
## [INDRE-ET-LOIRE]

Tiny market town in a pretty position where the little Claise and Egronne rivers meet, 33km SW of Loches, it is on a site important in the story of mankind. Excavations in 1862 revealed that it was one of the most important centres of prehistoric flint working. The flint is found in yellow clods and is ideal for shaping. In the Stone and New Stone Ages it was an industry. It was made mostly into blades which were exported all over Europe and into Africa.

In the Château you can see how Stone Age man made tools from the flint and split stone. The château is on a hill to the north and is in ruins but the Renaissance building with arcades between two courtyards is used for the museum. There is quite a lot of the château left, including a fine square twelfth-century keep, massive walls, with several fourteenth-century towers, and an unusual octagonal tower with a dome.

# LE GUÉ-DU-LOIR
## [LOIR-ET-CHER]

On the snaking river Loir 5km W of Vendôme, where the Loir meets the river Boulon amid willows, poplars, reeds and greenery. The pretty D5 skirts the surrounding walls of the Renaissance manor La Bonaventure, which belonged to the father of Henri IV, Antoine de Bourbon-Vendôme. Henri (le Vert Galant) forded the river carrying Gabrielle d'Estrées on his shoulders – not a habit of kings and princes. Later the manor belonged to the family of the poet Alfred de Musset.

# LE GUÉ-PÉAN – Château
## [LOIR-ET-CHER]

This little blue and white sixteenth-century château 13km E of Montrichard in a small wooded valley of Choussy forest deserves to be better known, but there are so many more important châteaux around here. You reach it through Monthou-sur-Cher at the end of a private alley. It was a hunting lodge for centuries, received many important guests, and now appropriately it is the centre for a riding school. It is built round a courtyard and two fine Renaissance pavilions are at the entrance, both with round towers in front of them, one taller and fatter. The pavilions have arcades facing the courtyard. Its guests included several kings, Fénelon, writer and priest, Lafayette and Balzac. The Keguelin family who bought it are descended from a family who owned it three hundred years ago. Their archives and mementoes in the library include documents and souvenirs of Louis XIV, Napoleon and great writers such as George Sand, Dumas, Balzac and the composer Chopin. Balzac wrote a novel about Jean Lambert, Baron Kainlis, who spent fifteen years here studying philosophy. Tapestries and pictures are splendid. The barrel organ and music boxes still play. There is a small museum of the Resistance. The Marquis de Keguelin was a leader of the Paris uprising and was decorated by de Gaulle.

The furniture is mostly Louis XV and Louis XVI and the walls have fine tapestries and pictures. (Open all year.)

# L'ÎLE-BOUCHARD
[INDRE-ET-LOIRE]

Spread along both banks of the river Vienne in a charming position 18km E of Chinon, this little town was once an important port on the river but seems to have been busy doing nothing ever since. Prettily placed among orchards and gardens it would seem to be a pleasant place to stay for a short time doing exactly the same thing. It was named after a man called Bouchard who built a fort in the ninth century on the mid-stream island. The town has three old churches – St Gilles (eleventh to fifteenth centuries), St Maurice, with an octagonal tower with a stone spire (1480) and St Leonard, once a church of a priory of which the eleventh-century Romanesque remains in white tufa on the lower slopes of the valley have a melancholy romantic look.

### RESTAURANT
*Auberge de l'Île*, 3 place Bouchard (47.58.51.07): the bait is good cooking and a wide terrace overlooking the river. MEALS D–E. Shut January, February; Sunday evening, Monday.

# INGRANDES
[MAINE-ET-LOIRE]

The left bank road beside the Loire from Angers west to Champtoceaux along the Corniche Angevine has many attractive villages but Ingrandes on the right bank is as pretty as most

of them. There is a suspension bridge across the river from
D210. The fine seventeenth- to eighteenth-century houses on its
deserted quays show that it was once a very important port. It
was for long a link between Brittany and Anjou, for it was at the
limit of what was then Brittany. Even after Brittany became part
of France, it was exempt from the salt tax.

Anjou had to pay the tax, and salting meat was the main
method of preserving it for winter. So a lot of smugglers
operated across the river. On the quays there is still an
eighteenth-century salt depot with arcades. The modern church
has an unusual bell tower and very brightly coloured modern
stained glass by Bertrand.

### HOTEL

*Lion d'Or*, rue Pont (41.39.20.08): 2-chimney Logis with above-
average cooking. ROOMS B–D. MEALS A–E. Shut late February–
mid-March; Sunday evening, Monday in winter.

# JARGEAU
## [LOIRET]

Little town which straddles the Loire 19km E of Orléans. Try to
take the little scenic road which follows the river bank to Sandil-
lon running parallel with the D951. The town, whose ancient
collegiate church dates from the twelfth and sixteenth centuries,
has a place in French history. On 12 June, 1429, Joan of Arc
won her first open field victory over the English here. When
things were not going well for the French, she mounted a scaling
ladder against the castle wall, carrying her standard. A rock hit
her helmet. She fell off but jumped up quickly and called for
another attack. The castle fell. The English prisoners included
the Duke of Suffolk, who had distinguished himself at Agincourt and been given Bricquebec Château in Normandy by
Henry V. Now he had to give it back to the French as part of his
ransom. Joan's mother, Isabelle Romée, lived after Joan's death
in a farmhouse nearby in the hamlet of Bagneaux, off D951.

TOURIST INFORMATION Syndicat d'Initiative, boul.
Carnot (38.59.83.42)

HOTEL

*Clair de Lune*, 5 boul. Carnot (38.59.70.25): simple Logis; pleasant bourgeois cooking. ROOMS B–C. MEALS A–D. Shut 15 December–15 January; Sunday evening, Monday.

# LANGEAIS
## [INDRE-ET-LOIRE]

Some drivers speak in horror about Langeais because of its heavy traffic, inevitable with such a useful bridge over the Loire, and its rather dingy, industrial appearance along the N152 road from Tours. We have stayed in gîtes among the countryside to the north and within 5–10km of the town you can escape to farming hamlets of small farms and cottages, old-fashioned shops and bakeries, bars and relais used only by locals where you can have a four-course lunch of good, old-style dishes, fresh vegetables, farm cheese and local fruit at prices of fifteen years ago.

Langeais's main square is hidden from the Route Nationale and the Sunday morning market there is a wonderful place to buy farm-fresh food and wine from makers of Vouvray, Montlouis, Bourgueil and Chinon. Piled high in season are the famous Langeais melons grown on local hillsides and claimed to be the best in France. Three of them are on Langeais's coat of arms. Some boats still fish in the Loire, and there are river bathing beaches over the bridge.

Most visitors stop just to see the extremely interesting fifteenth-century castle, up a hill surrounded by houses. It is one of the few châteaux which has hardly been altered over the centuries. Built in 1465 for Louis XI, it was strictly for defence. You enter by a drawbridge and the entrance is very stern. Three thick conical-roofed towers, a lower storey without windows and a wall passage with nearly 300 machicolations above its fourth storey show you that it would be no pushover for attackers. Yet the open garden side, with slender staircase towers and dormer windows, looks quite peaceful and welcoming – more like a big house than a fortress-castle, 'The Mask of War becomes a Mask of Peace', wrote Vivian Rowe. It was very suitable for the marriage of Duchesse Anne of Brittany and Charles VIII of France. Clever of him to bring her here. Warlike Bretons were still ready to kidnap her and take her back to her own Duchy of Brittany to foil the French take-over of their country, and the Austrians would have abducted her to get hold of Brittany.

The interior was superbly restored with the help of historians and artists by Jacques Siegfried, last private owner, before he left it to the Institut de France in 1904. Where original pieces were missing, he had exact copies made by artists and craftsmen in France and Italy, leaving Flamboyant Renaissance decorations and furnishings which tell us just how aristocrats lived in the fifteenth and sixteenth centuries. Chests and cupboards are lavishly decorated, carpets, hangings, sculptures and paintings are all lavish, too. Flemish and Aubusson tapestries, though faded now, are almost priceless. The fireplaces are ostentatious. One looks like a castle.

The great hall rises through two storeys to a chestnut timber roof. In a first-floor room is the marriage chest of Anne of Brittany. Her marriage to young Charles VIII of France was supposed to be secret. She was fifteen and already married by proxy to Maximilian of Austria whose daughter was already engaged to Charles VIII. But Anne of Beaujeu, Charles' elder sister who had been Regent of France and still had a lot of influence, sent Charles with a big army to besiege Anne in her capital, Rennes, and to persuade her to marry him. The people of Rennes were literally starving. They begged her to give in. Anne was 'persuaded'. Oddly, Anne and Charles liked each other right away. She was not attractive and had a bad limp but was strong-willed and intelligent. He was puny and unattractive, too, but a romantic who dreamed of great victories and conquests. Anne arrived for her 'secret' wedding in a litter covered in gold cloth and with a wedding dress with 160 sable furs. The sable was on her family coat of arms.

The kindly old soldier who lived in Langeais castle as a 'grace and favour' residence from the King, was Comte de

Dunois, son of Joan of Arc's companion in arms. He had been Anne's friend and protector when she was a young orphan. Alas, he was so excited to see her again that he died from a stroke.

TOURIST INFORMATION Syndicat d'Initiative at the Mairie (shut mornings low season – 47.96.58.22)

MARKET Sunday morning

HOTELS

*Hosten et Restaurant Langeais*, 2 rue Gambetta (47.96.82.12): owned by the Hosten family since 1904. With a few flirtations with fashion, it has always been loyal to classical cooking and it is good. Pricey. ROOMS D–F. MEALS F–G. Shut 20 June–10 July; 10 January –10 February; Monday evening, Tuesday.

# LASSAY-SUR-CROISNE
## [LOIRE-ET-CHER]

Always called the typical Sologne village, it is 8km W of Romorantin by D59 and D20. It has a fifteenth-century church with early sixteenth-century paintings showing St Christopher, and the delightful fifteenth-century Château du Moulin, which is really a manor house, built in a pleasant combination of brick and stone, surrounded by walls and defence towers, which are reflected in moats fed with water from the river Croisne. Even peaceful manors needed defence against roving bands of brigands. Period furnishings inside are interesting. The kitchen spit was pulled round by a dog – one way of giving Rover his exercise. The Château was built for Philippe du Moulin, captain of Charles VIII's guard who saved the King's life at the Battle of Fornova in 1495.

# LAVAL
## [MAYENNE]

A very pleasant town on both sides of the river Mayenne at the top end of the steep Mayenne valley. You can see the attractive old part best from the Pont Vieux, the thirteenth-century hump-backed bridge. It rises in tiers of half-timbered houses with slate roofs in narrow streets up to the old château. You can see it, too, from the old quays along the left bank, with the new château standing beside the old.

The eleventh-century Vieux Château contains a museum with a mixture of tools of medieval craftsmen to naïve paintings. Château Neuf, with a Renaissance façade, was restored and enlarged in the nineteenth century to serve as law courts.

Grande Rue, the old main street, is lined with half-timbered houses with overhanging storeys and decorated stone Renaissance houses. It reaches the river at the hump-backed bridge. Most attractive of the three Laval old churches is the Gothic–Renaissance basilica of Notre-Dame d'Avesnières, with large wooden statues of Jesus Christ and St Christopher and modern windows by Max Ingrand.

Beyond the old bridge is Jardin de la Perrine, a big garden set back from the river. Lawns, flowerbeds and a rose garden surround lakes and waterfalls, with lovely trees – Lebanese cedars, palms, chestnuts, limes and larches. There are good river views. It is just the place for a snack lunch of pâté, cheese, bread and a bottle of wine.

TOURIST INFORMATION place du 11 Novembre
(43.53.09.39)
FESTIVALS Fair-Exposition – mid-May

### HOTELS

*Gerbe de Blé*, 83 rue Victor-Boissel (43.53.14.10): good blend of classical and modern cooking. Long-standing reputation. Only 8 rooms. ROOMS D–F. MEALS D–F. Restaurant shut Sunday evening, Monday.

### RESTAURANTS

*Bistro de Paris*, 67 rue du Val de Mayenne (43.56.98.29): *not*

bistro cooking – light, dainty, flavoursome dishes. MEALS C–F.
Shut 4–27 August; Saturday lunch, Sunday.
*La Rouzine*, route Tours, 3½km by D21 SE (43.53.03.10): quiet
country position. Classic, modern or regional dishes – take your
pick. Menus range from cheap to fairly expensive. A good
restaurant. MEALS B–E. Shut 5–19 August; Sunday evening,
Monday.

# LAVARDIN
## [LOIR-ET-CHER]

A hamlet with yet another medieval fortress pulled down on
orders of Henri IV to discourage local and religious squabbles.
SW of Vendôme, it was a stronghold of the Counts of Vendôme
in the Middle Ages. The formidable ruins stand like a jagged
silhouette on a rocky spur high above the village. Some guides
call the ruins 'romantic' and they are being restored. Built in the
eleventh and twelfth centuries, the castle proudly fought off
attacks by Henry II of England and his son Richard Coeur de
Lion, probably because it was triple walled. From the sentry
walk, reached by a ladder, there are magnificent views. Lavardin
has one or two old houses and a very early Romanesque church,
originally part of a ninth-century priory, with some fascinating
wall paintings from the twelfth to the sixteenth centuries. Well
worth seeing.

The hamlet is on the south bank of the Loir river.

# LIGUEIL
## [INDRE-ET-LOIRE]

Small white stone old town on D31 at a crossroads 18km SW of
Loches. It is renowned for its creamery and its lively Monday
market, often attracting large crowds. Nice countryside around it.

HOTEL

*Colombier*, 4 place Gén. Leclerc (47.59.60.83): simple, cheap Logis known for good value meals. ROOMS A–C. MEALS A–E. Shut 1 January–early February; 1–15 September.

# LOCHES
## [INDRE-ET-LOIRE]

A delightful old town on the Indre, with riverside gardens, among very pleasant countryside 22km SE of Amboise, with the Loches forest to its NE. Though it has many visitors in season it refuses to be hurried and takes tourism in its stride, which is the apt phrase, for driving is almost impossible round its narrow lanes so you must walk. There is a big car park by the railway station.

To me, Loches is one of the gems of old France and I do suggest you spend at least one night there if possible, if only to see it when day visitors have gone.

The old château has been a sinister place. Richard Coeur de Lion lived there. When he was made prisoner in Austria on his way back from a crusade, the clever, conniving Philippe-Auguste of France persuaded Richard's brother John to hand over the château to him. Richard returned earlier than expected and was so angry that he stormed Loches and took it in three hours. Looking at the walls, the feat seems impossible with the equipment soldiers had in those days, but when he himself was aroused the Lionheart could rouse his loyal men to remarkable feats of fighting and building. Ten years later, when Richard was dead, Philippe-Auguste took a year to get the English out. Then it became a Royal prison, at its most sinister when the cruel and thoroughly nasty Louis XI kept little iron cages in Tours Ronde and Martelot for those who displeased him. The bigger cages were six feet square. They were suspended so that they swung with every movement. Some were so small that a man could neither stand nor lie down. Cardinal La Balue was behind the idea. Later Louis accused him of negotiating with the enemy in a war with the Burgundians and he himself spent eleven years in the cages but still came out alive.

Ludovico Sforza, Duke of Milan, captured by Louis's troops in fighting in Italy, spent eight years in an underground cell. He had been patron of Leonardo da Vinci, and he covered his walls with paintings. He died on his release – some say of sudden sunlight. Two bishops in a dungeon lit by a solitary ray of sunlight hollowed an altar out of the wall.

It is quite a breathless walk uphill to the château. If you go into the medieval city by Porte Royale, a thirteenth-century gateway backed by two fifteenth-century towers, you will find on the left two museums. Lansyer Museum contains works of a local nineteenth-century landscape painter Lansyer. The folklore museum allows you to see inside the Porte Royale, with a fine view of Loches.

Then comes the château itself, with Tour Agnès Sorel and Logis Royaux, living quarters of Charles VIII and Louis XII, who had it altered in Renaissance style to make it more comfortable. In the great hall, with a large fireplace and lovely tapestries, Joan of Arc, with her friend Dunois and the great soldier Gilles de Rais, came on 3–5 June, 1429, to persuade the Dauphin to go to Reims to be crowned King Charles VII of France. Gilles de Rais was later accused in Brittany of orgies in which small boys were killed and executed. Gilles was almost certainly framed because he was involved in arguments over ownership of property.

Perrault is said to have based the story of Bluebeard on him, but there is slim evidence. The story appears in folklore of many nations, and there was another French count who had been told in a curse that his son would kill him, so he killed his wives as soon as they were pregnant.

In the Charles VIII room is the alabaster tomb of Agnès Sorel, the beautiful mistress of the unattractive and weak Charles VII. She must have been one of the few people, apart from Joan of Arc, who really loved him. She lies down with her head supported by angels and two lambs lying at her feet, perhaps a pun on her name – Agnès, agneau. Alongside is a copy of the painting by her friend Jean Fouquet of the *Virgin and Child* for which she was the model for the Virgin. The original is in Antwerp's Beaux Arts museum.

She was certainly beautiful, and was called 'Dame de Beauté, another pun on the name of her home town of Beauté-en-Marne. Even Pope Pious II said that she had 'the most beautiful face one could see'. She was also gentle. But she spent the royal money very fast indeed, mostly on others or in gifts to the Church. Much of it she gave to the convent of St Ours, whose church you pass inside the Porte Royale gate.

The Dauphin, future Louis XI, hated her and at Chinon he slapped her face publicly. She moved to Loches out of his way. She died at twenty-eight, possibly poisoned at the Dauphin's command, and left her wealth to St Ours convent. The canons accepted it but did not want 'this immoral woman's' tomb in their church and asked Charles to remove it to the château. He agreed if they also sent back her money. They changed their minds. But in Louis XVI's reign they did get it moved to the château.

You can walk round the château ramparts (2km). Château shut Wednesday. The son-et-lumière is sarcastically called 'Charles par Grâce des Femmes' (Charles by Grace of Women).

In Loche's place de la Marne is a statue of Alfred de Vigny, the sensitive novelist, poet and philosopher, born here in 1797. He was moved away in his infancy. The fine Renaissance Town Hall with flowered balconies has been town hall since 1535.

TOURIST INFORMATION place Wermeiskirchen
(47.59.07.98)
MARKET Wednesday
FESTIVALS son-et-lumière June, July, August

## HOTELS

*Luccotel*, rue Lézards (47.91.50.50): modern, comfortable; pool, jaccuzi. In a park. Wide range of menus. ROOMS C–D. MEALS B–E. Shut mid-November–mid-January; Sunday evening in winter, Saturday lunch.

*George Sand*, 39 rue Quintefol (47.59.39.74): A pretty seventeenth-century inn with a flowery terrace overhanging the river. Small rooms nicely furnished, good value meals. ROOMS C–E. MEALS A–E. Shut 25 November–21 December.

# LE LUDE
## [Sarthe]

On some summer's nights you might think that the river Loir was alight as the floodlights of the biggest son-et-lumière in France blaze across the superb garden terrace of the Château du Lude at the edge of a magnificent park stretching 2km along the river. Three hundred and thirty local people in period costumes conjure up nearly five centuries of history amid changing lights, vivid sounds and three hundred luminous fountains. Henri IV appears on a white horse, Madame de Sévigné steps ashore from a barge, red-coated huntsmen blow fanfares, cavaliers and ladies dance the minuet. There are ballets. It is lavish and beautifully produced. They call it 'Les Glorieuses et Fastueuses Soirées au Bord du Loir', which they translate as 'Sumptuous Nights on the Banks of the Loir'.

By day, the château looks rather bewildering, with such a mixture of architectural styles.

Le Lude produces furniture and dairy products these days, but was an important military site for centuries, controlling two major routes and the Loir river. Foulques Nerra (971–1004), the fighting Duke of Anjou, inevitably put a wooden fort here in his lifelong fight with the Dukes of Blois. In medieval times a stone castle was built which kept out the English in the thirteenth and fourteenth centuries. They did hold it for four years from 1425. In 1457 Jean Daillon, one of Louis XI's few friends, acquired it. His son started to turn it into a home and each new owner built his own additions. The basic castle is a square fortress with a plump round tower at each corner. Henri IV altered the façades round the courtyard. The towers were given Renaissance decoration and pilaster-framed and dormer windows. To the north Gothic façade, built under Louis XII, stone balconies were added. The east façade of Louis XVI period in white tufa stone is surprisingly classical, symmetrical and severe.

The house is lived in and the inside is charming, richly furnished with the usual mixtures of a home. Most of the furniture and decorations are fifteen to sixteenth century but some modern pieces are blended in with them. The sixteenth-century Flemish tapestries on the dining-room walls and a seventeenth-century Gobelin tapestry on the library wall are very interesting. The ballroom has been delightfully restored in fifteenth- to sixteenth-century style. (Château gardens open daily all year, Château afternoons April–September.)

TOURIST INFORMATION High season 1 place F. de Nicolay; low season 8 rue du Boeuf (43.94.62.20 for both)

MARKET Thursday

FESTIVALS son-et-lumière Friday, Saturday from second weekend in June to last weekend in September; book (43.94.62.20)

### HOTEL

*Maine*, 24 ave Saumur (43.94.60.54): very good regional cooking by patron. ROOMS B–D. MEALS B–E.

### RESTAURANT

*Renaissance*, 2 ave Libération (43.94.63.10): good value. MEALS B–D. Shut Sunday evening, Monday.

# LUYNES
## [INDRE-ET-LOIRE]

From Langeais going towards Tours, branch off the busy N152 at St Étienne de Chigny onto D76 and you reach the photogenic little town of Luynes, which has an old port below on N152 by the Loire. Or you can take a road from N152 straight up to the village. If you can take your eyes off the road, there is a splendid view of the village with its nine cellars carved out of the rockface, clinging to the slope. In the village is a market place in wood with a high tiled roof, several half-timbered houses and, opposite the church, a house with carved beams showing the Virgin, a Pietà and St Christopher. The wine cellars were dwellings in ancient times. From the market stepped paths lead to the picturesque thirteenth-century castle – a formidable pile, with sheer tower walls which were not given windows until the fifteenth century. The four round towers and three tall build-

*Luynes*

ings joining them have no ornament whatsoever. They look really forbidding.

Continue through hillside vineyards up D49, then look back at the castle. Very impressive.

TOURIST INFORMATION Mairie (47.55.50.31)

HOTEL

*Domaine de Beauvois*, 4km NW on D49 (47.55.50.11): Relais et Châteaux. Charming and impressive. A big fifteenth- to seventeenth-century manor in 350 acres of woodland, with splendid swimming pool and huge fishing lake. Light dishes with regional touch, and old favourites like friture of Loire fish. Superb wine list. Lovely dining-room. Very expensive. ROOMS F–G. MEALS E–G. Shut 5 January–mid-March.

# MALICORNE-SUR-SARTHE
## [SARTHE]

In the Sarthe valley on a big river bend E of Sablé-sur-Sarthe on the riverside road to Le Mans, Malicorne is in a most attractive position. From the bridge are views of a mill and river banks lined with poplars. You can take pleasant boat trips from the old port.

The little town is renowned for rustic faïence pottery, including very nice reproductions of old pieces. The Tessier workshops E of the town, with a museum, are open daily except Sunday in winter and Sunday mornings and Monday all the year. The eleventh-century church has a few works of art. Downstream is a restored turreted seventeenth-century château, encircled by moats with a quaint hump-backed bridge, all in a fine park.

# LE MANS
[SARTHE – see Major Towns, page 73]

# MAYENNE
[MAYENNE]

On the slope of two hills astride the Mayenne river, it is not a very interesting town. William the Conqueror took it in 1064 by having burning brands thrown over the walls. It was almost totally destroyed in 1944 during the Allied advance in heavy fighting between the Americans and the Germans trying desperately to hold the bridge which was the last over the Mayenne river near the Normandy border.

TOURIST INFORMATION place du 9-Juin 1944
(43.04.19.37)
MARKET Monday

HOTEL

*Grand*, 2 rue Ambroise de Loré (43.00.96.00): Logis with 3 chimneys for outstanding cooking. ROOMS C–E. MEALS B–F. Shut 21 December–mid-January; Friday evening, Saturday in winter.

# MÉNARS – Château
[LOIR-ET-CHER]

Nothing was ever quite good enough for Madame de Pompadour, haughty, vindictive, witty and beautiful mistress of Louis XV, who let her run France for twenty years and run it into disaster. When she bought the handsome Château de Ménars, 6km from Blois on the water's edge of the Loire in 1760 she loved the garden but decided that the château itself needed complete remodelling and enhancing.

It was quite a small house when, in 1637, Guillaume Charron, a wine merchant, bought it. The family built onto it until it was a grand house and Louis XIV gave the Charrons the rank of Marquis, perhaps because Marie Charron was the wife of Jean-Baptiste Colbert, Louis' powerful chief minister. The gardens were already magnificent. A later Charron lost interest – or money – and sold it to Pompadour. In view of Pompadour's power, it may have been an offer he could not refuse.

Pompadour had better artistic sense than political. Wisely she chose the King's architect, Gabriel, designer of Blois bridge, to rebuild it. Only the first floor decoration was completed when she died in 1764. Her brother, the Marquis de Marigny, inherited it and hired Soufflot, architect of the Paris panthéon, to finish the work to Pompadour's plans. He also laid out the delightful gardens, with statues and monuments, including a temple of love, an orangerie and a grotto. The château has been shut recently for renovation, but should be open when you read this.

The gardens are still superb, with fine views from the terrace over the river. First you see the old outbuildings which housed the kitchen, bakery and butchery. From the kitchen is an underground passage for service. This not only made it easier to keep the food warm, which was always a problem in these old châteaux where the kitchens were often far away from the dining room, but it also kept the servants fairly invisible.

The interior is furnished and decorated mostly in eighteenth-century style.

# MENNETOU-SUR-CHER
## [LOIRE-ET-CHER]

A truly delightful, sleepy village 14km NW of Vierzon on N76, among attractive scenery. It has steep winding streets, old houses of the thirteenth to sixteenth centuries, and you can drive round the thirteenth-century ramparts which have kept three of their five original towers and three gates. Through one of those, la Porte d'En Bas, Joan of Arc passed on her way to Chinon to ask the Dauphin for an army.

# MEUNG-SUR-LOIRE
## [LOIRET]

The quietest, most attractive places can have the worst histories of crime, torture and violence. Loches is one. The photogenic old fortified town of Meung is another. Six kilometres up stream from Beaugency, it is much less crowded because it does not have quite such an important bridge or riverside beach. But it does have the little river Mauve, a Loire tributary whose channels run between its old streets. There are very pleasant walks beside these waterways past old mills which the Mauve used to drive. One mill is now an art gallery.

Down by the river is a pleasant *mail* (mall). The painter Ingres lived beside the river for several years. On the quayside is a statue of Jean de Meung, alias Clopinel, a poet and wit of the thirteenth century. He took a very long, already popular romantic poem written fifty years before, *Roman de la Rose* by Guillaume of Loris, and added eighteen thousand stanzas to the four thousand, turning the romance into a satirical criticism of conventions and people of his day. He even dared to satirize Royalty and the Church. Chaucer translated part of it and was influenced by it. When printing was invented one hundred and fifty years later, it was one of the first books published in French and became a bestseller.

François Villon, the vagabond poet (see Artists and Writers page 44) had less luck in Meung. For his usual crime of burglary (in a church!) he was imprisoned by the Bishop of Orléans and tortured, including forced water-drinking until near bursting point. Here he wrote his plaintive and haunting poem 'Épître à mes Amis' (Epistle to my Friends). For a time he was confined in the 'oubliette', down a well where the prisoners were kept in darkness on an unfenced ledge half-way down, with no hope of climbing up if they fell off. Each day a loaf and a pitcher of water were lowered to be shared among them. The leading churchmen of those days were nice Christian gentlemen! The oubliette was rediscovered in the château grounds in 1973.

Luckily for Villon, Louis XI, of all people, released him. Louis, who later invented the torture cells of Loches, was passing through on his way to his coronation in 1461 and declared an amnesty. Villon went back to Paris committed another burglary, was sentenced to banishment and never heard of again.

The château, now a mixture of twelfth-century fortress and eighteenth-century home, was a residence of the Bishop of Orléans and then a prison from the twelfth century to the Revolution. Then it was sold off. In 1970, when it was empty and falling apart, it was bought by a Channel Islander who had escaped from a German prison in the Second World War and worked underground for Allied Intelligence. He furnished it with his own pieces, from French fourteenth century to English Chippendale, and put in one room a collection of arms from crossbows like those used at Crécy to Bren guns, and helmets from the Middle Ages to 1945. He has also explored and opened up a network of underground cells, storehouses and corridors, including secret tunnels, torture chambers and an underground chapel. (Open daily May to 11 November; Saturday, Sunday rest of year.)

The church of St Liphard in place Martroi in the old town, is a fine example of eleventh to thirteenth-century Romanesque, with a huge plain tower. St Liphard was a Governor of Orléans who gave it all up to convert the area to Christianity, killing his dragon in the traditional manner.

The people of Meung had an ancient nickname of 'les ânes Meung' – the Meung asses. Locals claim that it started when Orléans had a famine and the men of Meung entered with a string of donkeys bearing flour to the cry of: 'Voici les ânes de Meung'. Others say that Silenus, the happy, drunken attendant of Bacchus, rode into town on a donkey and found the locals so miserable and unfriendly that he turned them into donkeys.

The town has a swimming pool by the Loire and an attractive suspension bridge leading to Cléry-St-André (page 172).

TOURIST INFORMATION 42 rue Jean-de-Meung
(38.44.32.28)


HOTEL

*Auberge St Jacques*, rue Gén. de Gaulle (38.44.30.39): 2-chimney Logis with simple rooms. Good value meals. ROOMS C–D. MEALS A–F. Shut Monday in winter.

# MEZANGERS
[Mayenne – *see* Evron, page 178]


# MONTBAZON
[Indre-et-Loire]

A meeting place of roads, from Routes Nationales and a motorway to little lanes, not very exciting except for its beautiful old
turreted manor house in a lovely wooded park high above the
Indre river, which has been turned into a delightful hotel. You
reach La Tortinière by turning off N10 just north of Montbazon
onto D287 and looking for the sign. It was Denise Olivereau-
Capron's family home until her father died and she made it into
an hotel. A handsome white Second Empire house, it overlooks
100 acres of woodland, meadows, flower beds and lawns running down to the river. A manor house has stood here since
1562 but no one remembers who planted the rare trees, which
include three-headed sophoras and two cedars of Lebanon.
Autumn wild cyclamen are superb. See also Château d'Artigny
(page 116).

TOURIST INFORMATION – ave Gare (June–September
47.26.97.87)


### HOTELS
*Domaine de la Tortinière* (47.26.00.19): see text. Lovely modernish
cooking. Try the round tower bedroom! Friendly welcome.
Pricey. ROOMS F–G. MEALS F–G. Open 1 March–20 December.
*Château d'Artigny*, 2km SW by D17 (47.26.24.24): see Artigny –
Château page 116.


### RESTAURANT
*La Chancellière*, 1 place Marronniers (47.26.00.67): simple,
creeper-clad village house hides pricey 2-star Michelin cuisine in
luxurious setting. MEALS F–G. Shut 1–8 September; mid-
February–early March; Sunday, except Sunday lunch, Monday
September–June.

# MONTGEOFFROY
[Château]

Especially delightful to me because this château just off N147, 26km E of Angers, is still the home of the de Contades family whose ancestor Marshal de Contades rebuilt it in 1775. He had furniture designed for it and if he walked in now he would find most of it still in the same place. Even the backgammon table on which Louis XVIII had a game when visiting the family, is awaiting a royal player. He would be fooled, perhaps, by the electric lights. The Marshal ordered all the furniture from Paris at the same time from leading makers. Their signatures, including Garnier, Durand and Gourdin, can be seen on some pieces. He was an orderly man, as befits a soldier, and he had an inventory made which still exists. He matched up perfectly his carpets, curtains, wall-panelling and tapestries. Perhaps he was *too* orderly. His enemies said that he was made a Marshal 'for successfully losing the Battle of Minden'.

There are fine pictures, including those of Desportes, specialist in hunting scenes, one of the many Van Loo family, Rigard, the portrait painter, and the younger Pourbus.

You can visit the large and small salons, billiard room, dining-room and Madame Hérault's apartments.

Madame is the key to the survival of all these treasures in the Revolution. The Marshal gave her these apartments. We are not told why! She had a son Marie-Jean Hérault whom Carlyle called 'one of the handsomest men in France'. Like a lot of 'natural survivors' among the French aristocracy, he became a member of the National Assembly after the Revolution, along with 'Philippe-Egalité', as the Duke of Orléans called himself. Hérault helped to draft the new constitution and was twice President of the Convention. He had the protection of Danton, one of the most powerful Revolutionaries. Like 'Philippe-Egalité', he came to no good in the end. Danton fell and he and Hérault met at the bottom of the guillotine. Danton nodded at the basket: 'Our heads will meet in there.' They did. The old Marshal died next year. The house was taken over by the Revolutionaries and sold. A local lawyer bought it to keep until the family returned.

The Marshal's cenotaph is in the 1543 chapel which he left unharmed when he rebuilt. It has a fine sixteenth-century stained glass window. He left, too, the moat and two round towers. One contains a lovely collection of the family's coaches and carriages. The handsome rebuilt château has a near-military symmetry. (Open daily early April–end October.)

# MONTLOUIS-SUR-LOIRE
## [INDRE-ET-LOIRE]

A wine village along the south bank of the Loire on D751 almost opposite Vouvray, its caves are cut in the cliffside and most of them offer 'Dégustations' (tastings) to lure you in to buy. On the corner of D751 and the D40 road to Chenonceaux the producers' co-operative has a modern tasting room above its fine old caves. (Open daily 8 a.m.–12 p.m., 2 p.m.–6 p.m.)

Montlouis produces white wines made like Vouvray, from the Pineau (Chenin) grape and until 1938 the wines were sold as Vouvray. They can be acidic when young, and do not become so luscious with age, but are cheaper than Vouvray and good value. A fully-sweet (liquoreux) wine is produced but much goes to producing semi-sparkling (crémant) and sparkling wines made by the Champagne method. Not much Montlouis reaches Britain.

MARKET Thursday
FESTIVALS Wine Fair, 3rd weekend of February and
15 August

### HOTEL
*Ville*, place Mairie (47.50.84.84): Logis with above-average cooking. ROOMS C–D. MEALS B–E.

### RESTAURANT
*Roc-en-Val*, 4 quai Loire (47.50.81.96): luxurious, in old house facing river. Attractive good-weather terrace. Choose between traditional dishes and subtle modern. Cheapest menu recommended. MEALS D–G. Shut Monday except evenings in season.

# MONTOIRE-SUR-LE-LOIR
## [LOIR-ET-CHER]

Nowadays Montoire is a pleasant leisure spot with excellent river fishing, swimming and boating. There are some delightful little roads around here, too, especially north of the winding Loir, arriving by a roundabout way at Vendôme to the NE. But Montoire's name brings very unhappy memories to Frenchmen of my generation. On 24 October, 1940, in a railway carriage at the station, Adolf Hitler, at the height of his power, met Marshal Pétain, First World War hero, now an embittered, pigheaded old man who thought he knew best for France. Pétain sold the North of France for an imaginary peace. He abandoned the people north of the Loire to Nazi occupation, the Gestapo, deportation to forced labour in Germany and concentration camp trains. The 'Government of France', unrecognized by Frenchmen in the north and many in the south, would run unoccupied France from the delightful spa of Vichy. The Germans knew that the peace was an illusion. They placed Hitler's train by the mouth of a tunnel in case the RAF joined in the party.

Stand on the bridge now and watch the delightful river running between banks of weeping willows and old houses decorated with wistaria, and find real peace.

There are some lovely Renaissance houses in Montoire. Beside one of them is the lane to an old priory chapel of St Gilles with some famous murals which experts date from early twelfth century. One of Christ sitting in judgement with details of the Apocalypse must have frightened even the most wayward medieval men and women into behaving themselves. From the keep of the ruins of an eleventh-century castle on a rocky spur you can have lovely views of the Loir, the countryside and Lavardin castle 2½km upriver (see page 198).

TOURIST INFORMATION Mairie (July, August –
54.85.00.29)
MARKET Wednesday

### HOTEL

*Cheval Rouge*, place Foch (54.85.07.05): 2-star, 2-chimney Logis.

ROOMS A–C. MEALS C–F. Shut February; Tuesday evening, Wednesday.

# MONTPOUPON – Château
### [LOIR-ET-CHER]

*A pigeon-house at Montpoupon*

Twelve kilometres SW of Montrichard on D764. The thirteenth-century fortress and fifteenth-century manor overlook fields and streams and still exist as a private house. Part of it, a hunting museum, is open to the public and the owner who lives there will let out three of her bedrooms. There is also a little grill-restaurant, Le Moulin Bailly, in the grounds.

Towers remain from the fortress. The main building has a gatehouse with Renaissance decoration. The house has Gothic-style mullioned windows and gables.

The owner still hunts. Musée de la Vénerie (the hunting museum) has trophies and hunting equipment from several centuries and recordings of hunting horns. You can see the interesting old cooking equipment in the ancient château kitchen still used until 1975. (Open daily 15 June–30 September, weekends only Easter–15 June and October – telephone 47.94.23.62 and 47.94.30.77.)

# MONTRÉSOR
## [INDRE-ET-LOIRE]

The village stands high above the Indrois river among delightful countryside and a wealth of pretty country roads 16km east of Loches. The D760 from Loches runs through the Loches forest, which has charming walks and drives.

It is worth spending time at Montrésor, not only to see its ivy-covered château, Renaissance collegiate church and old timbered market, but also because it is a really charming village with a true French village atmosphere. The villagers call it 'le plus beau village de France'. That's a very large and dangerous boast – but it *is* very attractive.

The sixteenth-century church shows how close-knit the village has been for centuries. From the white marble tomb of the sixteenth-century lord of the château, Imbert de Bastarnay, with his wife and son, to the portraits of families around the walls, the important local people are all there. Village life still revolves around the castle.

Foulques Nerra built a fortress on the château site in the

eleventh century. He couldn't see a hill overlooking a river without fortifying it. Ramparts and crumbling towers remain and there is a lovely view from them of the little river winding through meadows. Imbert de Bastarnay built the present château.

In 1849 an emigré Polish nobleman, Count Branicki, restored it. He went with Napoleon III to Constantinople in the Crimean War and later became a French Senator. One of his descendants, la Comtesse de Rey, lives there now in a sixteenth-century house by the gates, and the château is much as Branicki left it. His shooting trophies are in the entrance hall. There are military medals, souvenirs and nineteenth-century pictures by French and Polish painters, gold and silver plate which was buried during the Revolution, a bas-relief of battles fought by John III (Sobieski) of Poland who drove the Turks from Vienna in the seventeenth century. A spiral staircase came from the 1889 Paris Exhibition. (Open daily 1 April–31 October.)

### HOTEL
*France* (47.94.20.03): real local inn typical of the village. Nice little restaurant, good cheap meals, simple, comfortable rooms, some without bath. ROOMS A–C. MEALS A–C.

# MONTREUIL-BELLAY
## [MAINE-ET-LOIRE]

A delightful little town in a lovely position above the Thouet river, which joins the Loire at Saumur 18km N on N147. There are big attractive gardens by the river.

The town is very much dominated by its unusually interesting château whose turrets are reflected in the river way below when the river is not invaded by duckweed, which makes it look green and pretty but rules out swimming. The sturdy château is enclosed by a wall with thirteen towers and must look very much as it did in the fifteenth century when built by the d'Harcourt family. Foulques Nerra, Count of Anjou, had, of course, built a fortress on this prime hilltop site, but he gave it to a vassal,

Berlay, whose family revolted a century later. Geoffroi Plantagenet, descendant of Foulques and father of Henry II of England, knocked down its fortifications in 1150 after a siege and famine in the town.

Rooms in the Château Neuf are seven metres (23 feet) high. But first you go through the old château courtyard and into the medieval kitchen with an unusual central chimney rather similar to Fontevraud 20km away and designed for smoking meat and fish. To the right is the fifteenth-century canons' quarters, with four turreted staircases leading to four dwellings for the canons of the Lord's chapel, now Notre-Dame church.

Château Neuf was built in the fifteenth century. It has a lovely turret staircase with beautiful carved panels under the windows. The old vaulted cellar is still used for meetings of the Sacavins, the wine-growers brotherhood formed in 1904 by Georges de Grandmaison, then owner of the château, to publicize Anjou wine, little known outside the area. The little oratory is covered with fifteenth-century frescos of angels as musicians playing. Music written by a Scottish monk, Walter Frye, is played to you on a tape.

Anne, Duchesse de Longueville, daughter of the Prince of Condé, mistress of the philandering Duke of Rochefoucauld whose memoirs were so scandalous that he had to pretend that he had not written them, was exiled to Montreuil by Louis XIV for helping to organize the Fronde rebellion of aristocrats. You can see her bedroom here. Chamber music is taped into the music room. (Open 1 April–1 November except Tuesday.)

TOURIST INFORMATION Syndicat d'Initiative, rue Marché (May–September 41.52.32.39)

### HOTEL

*Splendid*, rue Dr Gaudrez (41.52.30.21): small, pleasant Logis in old house with trout pond in its courtyard; new annexe, four to five minutes' walk away with a swimming pool. Hotel rooms cheaper. ROOMS C–D. MEALS A–E. Excellent regional cooking.

RESTAURANT

*Hostellerie Porte-St-Jean*, 432 rue Nationale (41.52.30.41): rustic village hostelry renowned for local and regional dishes. MEALS B–F. Shut February holidays; Wednesday.

# MONTRICHARD
## [LOIR-ET-CHER]

This charming town of medieval streets and fine half-timbered houses of the fifteenth to sixteenth centuries around the Romanesque church of Ste Croix is very much a wine town now. Going out of Montrichard east to St Aignan are the huge J. P. Monmousseau caves, 13km long! They are especially renowned for sparkling Blanc de Blancs made by the Champagne method, matured in the bottle for eighteen months. It is called 'Cuvée J.M.93' because the founder, J. M. Monmousseau, lived to be ninety-three by drinking it! Now a fourth generation Monmousseau is still President, but the Champagne company Taittinger own it. You can taste the wine. Half-hour cellar tours are possible (tel. 54.32.07.04).

From the old bridge over the gentle river Cher you can see the old town with its old fort, yet another built by Foulques Nerra, Count of Anjou, in his non-stop arguments with the Counts of Blois. The keep is still there but is crumbling now. You can still climb to the top for splendid views and there is a little museum of local antiquities in its ticket office. (Open daily mid-June–early September. Late March–mid-June open Saturday, Sunday. Shut October–late March.)

No wonder it is crumbling. Philippe-Auguste of France drove Richard Coeur de Lion of England out of the castle in 1188 by using his famous 'Taupes du Roy' – the King's Moles. These sappers dug a secret tunnel under one corner tower, removed the stones, replaced them with wooden props and set light to them. The props burned through, the tower collapsed and the French rushed through the breach. The road opposite is still called rue de la Brèche. The Germans fired guns from the tower in 1940 at the French across the river.

Louis XI bought the fort to stay in safety while worshipping a miraculous painting of the Madonna in a church in neighbouring Nanteuil, a Montrichard suburb.

Louis was also one of the pilgrims who prayed for courage at the Montrichard church of Ste Croix. In the Middle Ages there lived in swamps near a spring a monster who fed on cattle or children who went too near. No one would go near the marshes until a young monk took a long cotton veil from the Virgin in the church, walked into the marsh and led the monster out. At the spring it died of convulsions. It was a huge crocodile. So the spring became holy and people prayed there for courage. One was King Philippe-Auguste, who had a reputation for riding away from the toughest action. Perhaps he was just wise. He was very successful in battle.

TOURIST INFORMATION rue Pont (Whitsun–September
54.32.05.10)
MARKET Monday

### HOTELS

*Bellevue*, quai du Cher (54.32.06.17): Modern, across the road from the river. Fine views from restaurant. ROOMS C–E. MEALS B–E.

*Château de la Ménaudière*, 2½km NW by route Amboise D115 (54.32.02.44): a château built in Henri II's reign, restored in the eighteenth century; elegant bedrooms, luxurious and expensive. ROOMS E–G. MEALS E–F. Shut 6 January–end February; Sunday evening, Monday in winter.

*Château de Chissay*, at Chissay-en-Touraine, 4km W by N76 (54.32.32.01): one of the splendid Savry family luxury hotels. Twelfth- to fifteenth-century turreted castle, entirely renovated in 1986. Pretty pool in wooded gardens. ROOMS F–G. MEALS E–G. Shut January, February.

# MONTSOREAU
### [Maine-et-Loire]

Charming little town with quays on the Loire, a little down-stream from where the Vienne flows into it. Strangely quiet and relaxed, with a few fishing boats and nearby sandy beaches. On a narrow road climbing up the hillside are the elegant houses of an old village decked with flowers in summer. From April to October the pleasure boats from Chinon land their passengers

*Montsoreau*

here, so for a short time it becomes more lively. But the visitors do not stay long. Steps take active visitors to a belvedere with wonderful views over the village and château to the meeting of the rivers.

For centuries this little hill road was the main road and until 1820 the castle walls were lapped by the river. Built in 1455 by Jean de Chambes when Charles VII reigned, it became a fortress with a more comfortable house inside. The Chambes family were a tough lot and their women were dangerous schemers. One of the women became mistress to Louis XI's brother, the Duke of Berry, and they formed the League of Public Good which aimed to put the Duke on the throne. A lot of the French public would indeed have been delighted to see Louis XI go. But Louis found out and had them assassinated. Another Chambes was one of the most dedicated killers during the St Bartholomew's Day blood bath of Protestant leaders in 1572.

The lovely, fickle Françoise de Montsoreau was the model for Alexandre Dumas' Diane de Méridor in his novel *La Dame de Montsoreau*, although he twisted her story a little. She fell for Louis de Bussy d'Amboise, a classic bully, braggart, formidable swordsman, notorious duellist and one of the planners with the Duke of Guise of the St Bartholomew massacres. He boasted of his conquest to Henri III who was overheard by her husband joking about it. Her husband forced her to arrange a meeting with de Bussy and killed him in front of her. Whereupon she lived happily with him and bore him six children.

Now the château has a museum moved here from the Moroccan capital, Rabat, when Morocco became independent again. It is devoted to the Conquest by the French of Morocco and of the Goums, the cavalry units of Moroccans recruited by the French. 'Goums' meant 'Knights'. They were certainly brave and were great horsemen but hardly gallant knights. Any woman they ran into they certainly did not treat in a chivalrous manner, as the Italian girls discovered in the Second World War. (Château shut Tuesday.)

### HOTEL

*Bussy et Diane de Méridor* (41.51.70.18): Diane de Méridor is a fine old friendly inn on the quayside, with pavement tables in summer, open fire in winter, excellent few-frills cooking. Good value. Simple bedrooms. Bussy is the annexe in an old house up the steep hill in the village. Better rooms. Book for meals. ROOMS B–D. MEALS A–E. Shut 15 December–31 January; Tuesday except in July, August: Monday in winter.

# NANÇAY
## [CHER]

A charming village on D944 NW of Bourges in the silent heart of Sologne forests and lakes, with a fifteenth- to sixteenth-century restored castle and workshops of craftsmen who display their work at Grenier de Vilâtre on Saturday and Sunday. The old world atmosphere is rather spoilt by a huge 'dish' 40 metres wide by 200 metres long to the north of the village. It is part of the radio telescope of the experimental research station in radio astronomy. It seems that the dish catches the Hertzian waves and reflects to points 460 metres away. And if you want to know what that means, a terrace at the entrance has explanatory boards and recorded explanations in English.

### HOTEL
*Les Meaulnes* (48.51.81.15): very old auberge, lovely setting, high quality cooking; advised to book. ROOMS E–F. MEALS C–E.

# NOUANS-LES-FONTAINES
## [INDRE-ET-LOIRE]

On the edge of the forest of Loches SW of St Aignan on D675, with the Indrois river flowing through it. In the 1930s a picture covered in the dust of centuries was found in the thirteenth-century church. It is a monumental painting on wood by Jean Fouquet or his school of painters dating from somewhere around 1470 and shows the body of Christ being taken down from the cross and placed by two bearded old men in the lap of

Mary. I am no amateur of medieval art, but experts regard it as one of the finest fifteenth-century French paintings and even I can see that it is a great work and well worth a diversion to go to see it. It shows the transition from medieval art to more modern. Fouquet is recognized as the greatest painter of portraits and miniatures of the fifteenth century and you can see his talent in the splendid animation of the faces in this picture. The mystery is how such a great painting lay forgotten in a remote village church.

## NOYEN-SUR-SARTHE
### [SARTHE]

Another delightful little town on the lazy Sarthe river between Sablé-sur-Sarthe and Le Mans. Here it is doubled by a canal. Noyen rises in tiers above the river's north bank. From the bridge you can see an island in midstream, a barrage, and the gardens and rooftops of houses.

## OLIVET
### [LOIRET – see Orléans, Major Towns, page 85]

## ONZAIN
### [LOIR-ET-CHER]

Just 2km from the north bank of the Loire between Amboise and Blois, it is a pleasant place on a little Loire tributary, the Cisse – good shops, wine caves and a superb eigthteenth-century hunting lodge, Domaine des Hauts de Loire, in a park. It is now a lovely Relais et Châteaux hotel, turreted, creeper-clad, with lawns overlooking a lake.

The wine caves sell the Touraine-Mesland wines from grapes grown at Mesland, 4km NW in the hills – Chenin,

Sauvignon, Cabernet and Gamay vines, making white, red and rosé wines, about 1 degree of alcohol stronger than most Touraines and with a strong individuality.

Mesland used to send to Onzain and to nearby Seillac something less welcome than wine – water. The 'Sorciers de Mesland', sorcerers, were supposed to have magic powers for diverting storms by ringing the church bells. The bell-ringer was the prettiest girl in the village who, at the threat of a storm, had to run to the church barefooted in her nightgown, and pull furiously on the ropes chanting, 'Clear off, wicked storm. Go and burst over Seillac. Go and drown Onzain.' Once, at least, the storm obeyed. One evening in 1856, when the Loire was threatening to flood, the storm burst over Onzain and the swollen river broke a 400-metre gap in its raised bank, the levee, and swept away twenty houses and the gendarmerie. The people escaped but their belongings and broken furniture could be seen floating on the wayward river as far away as Amboise. As late as 1890 local historians were blaming the Mesland sorcerers. The Marylebone Cricket Club should hire one for Lord's. So should the English Tourist Board.

FESTIVALS Wine, 3rd Saturday after Easter

HOTELS

*Domaine des Hauts de Loire*, route d'Herbault D1 (54.20.72.57): see text. Very luxurious, very expensive. ROOMS G. MEALS F–G. Open 1 March–1 December.

At Seillac, 7km N by D131 – *Domaine de Seillac* (54.20.72.11): quiet holiday hotel in attractive château with vast grounds. Tennis courts, fishing, pool. ROOMS E–G. MEALS D–F. Shut 20 December–5 January.

# ORLÉANS

[LOIRET – *see* Major Towns, page 85]

# LE PALLET
## [Loire-Atlantique]

A Muscadet wine town on N149, 7km NW from Clisson, producing one of the Muscadets most popular in Britain – La Galissonnière. It is made in a property of that name by Pierre Lussaud, who uses very modern methods of winemaking, with three or four weeks' fermentation (tastings – English spoken – 40.26.42.03).

Le Pallet was one of the earliest vineyards in this area, devastated by the Britons invading from Cornwall in AD 600, then by the Norsemen in 850. It was replanted in 1142 and has produced wine since. The Muscadet grape was not introduced here until 1709, when a heavy frost had devastated the vineyards. Another local producer, Futeul Frères, is at Château de Mercredière, named after a Roman temple to Mercury. The Romans made wine here. Winemaking restarted in 1350. (Tastings, except 10–25 August, 40.54.80.10.)

# PARCÉ-SUR-SARTHE
## [Sarthe]

One more of the delightful villages along the Sarthe, east of Sablé. The houses are grouped round a Romanesque belfry and there is a mill on the river bank.

# PINCÉ
## [Sarthe]

A very pretty village with delightful houses along the Sarthe river, flowery in season, along a lovely stretch of the D159 where it joins the river 6km SW of Sablé-sur-Sarthe, alongside the Forêt-de-Pincé.

# PONCÉ-SUR-LE-LOIR
## [SARTHE]

On D305, 7km NE of La Chartre-sur-le-Loir and a very attractive road all the way SW of Poncé to the N138. It has two craft
centres but they are not arty-crafty but very professional. The
Atelier de la Volonnière is for leatherwork, painted furniture,
painted silk antiques (open weekends). Moulin de Paillard, an
old paper mill, is for glassware, pottery, ironwork, weaving and
woodwork (open weekdays, afternoon on Sunday).

The sculptured Renaissance staircase of the Italianate
château is wonderful. It goes straight up, not in a spiral, with six
flights and the sculptured vaulting is decorated with 130 mytho-
logical and allegorical sculptures in fine detail. The château
gardens are open for lazing or walking along tree-shaded paths.
They have a terrace and a dovecote with revolving ladders
reaching 1800 nesting holes. A museum of Sarthe folklore is in
the outbuildings.

Louis XIII's first love, Marie de Hautefort, was banished
here from the Court by Richelieu.

Across the river (2km by D57) is the manor of La Possonière,
where the poet Pierre de Ronsard was born in 1524, son of a
scholarly soldier who built the house in the Italian style after
returning from a campaign in Italy. He also had Latin tags
carved in the white stone. I am told that some read: 'Sustain
your strength and be abstemious', 'Truth, the daughter of time'
(the truth will out?) and 'The eye of God is watching'. But I have
not seen them. It is a private house. I am also told that it is
possible, when the family are away, to get permission to enter
the garden by applying in writing.


# PONTLEVOY
## [LOIR-ET-CHER]

North of Montrichard, a small market town with a few nice old
houses and a former abbey (shut Mondays). The abbey was
founded in 1034. In 1644 it became a school which was famous

until last century, especially after 1776 when it added a Royal military college for boys from the aristrocracy, chosen originally by the King. Now it is a technical college of road transport, and the old riding school has a road transport museum with vehicles dating from 1900. In one building is a big stove in Delftware, one of four with which Marshal de Saxe hoped optimistically that he would heat Chambord Château. Chambord was notorious for cold and draughts.

The monastery buildings have a very handsome white stone façade, and the abbey church, started in the thirteenth century but never quite completed, is charming.

### HOTEL

*Ecole*, 12 route Montrichard (54.32.50.30): Logis with good cooking. ROOMS C–E. MEALS B–F.

# LES PONTS-DE-CÉ
## [MAINE-ET-LOIRE]

On the edge of rose-growing country, this town, 7km S of Angers by N160, grows orchids. The Loire divides into three here and three town bridges cross all three streams. The Authion, with flowers grown in its valley, is the most northern stream, the Loire is the centre stream, the Louet the most southerly.

The town has a bloodthirsty history. Under Charles IX 800 camp followers were thrown into the Loire to drown. In 1562 the Catholic Leaguers took it from the Protestants and drowned all the surviving Protestants. In 1793 many captured Vendeans were shot on the island surrounding the château. Another battle here was between forces of Henri IV's widow Marie de' Medici and those of her son Louis XII. The Queen's men were driven so easily from the town that the battle was called Les Drôleries des Ponts-de-Cé – the Frolics of Ponts-de-Cé. At the end, both sides shouted 'Long live the King' and their leaders held a party in Château de Brissac!

# QUINCY and REUILLY
## [CHER]

Reuilly is 16km S of Vierzon on D918 on the border of Cher and
Indre, a wine town which with Quincy produces what used to be
called 'the poor man's Sancerre', a dry aromatic and fruity wine
made with Sauvignon grapes. It has become more popular
recently and the price has risen. A little red and rosé are produced, both quite spicy wines. Young Claude Lafond at Le Bois
St Denis makes a beautifully fruity and fresh white for drinking
young and an elegant Pinot Noir red, as well as a very unusual
and delicate rosé from Pinot Gris grapes drunk as an aperitif
(54.49.22.17 – tastings).

Quincy is 9km NE by the Cher river, nearer to the Vierzon-
Bourges road. White wines have more finesse than Reuilly and
are dearer. Very aromatic and fruity. Drink young. Raymond
Pipet, fifth generation vigneron, offers tastings (48.51.31.17).


# RICHELIEU
## [INDRE-ET-LOIRE]

On the borders of Touraine and Poitou, 22km SE of Chinon.
Cardinal Richelieu, Louis XIII's Minister of State, a despot who
was one of the most powerful men in the world, planned the
town of Richelieu as his capital, to house his court and adminis-
tration close to the great castle he was building. It was the first
town-planned new town in Europe since the Romans. He commissioned Jacques Le Mercier, architect of the Sorbonne and the
Cardinal's Palace (now Palais Royal) to build him a palace and an
enclosed town. To get materials and to ensure that no one
nearby had a château to compete with his, he had knocked down
or stripped and allowed to decay nine other important châteaux,
including the great historic château at Chinon and the vast
fortress of Loudun. He filled his palace with magnificent works
of art, many looted. They included *The Slaves* by Michelangelo,
now in the Louvre in Paris, twelve paintings showing the victories of Louis XIII, now in Versailles, and works of Titian, Van

Dyck and Rubens. It is pleasingly ironic that his town, which was never finished after he died in 1642, is now a delightful little market town devoted mostly to cattle farmers and the terminus of the little steam railway which runs on summer weekends from Chinon (see Chinon page 164). And all that is left of his palace are three pavilions, one domed, canals and an orangery and wine cellars in formal gardens. During the Revolution the château was confiscated and most of the treasures were taken for the Museum of French Monuments. Major works are now spread around the Loire and Poitou. When Richelieu's family got it back they sold it to an asset-stripper who then sold it for building materials. The huge park remains, criss-crossed by canals and avenues of chestnuts and planes. His statue is just inside the gate. It used to have copies of antique statues and grottoes and here the first Italian poplar trees were planted in France.

When he bought the estate he was simply Armand du Plessis. He persuaded the King to raise it to a Duchy so that he could become Duc de Richelieu.

The town was planned with geometric precision in a rectangle, with all roads at right angles. The gatehouses are still there, so is Grande-rue with twenty-eight absolutely identical houses. Opposite the white church in place du Marché is a splendid market hall with fine beamed roof. In the town hall is a Richelieu museum (shut Tuesday). It remains a very pleasant town in attractive countryside, but unimportant because it is remote.

TOURIST INFORMATION Mairie (47.58.10.13 or 47.58.13.62 out of season)

HOTEL

*Le Puits Doré*, place du Marché (47.58.10.59): Logis with good value meals and rooms, which is also a seventeenth-century historic monument. ROOMS B–D. MEALS A–D. Shut mid-December–31 January; Saturday in winter.

# ROCHAMBEAU
## [Loir-et-Cher]

I wonder how many US citizens have heard of Jean-Baptiste Donatien de Vimeur, Marquis de Rochambeau? He was commander of the French forces in the American War of Independence and did a lot to help Washington win the Battle of Yorktown. He deserved more publicity than the flamboyant Lafayette. Château Rochambeau on the Loir 10km W of Vendôme was his home. Take the D5, an attractive road, to Le Coudray, just before Le Gué-du-Loir and a little road across a bridge reaches the château in 2km. It is marked on the local Michelin map. It has two classic pavilions joined by one more modern but it is a private home and cannot be visited. A pity – rumour has it that it contains some interesting historical documents. Rochambeau is buried in the cemetery of Thore, a picturesque neighbouring village with some troglodyte houses.

# ROCHEFORT-SUR-LOIRE
## [Maine-et-Loire]

On the attractive D751 south of the Loire from Angers to Nantes, the first little town you reach is Rochefort-sur-Loire, which is in fact on the river Louet, a side-stream of the Loire. Rochefort is a very pleasant little town at the beginning of the zig-zagging Angevine Corniche stretch of road. Several old houses with turrets or watchtowers line its square. The ruins of a castle on a spur of rock were once part of a river-pirate's lair called St Symphorien. The pirates had been soldiers fighting with the ruthless Catholic League, founded by the Duke of Guise and led in battle by the Duke of Mercoeur. Once Henri IV was on the throne, the League was on the run and these soldiers cut their losses, threw out the people from his little town and moved in with their families, preying on ships on the Loire and terrorizing local villages. They had such a well-organized defence that they withstood attacks by troops under the Prince of Conti in 1592 and then by Marshal d'Aumont. So Henri IV bought them out and demolished their stronghold. They moved down to the little village of Ste Croix, which they renamed Rochefort. There they seemed to have lapsed into domesticity.

Rochefort is now known for making Quarts de Chaume, best of the very good Coteaux-du-Layon sweet white wines. On good years, the wine can rival any sweet wine except Sauternes Château d'Yquem. It is made from Chenin grapes picked in October when overripe and attacked by *pourriture noble* (the 'noble rot'). Only 100,000 bottles are made even in the very best years. It is a truly luscious wine, rich on the palate, and has a honeyed and floral bouquet. Rochefort also makes a Coteaux du Layon-Chaume, a good sweet wine with 13 per cent alcohol.

### HOTEL

*Grand*, 30 rue René Gasnier (41.78.70.06): not *that* 'grand' – 2-chimney Logis with 8 bedrooms. Traditional, very French. ROOMS C. MEALS A–D. Shut Sunday evening, Monday out of season.

# LES ROCHES-L'ÉVÊQUE
## [LOIR-ET-CHER]

Troglodyte houses, some charmingly decorated with lilac and wistaria and with flowery terraces, and a troglodyte chapel above the Loir river, 4km N of Montoire-sur-le-Loir. They are unusual because most were cut out of the rock deliberately – no doubt because of a housing shortage.

# ROMORANTIN-LANTHENAY
## [LOIR-ET-CHER]

Metropolis of the Sologne, with twenty thousand inhabitants, it is 41km SE of Blois and in the heart of the Sologne lagoons (étangs) and is a very pleasant town. It used to be a French national joke – comedians, humorous writers and newspapers poked fun at it as the typical dull small provincial town. But now new suburbs and industries have changed it. It is an industrial town making refrigerators, ciné-cameras, electronic equipment, sheet iron and has steel plate rolling mills. Its Matra cars won the Formula One World Championship in 1969 and to celebrate victory the town set up a motor-racing museum in Faubourg d'Orléans, showing how racing produced technical advances. This has a motor-sport library (open all the week except Tuesday and Sunday morning).

The old town straddles the river Sauldre where it divides into arms and its banks are rich in flowers in season. So are the island with a creeper-clad mill and the very attractive public gardens beside the river. The gardens have footbridges crossing branches and reaches of the river. There is a splendid old street market on Wednesdays and the town is proud of its two-star Michelin Relais et Châteaux hotel, until quite recently a posting inn called Lion d'Or, now quite rightly called Grand Hôtel Lion d'Or. But most of the townspeople can no longer afford to go there. Lanthenay, joined to the town quite recently, is quieter.

François I spent his childhood in Romorantin and kept his affection for it. It was in excellent hunting country! In 1517 he commissioned Leonardo da Vinci to design a palace astride the river for his mother, Louise de Savoie, but she died and the idea was dropped. A pity – I should have loved to have seen a palace designed by the master, especially as he planned to use prefabricated units. He also planned to link Romorantin to the Loire by canal.

During Twelfth Night celebrations in 1521, François joined in a mock battle with snowballs, apples and eggs. A drunk threw a lighted log from Hôtel St Pol and it landed on François's head. To treat the wound, doctors shaved his head, so he compensated by growing a beard. That started a fashion at court.

In the town hall is a museum presenting a picture of the Sologne – from its traditions, costumes and crafts to geology, soil, vegetation and wild animals. Two very interesting recreated interiors show a peasant's cottage and a wooden sabot (clog) maker's workshop. Sabots are made by hand to sell to tourists and wheelwrights, coopers and charcoal burners are still at work.

TOURIST INFORMATION place Paix (54.76.43.89)
MARKETS Wednesday, Saturday
FESTIVALS Gastronomic Fair, end October

### HOTELS

*Grand Hôtel Lion d'Or*, 69 rue Clemenceau (54.76.00.28): see text. Both a Logis *and* a Relais et Châteaux hotel. Lovely rooms, excellent individual cooking; prices have rocketed. ROOMS G. MEALS G. Shut early January–early February.

*Colombier*, 18 place Vieux-Marché (54.76.12.76): good value meals. Traditional cooking. Pretty terrace, nice garden. Try to book. ROOMS C. MEALS B–D. Shut 16–22 September. Restaurant also shut mid-January–mid-February.

# LES ROSIERS
## [MAINE-ET-LOIRE]

Very likeable little town along the Loire, fifteen kilometres from Saumur, with a bridge over to Gennes (see page 185). Busy town square with nice little shops and with a famous hotel-restaurant Auberge Jeanne de Laval, which used to be the favourite restaurant of the Queen Mother when she came this way to look at horses and which I seem to have known for ever. The chef-owner for very many years, Albert Augereau, was one of the great old-fashioned classical chefs of France. Alas, he is dead, but his son Michel continues the great tradition.

### HOTELS

*Jeanne de Laval et les Ducs d'Anjou*, 54 rue Nationale (41.51.80.17): see text. Not cheap but really superb. Most bedrooms in old house, which was once run separately, open onto a flower garden or the river bank. ROOMS F–G. MEALS F–G. Shut 8 January–mid-February. Restaurant shut Monday.

*Val de Loire*, place Église (41.51.80.30): dull-looking but good value; favourite of locals and regular visitors. Rooms simple. ROOMS B–C. MEALS A–D. Shut 1 February–mid-March; Monday. Restaurant also Sunday evening.

# SABLÉ-SUR-SARTHE
## [SARTHE]

A delightful place in a pretty spot on the superb stretch of the Sarthe from Le Mans – one of those almost hidden areas of France. The Vaige and Erve flow into the Sarthe here. The Colbert castle is gloomy but there are some fine old houses on the way up to it, the town itself is friendly, the river very attractive, so are the gardens above it, and you can take boat trips from the port on the canalized side of the river once used by barges bringing sand from the Loire.

Sablé now has small metal industries and food manufacture (cheese, biscuits called Sablé and milk products). The black marble, veined with white, from nearby quarries was used in building Versailles.

Louis XIV's extremely efficient and dictatorial Minister, Jean-Baptiste Colbert, who was very unpopular for his punitive taxes but had saved Louis from bankruptcy when the King had ruined France by making unsuccessful war against England, bought a half-wrecked château at Sablé for the title of Marquis which went with it. The irony was that Louis had appointed him originally to combat the power of the aristocrats, but he wanted to be one himself. His nephew rebuilt the castle. It now houses the Bibliothèque Nationale, where old documents are restored.

Cruise boats, which are flat-bottomed, run from Sablé (Sablésien, quai National – 43.95.14.42).

The famous Solesmes Abbey, 2km up river, looks to me like a granite medieval prison. It was built mostly between 1896 and 1901 to what was said to be a twelfth-century design. But it is in a lovely riverside setting, is a centre of religious art and music, and the monks have been behind the restoration of several other great old abbeys, including St Wandrille in Normandy, and the building of others, including Farnborough in Hampshire. You cannot enter the monastery, but you can go to services at the church (Mass at 10 a.m. Sundays, 9.45 weekdays and Vespers at 5 p.m.). It is famous for the rebirth in France of the Gregorian chant, and here it is said to be the greatest in the world.

TOURIST INFORMATION place R.-Élize (43.95.00.60)

MARKETS Monday, Wednesday
FESTIVALS Sablé Festival of Music and Dance – 2nd
fortnight of August

### HOTELS

*Grand*, 3km NE by D221 at Solesmes (43.95.45.10): very comfortable modern hotel, balconies overlooking garden. Regional–
modern blend of cooking. ROOMS D–E. MEALS C–F. Shut February; Sunday evening in winter.
*Aster*, 3km SE route La Flèche (43.92.28.96): small, modern
rooms, cheap. ROOMS C. MEALS A–C. Restaurant shut Sunday
evening.

# SACHÉ
## [INDRE-ET-LOIRE]

In charming countryside among orchards and watermills on the
river Indre 8km E of Azay-le-Rideau.

Honoré de Balzac (1799–1859), the great French novelist,
had close friends living at the Château de Saché, the big manor
house, and there he fled to find peace, write books and escape
his creditors. He used to walk there from Tours, his home town,
and there he wrote some of his books including *Le Père Goriot*,
his huge novel *La Comédie Humaine* and his greatest *Le Lys dans la
Vallée*, which was almost entirely set in this area. It includes a
beautiful description of the river, the mills, the farms, and their
animals and the flowers. And it is all made more poignant by the
typical nineteenth-century plot of unfulfilled love for a girl who
puts family 'duty' first. His host at Saché, Jean de Margonne, is
believed to have been his mother's lover.

You must follow the guided tour of the Château now
because in 1982 someone stole the bust of Balzac by Rodin
(closed Wednesdays low-season and January, February). But it is
well worth seeing. If you have no interest in Balzac, a visit might
well arouse one. You see the salon where he read his day's work
to his hosts, a museum upstairs with portraits of some of his

mistresses, including Laure de Berny, and of Balzac himself. I had never thought of him as pot-bellied! I like Picasso's cartoon-like drawing of him.

His bedroom is furnished as it was around 1850, with his quill pen, ink-well and coffee pot, even a copy of the original wallpaper. It seems that he often got up or started to write in bed as early as 2 a.m. and worked for about twelve hours by candlelight with shutters closed, keeping going on black coffee. The bed is very short. As John Ardagh points out in his delight-ful book *Writers' France* (Hamish Hamilton), many people in those days slept sitting up – 'possibly because they all had diges-tive problems'. Presumably he and his mistresses besported in the girls' bed.

A scene which Balzac described beautifully was Pont-de-Ruan, a village with a bridge across the Indre 4km NE. It is still a superb site with its flower gardens and three mills, two on river islands in a lovely green setting. Over the river is Vonne, an ancient manor which was called Clochegourde by Balzac in *Le Lys*. His heroine the Comtesse de Montsauf lived there. She was based on his mistress Laure de Berny. There are fine views from the terrace.

No one has yet stolen any of the mobiles and stabiles of their originator, the American sculptor Alexander Calder (1898–1976). Several outdoor stabiles can be seen at Le Carroi, north of the village. Calder lived at Saché. I can understand why. It is a charming area.

**RESTAURANT**
*Auberge du XIIe Siècle* (47.26.86.58): at foot of Saché Château. Excellent cooking, seasonal dishes. Pricey. MEALS E–F. Shut February; Tuesday and Wednesday low season.

# ST-AIGNAN
## [LOIR-ET-CHER]

One of the most delightful little towns in the whole Loire area, it is on the Cher, 16km SE of Montrichard, among forests and vineyards, running down through narrow cobbled streets from a splendidly photogenic Renaissance château to a river port which has become a little pleasure resort. It has excellent natural sandy beaches, rowing boats, pleasure craft and pedalos for hire, and very good fishing in the Cher and in the Ancien Berry canal. There is a camping ground by the river.

You cannot enter the château but do climb the monumental staircase opposite the porch of the eleventh- to twelfth-century church and wander the courtyard and terrace for views over the rooftops, the Cher and its bridges and to walk round the park.

The church is a delight. Through its Romanesque doorway with delicate sculptures is a high nave with capitals showing fantastic animals. The Romanesque crypt has beautiful twelfth- to fifteenth-century frescos which have kept a lot of colour remarkably well, considering their age. In the old streets and secret little squares are half-timbered and sculptured houses. At Par de Beauval (just off D675 S) are one thousand rare exotic birds bred and raised for protection and preservation (open daily).

TOURIST INFORMATION Office de Tourisme (July, August – 54.75.13.31 – rest of year 54.75.22.85)

FESTIVALS son-et-lumière in season

### HOTEL

*Grand Hôtel St-Aignan*, 7 quai Jean-Jacques Delorme (54.75.18.04): not grand or pretentious but very nice indeed. Old-style French hotel with gardens to the river. Meals excellent value. ROOMS A–D. MEALS A–E. Shut 11–24 February; 19–24 November; Sunday evening, Monday in winter.

### RESTAURANT

*Relais de la Chasse*, 8 ave Gambetta (54.75.01.89): old beamed inn; good cooking; try river fish. MEALS A–E. Shut mid-December–2 January; fortnight late June–early July; Wednesday.

# ST-BENOÎT-SUR-LOIRE
## [Loiret]

We know St Benoît as St Benedict, founder of the Benedictine order. At this site 10km SE of Châteauneuf in Gaulish times Druids from afar met annually in council. After St Benedict died in the sixth century, monks of his order founded an abbey named Fleury here in the seventh century. The monastery is still active. Around 672 the Abbot heard that the Barbarians had destroyed the great monastery of Monte Casino in Italy where Benedict was buried and that his body and that of his sister, St Scholastica, were still under the rubble. He sent monks to go there secretly and bring back the precious remains. Their return journey was something of a nightmare. St Scholastica's body was wrapped and propped up on a horse. The party beat off attacks, finally with the help of the monks of Le Mans, who were given St Scholastica as thanks for their help. The abbey became 'St Benoît', pilgrims flocked in, so did their gifts. The Italian monks were furious and legal actions continued until the Pope said that St Benoît must stay where he was, in France.

In the ninth century the Bishop of Orléans, St Théodulf, founded a monastic school that became one of the greatest education centres in the world. Apart from theology, more worldly subjects were taught – history, grammar, logic, rhetoric, arithmetic, geometry, astronomy, art, music, medicine and agriculture. Branch monasteries included one at Minting in Lincolnshire.

When Norman raiders came the monks had time to flee behind the walls of Orléans with their relics and treasures. They went back to repair their buildings when the invaders had gone. The present church was built between 1067 and 1108.

In the fifteenth century French kings introduced the system of 'commendatory' abbots to reward their favourites and curb church power. The 'abbots', often laymen, were given the abbey incomes but usually took no part in abbey life. Richelieu had a string of them. The monks of St Benoît went on strike when one was appointed until François I arrived with troops as strike-breakers. With an absentee abbot the abbey declined as the monks became lax. Then in the Religious Wars the abbot Odet de Coligny, brother of the Protestant leader Admiral Gaspard de Coligny, a French patriot rather than a religious zealot, became a Protestant and told Condé's Protestant forces where the best treasures were hidden. They were all sold, even the library collected over seven hundred years. Some manuscripts are now in Oxford, Rome, Moscow and Berne.

Everything except the church was knocked down under Napoleon, and the church became a wreck. But the State restored it in 1835 and the monks returned in 1944, when the poet and artist Max Jacob retired there, only to be arrested by the Gestapo (see Artists and Writers page 46).

It is an imposing building, not austere. The upper part of the church tower looks unfinished but in fact François I took the top off to punish the monks for refusing to have his nominee as abbot.

About forty monks live there. They perform the Gregorian Chant and you can attend Mass at noon on weekdays, 11 a.m. on Sundays. Otherwise the church is open when there are no services.

There is a little old village port by the river and a beach of sorts.

HOTEL

*Labrador* (38.35.74.38): opposite the abbey, modest, quiet. No restaurant. ROOMS C–D. Shut 1 January–mid-February.

# ST-CALAIS
[SARTHE]

Thirty-two kilometres NW of Vendôme, a farming market town with narrow streets containing old gabled houses. It bestrides the river Anille with five bridges over it. An old monastery was destroyed in the Revolution. Surviving buildings are used now as the theatre, town hall and museum. In the Renaissance church (1549), hidden in a cupboard, is the shroud of St Calais.

Walking along the tree-lined quays you have pleasant river-side views of gardens and river.

Each year since the end of the Plague in 1581 the town has commemorated it with a happy and amusing Fête de Chausson aux Pommes (an apple-turnover festival). It is held on the first Saturday and Sunday in September.

TOURIST INFORMATION place Hôtel-de-Ville
(43.35.82.95)
MARKET Thursday
FESTIVAL see text; also Folk Festival – September

HOTEL

*Angleterre*, rue Guichet (43.35.00.43): good regional cooking. ROOMS B–C. MEALS A–D. Shut 22 December–7 January; Sunday evening, Monday.

# ST-FLORENT-LE-VIEIL
## [MAINE-ET-LOIRE]

On the south bank of the Loire 14km E of Ancenis, a very pleasant little town with hilly cobbled streets, built around a church on a rocky spur beside a swing bridge over the river. In the brutal Vendean War, when some Royalists tried to overturn the Revolution, the Royalist leader Marquis de Bonchamp, who had fought in the American Revolution, was mortally wounded at the battle of Cholet and retreated to St-Florent. Eighty thousand Royalists – soldiers, old men, women, children, crossed the Loire on a bridge made of any wood they could find, including doors and window frames. The Royalists had imprisoned four thousand Republicans in a church and proposed to massacre them. The dying Bonchamp persuaded them not to do it. Among the prisoners was the father of the Loire sculptor David d'Angers, who in thanks made the beautiful memorial in front of the church. He also designed the white marble tomb of Bonchamp inside the church. An attractive tree-lined esplanade round the church gives wide views of the Loire valley and of the river island Île Batailleuse, a base of invading Norsemen for eighty years from 853 when Cidroc had his fleet of two hundred ships here for raiding up the Loire, pillaging, murdering, burning every town up to Roanne until the Breton Alain Barbe-Torte returned from England to drive them out.

### HOTEL

*Hostellerie de la Gabelle* (41.72.50.19): on the cobbled quayside where men sit fishing. A simple Logis with small simple rooms and good value lower-priced menus. ROOMS C–D. MEALS A–E. Shut 30 October–3 November; 23 December–3 January.

# ST-GEORGES-SUR-LOIRE
## [MAINE-ET-LOIRE]

On N23 N of the Loire 18km SW of Angers, with a Loire rivulet running through it to a lake, it has two buildings of a former abbey, now the town hall and presbytery. Nearby is the great Coulée de Serrant vineyard and the historic Château de Serrant. This château is one of the finest in the Loire valley – remarkable architecturally for its symmetry, uncluttered elegance and unity of Renaissance style, often reflected in the waters of its moat. Yet it was built over three centuries, from the sixteenth to eighteenth.

In 1546 the great Philibert Delorme, who designed Fontainebleau and the Tuileries, started this château for Charles de Brie, but when it was half-finished, the cost bankrupted de Brie. It was bought in 1636 by the comedian–diplomat Guillaume de Bautru, who could even make Richelieu laugh. He became ambassador to England, Spain and the Netherlands. He followed Delorme's building plans and his granddaughter finished it. She also added a chapel and white marble mausoleum in memory of her soldier husband, the Marquis de Vaubrun, sculptured by Antoine Coysevox.

The château is very striking, with its thick round towers and contrasting stone in dark schist and white tufa, all surrounded by moats. The only alterations were made in the eighteenth century by the Walsh family, originally Irish Jacobites. They came from the Nantes area, and were almost certainly descended from Captain Francis Walsh who provided and captained the ship for James II's escape to France after the coup in 1688 by William III of Orange, and thought it prudent to stay in Nantes. He became a successful shipbuilder and owner and his son Antoine provided the ships for Charles Stuart (Bonnie Prince Charlie) to cross to Scotland for his abortive and disastrous uprising in 1745. He had already bought Serrant and when Louis XV made him a Count for helping Charlie, Antoine de Walsh, as he called himself now, became Count of Serrant. He had no right to the prefix 'de', but nor have some Frenchmen to this day. A descendant, Theobalde, created the lovely gardens with lakes and chestnut and cedar trees which are now old and gorgeous.

Over the library fireplace is a picture of Charlie talking to Antoine de Walsh.

The château, owned by the de Ligne family, descendants of the great Austrian soldier, Charles de Ligne, is lived in but open for guided tours from Palm Sunday to the last Sunday in October (closed on Tuesday except in July and August). It has a beautifully panelled staircase, a bedroom in Empire style especially decorated for a visit in 1808 by Napoleon I, with a bust of Empress Marie-Louise by Canova, the great Neoclassical Italian sculptor. Another bedroom has a bathroom concealed in a big rustic closet. The gloriously furnished green-decorated drawing room has a splendid carved wooden ceiling. The library has around ten thousand books.

RESTAURANT

*Relais d'Anjou*, rue Nationale (41.39.13.38): MEALS B –F. Shut 1–13 July; 2–18 January; Sunday evening, Monday.

# ST-HILAIRE-ST-MESMIN
## [Loiret]

An old fishermen's hamlet on the green banks of the Loiret river, 7km W of Orléans and a short distance from the meeting of this little river with the Loire. Since the end of the century, people from Orléans have retired here, building pleasant little houses or bungalows, cultivating their gardens which stretch to the river towpath where the flat-bottomed wooden boats they use for peaceful fishing are still tied up. Now there are a few commuters to Orléans, too, so the hamlet and river are livelier at weekends.

On a fine day you can sit on the white-painted terrace of the little hotel–restaurant with an aperitif bottle of Loire wine on the white table and be mesmerized into delightful dreams by the fast-flowing river and the gentle movement and sound of the lime trees, big willows and tall birches. Swallows dive and weave over the water, ducks hug the banks seeking worms, wavelets slap against the flat-bottomed boats. Or if the weather is not so good, you can sit in Hotel l'Escale du Port Arthur's glass-enclosed addition to its cosy dining room and still see the river over the terrace and towpath. It is a world away from Orléans.

### HOTEL

*L'Escale du Port Arthur* (38.76.30.36): charming, friendly atmosphere, excellent cooking. Renovated rooms are very good value. Rooms C–D. Meals C–E. Shut 1–14 January; 1–7 February; Sunday evening, Monday in winter.

# ST-SATUR
## [Cher– *see* Sancerre, page 244]

# ST-THIBAULT-SUR-LOIRE
## [Cher – *see* Sancerre, page 244]

# ST-VIÂTRE
[LOIR-ET-CHER]

Pretty village in the Sologne 25km NE of Romorantin, named after a hermit who hid here in the sixth century. The sixteenth-century painted panels in the church show his life story. The village became a place of pilgrimage for people to pray for a cure for 'Sologne Fever', which was malaria. Then Napoleon III started to drain the marshes, quinine was discovered to be an antidote, and so pilgrimages stopped. There are many étangs from here southward to Salbris and to Romorantin SW.

HOTEL
*Auberge de la Chichone*, place Église (54.88.91.33); 2-chimney Logis. Good regional cooking. ROOMS D. MEALS D–E.

# SANCERRE
[CHER]

Sancerre is a true wine village, standing on top of a hill with views across its vineyards and down its narrow steep streets lined with gables and turreted houses. On top of the hill is an enormous tower, last remains of a castle, and from its lime-shaded terrace you can see not only the vineyard slopes but the river Loire and a curved viaduct taking a road to bypass the ancient village of St-Satur. You can see into Burgundy, too, and way back in 1844 Balzac wrote that the wine was 'like enough to the wines of Burgundy to deceive the vulgar palates in Paris'. I don't think that it would now deceive even Parisians, though they are well known in French wine-growing areas to know nothing about wine! But I do not think the smoky flavour (pierre à fusil or gunflint) is as definite as it was. That may be my age, but the trouble is that modern producers don't keep their white wine in oak casks for several months as they used to. They want the cash to flow.

White wine is 80 per cent of production, and must be made

from Sauvignon grapes. Three types of soil produce slightly different wines. White, chalky soil on steep slopes around Chavignol produces elegant wines that can be kept. The stony lower slopes around Bué make very fruity wines for drinking young. The clayey soil on a chalk base from around Ménétréol produces less fruity but softly elegant wine. Pouilly, across the river, makes only half as much Fumé white as Sancerre. They are ardent rivals and will not admit that their wines are similar. Sancerre is usually fruitier. Sancerre also makes a red, recently fashionable in Paris for drinking young. It is made from Pinot Noir grapes and has been called 'a misplaced Burgundy with Loire Valley charm'.

In 1534 Sancerre was a Protestant stronghold and withstood several Catholic attacks. In 1573 the Marshal de la Châtre laid siege to the town with seven thousand men. He pounded the town with artillery, knocked holes in the wall and attacked. But the people of Sancerre threw them out. The siege lasted seven months and the people were reduced to eating powdered slate and leather. When the siege ended, they were given military honours and allowed to practise their religion.

The old town is delightful. So are neighbouring wine villages. St-Satur, 4km N on D955, was an old town in the eleventh century, has a fourteenth-century church and even older houses. Monks from an Augustinian monastery at St-Satur started the Sancerre vineyards and grew rich on the wine. They started to build a Gothic church but English marauders arrived and demanded one thousand gold écus. The monks did not have that much so the English locked the senior monks in a tower and set light to it. They tortured younger monks to find out where the treasure was hidden and when this failed, drowned the monks in the river. The monastery never reopened but the vineyards thrived. St-Satur is still a port on the Canal Lateral.

Chavignol, 3km NW by D183, produces one of the best Sancerre wines, Côtes de Mont Dâmnés, and the superb goats' milk cheese with a less-than-superb smell – Crottin de Chavignol (goats' droppings of Chavignol). The Mont Dâmnés wines from south-facing slopes have been known since the eleventh century, and for long the local lords squabbled over them. Then they became Bourgeois-owned, part of Domaine Henri Bourgeois, which has been in the family for ten generations. The wine is strongly fragrant and delicious. They also produce Vigne Blanche, a fresh wine with a flowery smell and Duc Étienne de Laury, which needs to be kept in bottle for two or three years. La Bourgeoise white, a powerful wine, has to be kept, too. Red La Bourgeoise from vineyards planted fifty-eight years ago with Pinot Noir, is matured in oak barrels, is full-bodied and fruity, and must be kept for four to five years. Perfect for drinking with Crottin. You can taste at the caves and English is spoken (8–11 a.m., 2–6 p.m.); (48.54.12.67).

St-Thibault-sur-Loire, almost adjoining St-Satur, is on a canal and the Loire river and was a thriving port until 1860 for shipping Sancerre. The canal has been turned into a pleasure craft centre and the water of the Loire runs slowly between islands for bathing. There is a sailing school.

TOURIST INFORMATION Hôtel-de-Ville (48.54.08.21)

MARKET Saturday, also Tuesday March–November

FESTIVALS Fête 15 August; Crottin Cheese Festival weekend nearest to 1 May; Wine Fair 1st weekend June; Fête du St Roch at St Satur mid-August; Witches' Fair at Bué 1st Sunday August.

### HOTELS

*Panoramic, Restaurant Tasse d'Argent*, rempart des Augustins (48.54.22.44): modern, not my type but comfortable and superb views. Reliable cooking. ROOMS C–D. MEALS B–F. Restaurant shut January; Wednesday in winter.

At St Thibault – *Étoile*, quai Loire (48.54.12.15): lovely position overlooking Loire. Elegant restaurant. Good local cooking, including charcoal grills. Restaurant very popular with my *Travellers' France* readers. Rooms in old building opposite are *very* simple and cheap but not recommended. ROOMS A–C. MEALS B–F. Open 10 March–15 November.

*Auberge St Thibault* (48.54.13.79): built 1610. Five basic rooms. Meals great value family cooking. Local favourite. ROOMS B–C. MEALS B–E. Shut 25 January–15 February; restaurant shut Tuesday except high season.

### RESTAURANTS

*Tour*, 31 place Halle (48.54.00.81): best restaurant around here, but Daniel Fournier, great classical chef, has become a little more modern. Lovely old building. MEALS C–F. Shut part March; mid-December–mid-January; Monday evening, Tuesday.

*Auberge Joseph Mellot*, 16 place Halle (48.54.20.53): Mellot family has made wine in Sancerre since 1513 (La Châtellerie). This is 'an auberge for wine-tasting'. Wines with snack meals of terrine, ham, omelette, Crottin cheese. MEALS A.

# SAUMUR
## [MAINE-ET-LOIRE]

A very interesting town, famous now for horses, wine and mushrooms but once extremely important for its massive fourteenth-century castle standing in a truly commanding position on a sheer cliff overlooking the town and the Loire. Its solid martial appearance is softened now by terraces of lawns and flowers, garlanded with vines that step down the castle slopes.

It is a very pleasant provincial town now but was a booming town under the Protestants until that faith was made illegal by the revoking of the Edict of Nantes.

Such an important position with its heights overlooking a good river crossing was certain to be coveted and the Counts of Blois and Anjou fought over it for centuries. Then the fearsome Foulques Nerra heard that the Count of Blois had left it to go out and attack one of Foulques' own fortresses. He rushed all his troops to Loire and attacked. There were too few defenders to hold every gate, so monks suggested, with more faith than military sense, that the holy shrine of St Florent should be left to defend the east gate. Foulques' men removed the shrine to safety, then marched in. So the Counts of Anjou owned Saumur and when the title was inherited by the Plantagenets the English ruled it. Philippe-Auguste took it for the French crown. Then it became a centre of Protestantism and Henri of Navarre (later Henri IV) appointed as Governor Philippe de Mornay, Seigneur

*Saumur*

du Plessis-Marly. Known as 'Duplessis-Mornay', he was a great statesman, great soldier, great scholar and ardent Reformer. The Catholics called him the 'Pope of Protestantism'. He fortified the fourteenth-century château, court of the Dukes of Anjou, then he set up a Protestant Academy, which drew scholars from all over Europe and rivalled Geneva. Protestant craftsmen took sanctuary in Saumur and it prospered and became a rich town. But when Henri IV's Edict of Nantes guaranteeing freedom of religion was revoked by Louis XIV in 1685, these craftsmen fled abroad, mostly to England and Holland. Saumur was half-deserted and poor. One trade which did continue was the export of Anjou wines to England and Holland.

The château became a prison, then barracks. When the town authorities took it over, it was in a bad state, but it looks formidable still, with its pointed towers and roofs with dormer windows breaking the skyline, and there is a lovely panoramic view from the Guet tower of the town and the valleys of the Loire and Thouet rivers.

It contains two interesting museums. The Museum of Decorative Arts has a rich collection of Renaissance pieces, left to it by a rich local scholar, Comte de Lair, in 1919. You can see old Limoges enamel, furniture, paintings, pottery and porcelain of the seventeenth to eighteenth centuries and superb fifteenth- to sixteenth-century tapestries of secular subjects moved from the ancient Romanesque church of Notre-Dame-de-Nantilly. The church still has religious tapestries just as good and well worth seeing. An unusual exhibit in the museum is a carpenter's workshop from the Gallo-Roman period, dug up at Just-sur-Dive.

The Museum of Horses is delightful. As well as horseshoes and harnesses there are prints, paintings and fine engravings by George Stubbs (1724–1806), the Liverpudlian who taught anatomy to medical students and painted superb horse pictures, especially of racehorses. The prize exhibit is a remarkable glass model showing Saumur's cavalry school in the nineteenth century, made by an enamel-craftsman who lived to be a hundred. And there is the skeleton of one of the world's greatest seducers, who died in 1911, aged fifteen. Flying Fox was a long-striding horse belonging to the Duke of Westminster which won the 1899 Derby, St Leger and Two Thousand Guineas. Next year the Duke died and his heir was in Army service in Africa and could not be found. The stupid executors put Flying Fox up for auction. Edmond Blanc, who owned Monte Carlo Casino, bought him and made a fortune out of stud fees. Many great French horses were descended from him. (Château and Museums shut Tuesday in winter.)

Saumur's cavalry school was started in 1763 as a crack cavalry regiment picked from the best horsemen in the French army. In 1814 Napoleon called it the Cadre Noir and dressed it in black uniforms, decorated with gold, with curious two-cornered hats. The great buildings of the Cavalry Academy are now used for training officers and NCOs in armoured warfare. Since 1972 the Cadre Noir has been part of the National Riding School at St-Hilaire-St-Florent for training civilian and army riding instructors. The stables there for 120 horses are modern and automated, with automatic grain-feeders and a conveyor belt for removing dung. You can visit it (book with tourist office 41.51.03.06).

The horsemen still take part in the great annual tattoo on place du Chardonnet in July, with a rodeo of tanks, armoured cars, jeeps, motorbikes and helicopters. At the north end of place du Chardonnet is Musée des Blindés (Tank Museum) with over 150 fifty armoured vehicles, including France's first Renault tank (1918), the famous German 'Panther', the big British 'Conqueror' and the Soviet T34.

In the old Cavalry Academy buildings on avenue Foch is the Cavalry museum, giving the history of the Cadre Noir and armoured corps. Among swords and sabres, some jewelled, are super uniformed figures in Sèvres and Meissen porcelain of Napoleon's soldiers and Imperial Guard. (Open afternoons 15 April–15 October except Monday and Friday and on Sunday mornings.)

Saumur is surrounded by tufa cliffs honeycombed with galleries and vast caves in which wine is champagnized. At St-Hilaire-St-Florent (3km along D741 towards Angers) are the caves of Ackerman-Laurence where in 1811 Jean Ackerman introduced the Champagne method of making sparkling wine – the first time it had been done outside Champagne. (Open for guided tours 1 May–30 September, including weekends.) For wine information apply at Maison de Vin, 25–27 rue Beaurepaire, Saumur.

Other caves are used for growing mushrooms, known as Champignons de Paris because suburbs spread over the Paris caves and the growers moved to the Loire. There are now 800km of growing tunnels, producing over 120,000 tonnes of mushrooms a year. Musée de Champignon (Mushroom Museum) is 2km W of St-Hilaire. A tour shows you different methods of growing. (Guided tours 15 March–15 November.)

TOURIST INFORMATION Tourist Office, place Bilange
(41.51.03.06)
MARKETS Saturday, Tuesday, Wednesday morning,
Thursday
FESTIVALS Grand Carrousel Militaire and Reprise du
Cadre Noir – end July; Gala des Amis du Cadre Noir –
April; Festival of Military Music – 4th weekend July;

Wine Fair – mid-February; Fair–Exposition – early May

*La Gare*, 16 ave David d'Angers (41.67.34.24): facing station. Long-time favourite of *Travellers' France* readers, in the same family since 1919. Simple, impeccably clean rooms. Meals range from 'dish of the day' to gourmand. ROOMS B–D. MEALS A–E. Shut 1 November–1 April.

*Anne d'Anjou*, 32 quai Mayaud (41.67.30.30): restored eighteenth-century mansion overlooking the river. No restaurant. ROOMS C–E. Shut 23 December–3 January.

*Delices du Château*, courtyard of the château (41.67.65.60): fourteenth-century building, modern cooking. MEALS D–F. Shut 15 December–15 January; Sunday evening, Monday in winter.

*Gambetta*, 12 rue Gambetta (41.67.66.66): chef who was at the Savoy and Park Lane hotels, London, cooks excellent traditional meals. Terrace, garden. MEALS C–F. Shut early January–early February; 1st week October; Sunday evening, Monday except in July, August.

# SEGRÉ
## [MAINE-ET-LOIRE]

Unassuming regional capital on the Oudon 40km NW of Angers on D863, it has an old hump-backed bridge, picturesque quays and old houses by the river, with the town rising in tiers behind it. Around it is wooded farmland with mixed crops and pigs, cattle and horses.

Château de la Lorie, 2km SE, is reached by a lovely shadowy avenue, then formal gardens. It is an important-looking eighteenth-century manor with a courtyard protected by buildings on three sides and by a now-empty moat on the fourth. James, Duke of Alba and Berwick, lived there. He was the illegitimate son of James II and Arabella Churchill, sister of the

Duke of Marlborough, Winston Churchill's ancestor. Born in 1670, he was a successful French general, although he was with his father in his Irish Campaign failures against William of Orange. He was killed by a cannonball in 1734. (Château open 1 July–30 September except Wednesday.)

# SELLES-SUR-CHER
## [Loir-et-Cher]

With the towers of its château reflected in the waters of the Cher, which wanders gently round a bend beside the town, this small agricultural town of old buildings in the Sologne has a quiet charm. It was not always so peaceful. It grew from an abbey that was built after a hermit-saint, St Eusice, died here in the sixth century. The abbey was destroyed by invading Norsemen but the church was rebuilt in the twelfth century, burned out in the Religious Wars, partly restored in the seventeenth century and completed in the nineteenth century. It is a fine building and St Eusice's tomb is still in it. But it is empty. His remains are walled up in a pillar of the choir.

There are two châteaux in one – the remains of a thirteenth-century fortress and a handsome house of Renaissance elegance built in the seventeenth century. The rectangular wall of the medieval fortress is on the banks of the Cher and surrounded by wide moats with water in them. Across the small park shaded by great old cedar and mulberry trees is Pavillon Doré – the gilded pavilion built in 1604 by Philippe de Béthune, brother of Henri IV's great Minister, Duc de Sully. The superb fireplaces decorated with gilt murals and coffered ceilings are in remarkable condition. Philippe lived there while he built the grander château in red brick outlined in white stone – a vast house. You can see the guardroom with a huge fireplace, an attractive games room and the bedroom of Marie Sobieska, Queen of Poland, with her four-poster bed on a dais. (Tours 1 July–15 September – shut Sunday morning; also Saturday, Sunday and weekday afternoons Easter–30 June.)

TOURIST INFORMATION Mairie (June–September
54.97.40.19)
MARKET Thursday

### HOTEL

*Lion d'Or*, 14 place de la Paix (54.97.40.83): Logis – one-star comfort, 2-chimney cooking. ROOMS C. MEALS A–E. Shut Sunday evening, Monday.


## SERRANT – Château
[MAINE-ET-LOIRE – *see* St-Georges-sur-Loire page 241]


## SILLÉ-LE-GUILLAUME
[SARTHE]

D304 NW from Le Mans leads to this small town on the border of Mayenne, alongside the delightful Sillé forest in the Parc Régional Normandie–Maine. William the Conqueror added his name to it when he captured the castle. The replacement, a massive fifteenth-century château, is now used as offices. You can walk, hire horses to ride, or drive through the woods. Four kilometres into the forest is a lake, Étang du Delais, with beaches, bathing and fishing, and windsurf boards, boats and pedalos for hire. The sailing school offers board and lodging. There is a 3-star camp-site – Les Mollières (43.20.16.12).


### HOTEL

*Pilier Vert*, 1 place Marché (43.20.10.68): simple rooms, family cooking. ROOMS B–C. MEALS A–D. Shut Monday; also Sunday evening in winter.


### RESTAURANT

*Auberge Forestière*, Étang du Delais (43.20.17.16): lakeside. Choice of simple, cheap meals to gourmand. MEALS A–E. Shut early November–1 March except weekends; Tuesday except mid-summer.

# SOUVIGNY-EN-SOLOGNE
## [LOIR-ET-CHER]

Eleven kilometres NE of Lamotte-Beuvron by D101, a very pleasant flowery village with two good restaurants.

### HOTEL
*Auberge Croix Blanche*, place de l'Église (54.88.40.08): two-star Logis, above-average cooking. Regional dishes of regional food. Garden. ROOMS C–D. MEALS B–F. Shut 15 January–1 March; Tuesday evening, Wednesday.

### RESTAURANT
*Perdrix Rouge*, 20 rue Gâtinais (54.88.41.05): becoming well known in far-away places for fine individualistic and regional dishes. Wide range of menus. Garden. MEALS B–G. Shut 2–10 September; 26 December–1 January; Monday evening, Tuesday.

# SULLY-SUR-LOIRE
## [LOIRET]

Visiting this serene little town with a happy atmosphere, it is difficult to realize what a terrible mess it was in after the Second World War. The old town was half-destroyed by German shells in 1940 and the job was finished by US Flying Fortresses in 1944 when they were aiming to cut the bridge. It still looked like a bomb site in the early 1960s. The proud spire of St Germain's, 38 metres (125 feet) high, stands above the still-ruined church. The Loire, spanned by a graceful suspension bridge, is attractive here, there is a pleasant river beach, good fishing from across the river, and quiet tree-lined walks on the river banks.

Sully becomes a little over-run with hunters at the beginning of the season, for it *is* on the edge of the Sologne hunting lands, 18km SE of Châteauneuf-sur-Loire. It is a fine fishing centre, too, rich in streams and lagoons for miles around. But it is the castle and a man who lived in it that brought fame to Sully. The château stands alongside the Loire by the town among trees and lawns, surrounded by water, and looks very formidable, with splendid towers at either end. It used to stand in the middle of the Loire. Maurice de Sully, the Paris bishop who built Notre-Dame, was born here in 1120. Charles VII hid here with his mistress while Joan of Arc and Dunois fought the English for him at Patay in 1429. Georges de Trémoille owned it. The Burgundians had taken it from him but handed it back in rather suspicious circumstances. Trémoille thought that Joan was a bad influence on Charles. But she came back from Patay and persuaded Charles to go at last to Reims and be crowned. Joan went off to try to take Paris. She failed, and on her return to Sully she was kept there as a virtual prisoner. Trémoille had great influence with Charles. It is still suggested that Charles was plotting an accidental fall in the river for Joan. But she and her page D'Aulon slipped away in the night and a few weeks later she fell into the hands of the enemy.

The most celebrated owner of Sully was the man who bought it from the last Trémoille in 1602 and took its name – Maximilien de Béthune, Chief Minister to Henri IV, Protestant commander at their victories at Coutras and Ivry and one of the greatest statesmen in French history. He was the man who saved France's finances by persuading even the French to pay their taxes. Henri made him Duc de Sully. He was a fussy, meticulous man who even made a written contract with his odd-job man for the building of three rabbit hutches. He had a love of trees and laid out a fine garden and park. He rescued the château from dilapidation and brought it ashore by building flood banks and putting moats around it. He built the Petit Château within the walls of the old one and you can see his office there.

When Voltaire was exiled from the Court in 1716 for his barbed witticisms, the great-great-grandson of the first Duke gave him shelter at the château and turned the salle d'honneur on the first floor into a theatre for him. He was only twenty-two and still called by his real name, François-Marie Arouey. He wrote his first play there, *Oedipe*. He left verses on people's plates before dinner – especially the young women guests whom he used as actresses in the theatre. One of them, Suzanne de Livry, wanted to be an actress, so she deliberately became his mistress.

When he was allowed back to Paris, he took her with him and let her play the lead in *Oedipe*. The comedy was a huge success, with a lot of the laughs coming from Suzanne's bad acting. He then let her take the lead in his next play, *Artemire*, which he had also written at Sully. This time she was booed off the stage. She fled to London and was booed off the stage there. But she married the Marquis de Gouvernet, the French Ambassador. (Château shut December, January, February.)

TOURIST INFORMATION place Gén. de Gaulle
(38.36.23.70)
MARKET Monday
FESTIVALS Fête of St Hubert, patron of hunters, last
Sunday in October; Music Festival June and July

HOTEL

*Grand Sully*, 10 boul. Champ-de-Foire (38.36.27.56): old country hotel completely restored. Excellent cooking according to seasons, not fashion. ROOMS D–E. MEALS D–F. Shut 24–31 December.

# TALCY
## [LOIR-ER-CHER]

Talcy is one of the gems of the Loire valley. Forget the severe, warlike looks of its château – go inside and see its beautiful rooms and dream of the beautiful Salviati women who were born and bred here and who inspired great poets.

But first be sure to come to it from along D15 from the pleasant little old town of Mer on the Loire's north bank 16km NE from Blois. There you pick up the little D15 which runs under the A10 motorway. It is flanked for 9km by ten thousand roses.

The little hamlet with the great château is almost isolated out on the Beauce plains. A feudal fortified manor of the thirteenth century, it was bought around 1520 by a rich Florentine banker, Bernardo Salviati, cousin of Catherine de' Medici, and he seems to have gutted the inside. The courtyard with a domed well is very attractive. So are the beautiful Salviati-family furniture and tapestries. The kitchen still seems to live in the sixteenth century. Another courtyard has a dovecote with revolving towers, like the one at Boumois, and under the trees is a huge seventeenth-century winepress which still works.

Bernardo Salviati had a sixteen-year-old daughter who lived at the château. Young Pierre de Ronsard, the poet, came to stay and fell immediately for the little blonde beauty. He wrote beautiful poems to her. As a poet, he should surely have been wary of a girl called Cassandra! She married a man called Jean de Peigny. Ronsard met her again twenty years later. She was a widow. She still turned him down. But he dedicated to her 183 sonnets – *Les Amours de Cassandre*.

Her brother Jean, who had inherited Talcy, had an attractive and, it seems, a warmer-hearted daughter, Diana. A young wounded Protestant was brought to the château, had an operation on the kitchen table and stayed to recover. Diana nursed him – very lovingly indeed. He was the poet Agrippa d'Aubigné, friend and comrade-in-arms of Henri of Navarre. But her father, a Catholic, found out about their affair and threw him out of the house. By the time she caught up with him again, he was married. Legend says that she then 'languished in sorrow and died'. The love poems he wrote to her were not published until after his death.

Cassandra's daughter married Guillaume de Musset and one of her direct descendants was the great poet of the nineteenth century Alfred de Musset.

In 1562 Catherine de' Medici tried the impossible at Talcy. She called together the bloodstained Catholic Guise clan and the stubborn Protestant Condé clan to try to find a solution to the Religious Wars. As Vivian Rowe wrote in 1969: 'When two sides are equally determined that the other is not to be trusted in any peaceful situation, it takes more than even a Queen of France to bring their quarrel to a close.'

# TOURS
[INDRE-ET-LOIRE – *see* Major Towns page 93]

# TRAPPE DU PORT-DU-SALUT
### [MAYENNE]

Seven kilometres S of Laval by the Mayenne river where the monks produced from 1810 the famous Port-du-Salut cheese until 1959. They sold the right to a commercial company in Entrammes, where it is now made. They still make a little cheese at the monastery.

# TRÈVES
### [MAINE-ET-LOIRE – *see* Cunault and Trèves page 176]

# TROO
### [LOIR-ET-CHER]

A hamlet on the Loir 26km W of Vendôme, it is still called the 'cave-dwellers' town' after the troglodyte houses on its steep slopes, built right into the tufa rock, which are still used. Equipped with modern conveniences, many have terraces with flowers growing in pots. Their chimneys do look odd sticking from the rock. They rise in tiers, linked by stairways, narrow alleys and passageways. The rock has a labyrinth of galleries, called caforts (*caves fortes*) because they were used as hideouts during medieval wars. Troo has three medieval religious buildings. Collegiate Church of St Martin was founded in 1050 and altered a century later. It has a dominating square tower. Just below it is La Butte, a Gaulish burial mound from which you can see the winding Loir river valley. Maladrerie Ste-Catherine from the twelfth century was a lazar house – a medical hospice on the pilgrim routes to St Martin in Tours and St James's shrine at Santiago de Compostela in Spain. St Jacques-des-Guérets is a small twelfth-century church with very interesting wall-paintings in fresh colours made between 1130 and the fifteenth century.

# USSÉ – Château
## [INDRE-ET-LOIRE]

Whether Charles Perrault was really inspired by the château to write the *Sleeping Beauty* we do not know but Ussé is magnificent, and having seen it in a white mist swirling off the Indre river right across to the dark firs and cedars of the Chinon forest behind, I can believe that he was.

From the bridge over the Indre 180 metres away it has a truly dream-like look.

Topping a ridge overlooking the river, it is built in white

*Chinon forest*

stone in a medley of styles from the fifteenth to the seventeenth
centuries – an attractive mixture of towers, pointed rooftops,
beautiful curves, lofty pinnacles and tall chimneys. It started as a
fort, then became a comfortable home, which it still is.

It belonged first to the Bueil family, who had made good in
the Hundred Years War and wanted a château worthy of their
importance. One of them married the daughter of Charles VII
and Agnès Sorel, but these two sold it. Perhaps it was not good
enough for the daughter of a king – even an illegitimate one.

The Duchess of Duras, who owned it from 1807, had no
fairy-story love affairs. Her husband was beheaded in the
Revolution. Then she fell for the writer and politician Châteaubriand, an unscrupulous man. Her son was influential at Court
when the monarchy was restored and Châteaubriand used their
influence to get himself made Ambassador to London. In return
he gave her the row of cedars lining the avenue. Then she
helped him to become Foreign Minister. Having no more use
for her, he left her for younger mistresses. The poor Duchess
was heartbroken. 'I have stopped the hands of all my clocks so as
to hear no longer the striking of the hours at which you will no
longer be coming', she wrote to him.

Parts of the château are open to the public from mid-March
to 1 November. There are waxwork figures in a tower to re-
create the Sleeping Beauty story but getting round the narrow
passages is a scramble. In the main part is a collection of Charles
X's sporting guns and swords, a fine Mansard seventeenth-
century staircase worthy of the fairy tale and a Royal bedroom
hung with red and white Chinese silks and with a great four-
poster bed canopied like a crown. It was intended for a visit by
Louis XVI and Marie Antoinette, but they never came. In the
pleasant park is a lovely Renaissance-style chapel of 1520 with
magnificent Italian wood sculptures and a Virgin by Della Robia.
I did not see the famous Aubusson tapestries. Stolen in 1975,
they have not been seen since. They will turn up at an auction
some time – but not yet.

# VALLET
## [LOIRE-ATLANTIQUE]

Busy little Muscadet wine town where the new dual carriageway N249 from Nantes meets D763 from Clisson to Ancenis. Olivier de Clisson, Marshal of France and 'Butcher of the English' inherited it in the fourteenth century (*see* Clisson page 173). Vallet has a Fête du Muscadet in November and a wine trade fair in the 3rd week of March. On the old D756 road towards Nantes are many little wine growers with boards marked 'Dégustations et Vente' (Tasting and Direct Sales).

TOURIST INFORMATION 4 place Charles-de-Gaulle
(May–September 40.36.35.87)
MARKET Sunday
FESTIVALS see text

### HOTEL

*Don Quichotte*, 35 route Clisson (40.33.99.67): good restaurant deservedly becoming popular. ROOMS C–E. MEALS B–F. Shut 1–7 January. Restaurant shut Sunday evening.

# VASS
## [SARTHE]

Little town upstream from Le Lude has a riverside beach well known for watersports. Its medieval castle was almost as important as Le Lude and kept changing hands between English and French. Some older women still use its riverside lavoir, harder work than a launderette but not so noisy.

# VENDÔME
## [LOIR-ET-CHER]

Little bridges crossing narrow streams into which the meandering Loir river divides in the charming centre of Ven-

dôme, give you a feeling that you are wandering round a park.
The city becomes a series of islands. One of the bigger arms laps
the public gardens, which give a pleasant view over the city. Men
fish under the little bridges, ignoring the town above.

Vendôme has become more industrialized recently, making
machinery, car parts, instruments and plastics, with a population
of eighteen thousand, but it has an attractive unhurried atmosphere, and it is a very interesting place.

The novelist Balzac did not like it. At the age of eight, in
1807, he was sent to the Oratorians' College, which had been
founded in 1623 by César of Vendôme, son of Henri IV and
Gabrielle d'Estrées. He was constantly in trouble for indiscipline
and spent much time in a a punishment cell, reading in peace.
He got his revenge by describing the school in his book *Louis
Lambert*. Now it is a lycée. Not surprisingly, it is not named after
him but after the local poet Ronsard.

Foulques Nerra's son Geoffroi Martel, Count of Anjou,
founded a monastery here in 1040 after he had seen three
flaming swords fall into a fountain. Now the abbey church is a bit
of a hotchpotch of eleventh- to sixteenth-century styles. But its
free-standing bell tower is said to have been the model for an old
tower at Chartres Cathedral. It doubled as the keep to which
people fled for safety in times of attack, which is why there are
no windows at the bottom, but they become bigger towards the
top and the shape changes from square to octagonal to make
room for corner turrets. It is 80 metres (262 feet) high, with a
big iron cross at the top.

The stone lacework of the Flamboyant façade is exquisite.
This was built in the sixteenth century by Jean de Beauce before
he built the new tower (*Clocher Neuf*) at Chartres Cathedral. In
one of the chapels is a famous twelfth-century stained glass
window of Virgin and Child, which has a strangely modern look,
and there is more fine sixteenth-century glass in other chapels.

The monastery buildings have not been the same since the
Rochambeau Regiment of Light Cavalry were billeted in them.
But they have a fine staircase and a little museum with interesting wall paintings, a harp which was played by Marie-Antoinette
(something of an omen, perhaps), and a wonderfully lifelike
reconstruction of a peasants' cottage with big fireplace, canopied

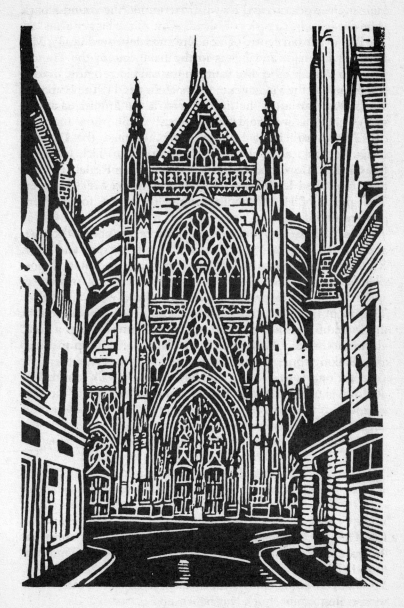

*Abbaye de la Trinité*

bed, and the peasant and his wife in costume. She is preparing a meal.

Part of the old centre of Vendôme was destroyed by German bombers in 1940, and it was in the front line in the Franco-Prussian War in 1870. But it was in the wars long before that. It was owned by the Plantagenet Kings of England in the Hundred Years War, but after the French took it the English sacked it in 1361. It was inherited by the House of Bourbon and so it came down to Henri IV. When he inherited the Catholic Leaguers had taken it. He recaptured it in 1589, hanged the Catholic Governor and knocked down the castle. Its ruins on a hill called La Montagne give lovely views over the river. The graves of Henri's mother and father were found there quite recently.

César, Henri's son by Gabrielle d'Estrées, was given the town and became Duke of Vendôme. When his father died and Louis XIII and Richelieu ruled in France, making life almost impossible for Protestants, he used the town as a centre for conspiracy, spent four years in prison in Vincennes, and was then exiled. The last of his family, Louis Joseph, a great soldier who fought the Duke of Marlborough and was equally renowned as a great glutton, died in 1712. Some say he died after a massive eating and drinking spree. Vendôme became royal property.

Vendôme is small and a wonderful place to walk round. The old town gate at St Georges bridge over the main arm of the Loir is superb. It was built in the fourteenth century. Two towers and amusing gargoyles were added in the sixteenth century.

TOURIST INFORMATION Hôtel Belay-Le-Saillant, 47 rue Poterie (54.77.05.07)

MARKET Friday (a good market)

FESTIVALS son-et-lumière in mid-summer

### HOTELS

*Vendôme et Restaurant Cloche Rouge*, faubourg Chartrain (54.77.02.88): traditional cooking, very popular with *Travellers' France* readers and locals. Bedrooms modernized. ROOMS C–E. MEALS B–F. Hotel shut 15 December–5 January; weekends in winter. Restaurant shut 1 November–28 February.

*Jardin du Loir*, place Madeleine (54.77.20.79): simple bedrooms.

Family cooking; also outside grill for summer. ROOMS C. MEALS
A–E. Shut February holidays. Restaurant shut Wednesday.


RESTAURANTS

*Petit Bilboquet*, route de Tours (54.77.16.60): small with flowery
terrace. Classic cooking. Rather pricey. MEALS E–F. Shut
Sunday evening, Monday.
*Paris*, 1 rue Darreau (54.77.02.71): very good cooking of classic
dishes. MEALS B(weekends), C–F. Shut 1–21 August; 25–31
January; Sunday evening, Monday.


# VERNEUIL-SUR-INDRE
## [INDRE-ET-LOIRE]

Twelve kilometres S of Loches by N143 and D41 in Bois de
Verneuil. You can visit the gardens of the château (remodelled
in 1820 in fifteenth-century style) which are a horticultural
centre (June–October only).


# VIERZON
## [CHER]

A strange mixture of industrial town, making agricultural
machinery, porcelain and glassware, and of pleasant old town
with old houses looking down on lovely river banks of the Cher
and Yèvre, which meet here. It has a port on the Berry canal,
too. Vierzon is on the N20, but a superb stretch of it that passes
through the Sologne all the way from just south of Orléans
through Lamotte-Beuvron to the Forêt de Vierzon on the town's
doorstep. So does the A27 motorway which skirts the town.
Quincy vineyards (page 228) are 10km upstream on the Cher.
TOURIST INFORMATION 1 place Maurice-Thorez
(48.75.20.03)
MARKETS Tuesday morning, Saturday, Sunday

### HOTEL

*Château de la Beuvrière*, at St-Hilaire-de-Court, 7km SW by N20 and D90 (48.75.14.63): fine old turreted manor, restored, family-run; big rooms. In big park with lake (fishing). ROOMS D–F. MEALS D–F. Shut one week mid-August; mid-January–mid-February; Sunday evening. Restaurant also Monday.

### RESTAURANT

*Grange des Epinettes*, 40 rue Epinettes (48.71.68.81): good value; wide range of menus. MEALS A–F. Open all year.

# VILLAINES-LES-ROCHERS
## [INDRE-ET-LOIRE]

Village 5km SE of Azay-le-Rideau on D57 where wickerwork articles have been made for centuries. Green rushes and black and yellow osiers are cut in winter and steeped in water until May, when they are taken out, stripped and woven. If you are there during the weaving period it is very interesting to watch the speed and skill of the villagers. You can see and buy finished products – bags, baskets, etc, at the Co-operative, signposted in the village.

# VILLEBERNIER
## [MAINE-ET-LOIRE]

Just over the bridge from Saumur on the right bank of the Loire, 3km E along N152 is this village with a lane leading to its manor house, the picturesque Manoir de Launay. It is an unassuming old mansion. Its little fat stone tower has a pepperpot slated roof and a chimney obviously added later. The oblong house below it is quite small. This is where good King René (1409–80) used to hide with a few friends from the problems and squabbles of being Count of Anjou, Count of Provence and technically King of Naples. He much preferred it to his big

castles at Angers and Saumur. He and his friends held friendly
tournaments in the surrounding fields and sat around in the
sunshine playing music, singing and listening to each other's
poetry. He was one of the most cultured men of his time, a
friend of the poet Charles d'Orléans whom he visited at Blois.
He did not try very hard to take up his crown of Sicily nor fight
when his nephew Louis XI annexed Anjou for the French
crown. He retired happily to Provence to improve local agriculture and write Provençal poetry.

Unfortunately his daughter Margaret was married to Henry
VI of England, who was weak and had fits of insanity, and she
had a tough job looking after her husband and ruling a foreign
land. She became extremely unpopular in England where she
was not only blamed as a foreigner for England's ills and the
Wars of the Roses but for the loss of Normandy in a war, and for
Louis getting control of Anjou and Maine, which had been
English. She continued to fight for the House of Lancaster
against York even when Henry was totally insane but she lost
finally at Tewkesbury and spent four years in the Tower before
the mean Louis XI would pay her ransom, though he had
'annexed' her father's wealth.

She was called 'unhappiest of mothers, unhappiest of wives,
unhappiest of queens'. Her reputation in England was totally
blackened by Shakespeare in *King Henry VI* ('she-wolf of France')
who even disparaged her father for having 'less wealth than an
English yeoman'. No way to libel a fellow poet!

# VILLEDIEU-LE-CHÂTEAU
## [LOIR-ET-CHER]

I wonder how many places called 'Villedieu' there are in France?
This one is a very attractive village 4km south of the river Loir in
a delightful setting of slopes covered in vines and fruit trees
which surround houses with pretty flower gardens, ruined ramparts and an ancient belfry. There are still cave-houses in the
slopes. It is a few kilometres east of La Chartre-sur-le-Loir. The

D80 takes you to the river and across a bridge to the wine village of Ruillé.

# VILLESAVIN CHÂTEAU
[LOIR-ET-CHER – *See* Bracieux page 140]

# VOUVRAY
[INDRE-ET-LOIRE]

I heard an American guide telling her flock that there was nothing to do or see in Vouvray. Well, first of all, when you are driving along the N152 on the north bank of the Loire you go east under the motorway at Tours and drive on for 6km watching for a tiny road on the left marked 'Vallée Coquette'. This is the road to a little white wine-lover's paradise. A thousand metres up on the right, past the Cave Co-operative des Producteurs des Grands Vins de Vouvray, is a cave in a hamlet called La Caillerie. Here, probably in blue overalls and a flat cap, you will find my friend Daniel Jarry, wizard winemaker. And what you do is taste his wine. His cave looks nothing until you step inside. Then you will see that it is a *real* cave, cut into the white stone of the hillside. And there you will see long corridors lined with old oak casks with shelves cut into the stone above them lined with bottles. More long corridors are lined all along with bottles of his nectar mixed with fruit which is called demi-sec, his superbly refreshing and clean but still delicate sec, to quench your thirst without assaulting your palate with too much acid, and his luscious, honeyed and intensely flowery moelleux – a precious sweet wine which should be kept for ten years, can be kept for thirty or even fifty years, and gives fresh summer fruit, especially strawberries, a taste of heaven. As a mid-morning reviver his old moelleux puts flowers into your jaded mouth.

You can call and taste between 9 a.m. and 7 p.m. – but try to avoid 12 p.m.–2 p.m. (tel. 47.52.78.75). Winemakers still eat lunch in the Loire. There are many other winemakers on whom you can call, too. Then I suggest that you seek out the sleepy country village of Vernou-sur-Brenne, 4km along the pretty D46. Stop at Hostellerie les Perce Neige and plead for a bed for the night. I cannot think of a better place to sip an aperitif bottle of Vouvray than its peaceful garden. This time you swallow the wine. Then you can eat a good meal of good bourgeois dishes at a price which won't bankrupt you with a bottle of whichever Loire wine you wish and fall into a comfortable bed in the old creeper-clad family house. The châteaux of the Loire can wait until tomorrow.

FESTIVALS INFORMATION Vouvray Wine Fairs – last Saturday in January and 2nd week August

### HOTELS

*Auberge du Grand Vatel*, 8 rue Brulé (47.52.70.32): old-fashioned meals. Rabelaisian murals help you to enjoy generous portions. Logis. ROOMS C. MEALS C–E. Shut 1st fortnight December; 1st fortnight March; Sunday evening, Monday.

*Hostellerie les Perce Neige*, 13 rue Anatole France, Vernou-sur-Brenne (47.52.10.04): see text. ROOMS C–D. MEALS B–D. Shut 2 January–1 February; Sunday evening and Monday low season.

# M A P S

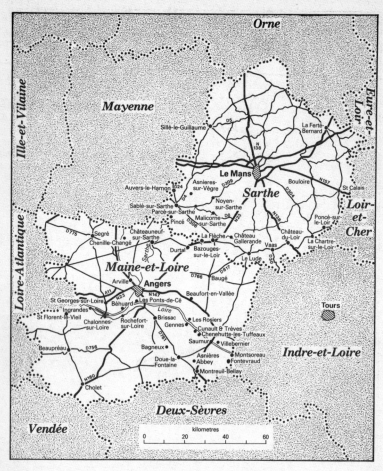

2  *Sarthe, Maine-et-Loire*

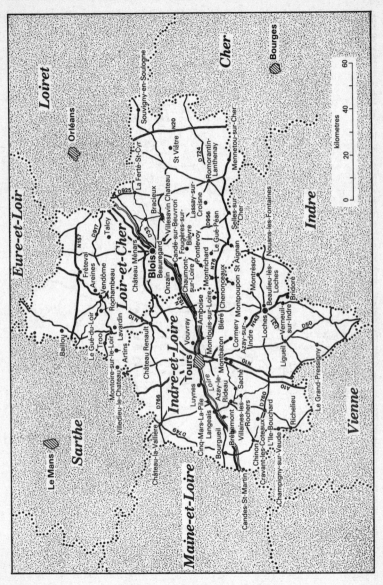

3 *Loir-et-Cher, Indre-et-Loire*

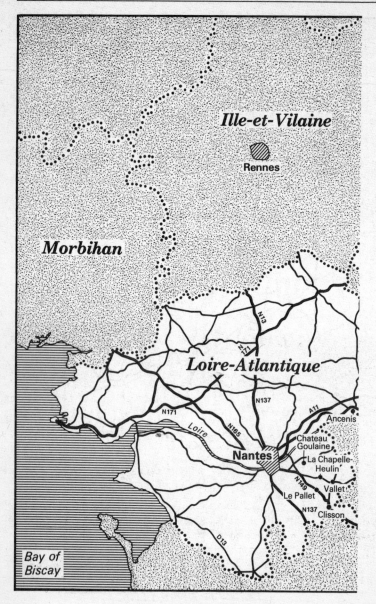

4  *Loire-Atlantique, Mayenne*

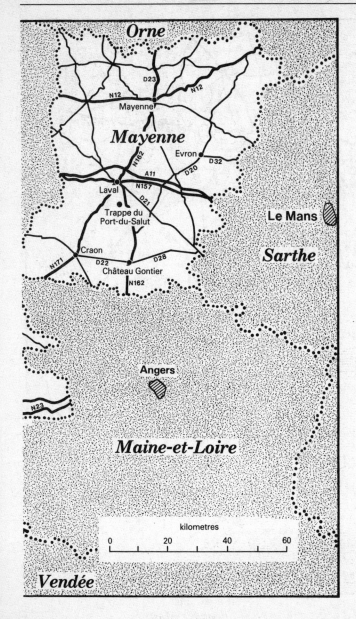

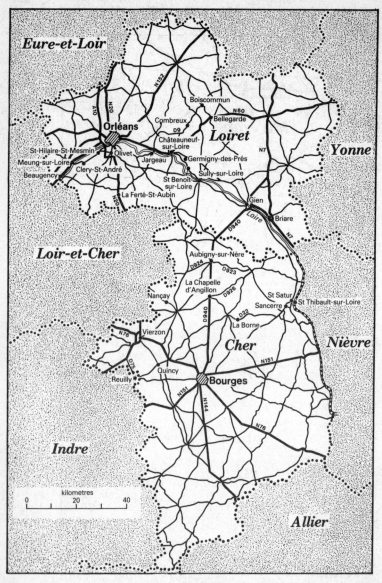

5 *Loiret, Cher*

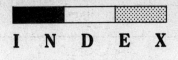

# INDEX

Names of hotels and restaurants appear in *italics*.